"SAY NOTHING"

My Brief Career in an Irish Asylum

By Christine Lacey

Cover Photo, Concept and Design by Christine Lacey

Layout Design by Francesca Giannotta

Twitter.com/ShebaofChennai

©Christine Lacey 2018

Paperback ISBN: 978-1-9993545-9-6

Ebook ISBN: 978-1-9993545-8-9

Disclaimer

This is a work of creative nonfiction.

During the entire tenure of this memoir, I kept an ongoing journal of notes; a documentation of events, places and conversations.

In deference to those who may currently be inhabiting my subterranean bedsit with its crop of toilet toadstools, the address of No. 292 as well as the name of the landlord are fictitious. To the best of my knowledge, neither one of them exists.

I have tried to recreate events, locales and conversations from my notes and memories of them. In order to maintain their anonymity in some instances I have changed the names of individuals and places, I may have changed some identifying characteristics and details such as physical properties, occupations and places of residence.

Names have been changed with the following exceptions:
- Leo, My Dub of a California Neighbor
- Mary, my most grounded boss
- Mary, my grounded replacement
- Dr. Connor
- Buck
- George the Bartender
- Pat the Yank
- Madame Lee
- Kitty O'Doherty

Dedication

Pasadena, California; summer school for kids with special needs. My class is all boys, ages 8 to 10. Fifteen bodies emitting pure energy. In the corner, I write my notes, trying to keep the noise from puncturing my brain. I see Fernando, rocking and stimming, his fingers quietly whirring away. He sees me, too. He stops. His big brown Mexican eyes lock on my Portuguese ones. He leans forward, elbows on desk, cupping his chin in his hands while his fingers thump away on his cheeks.

"What's up?" I whisper.

He sighs, "I just need to change my life."

****

"Say Nothing" is dedicated to Leo and Delia Black, true Dubs who made their way from Fairview, to Pasadena, to changing my life..

Table of Contents

Chapter 1 - A Public Display of Affection

In 1994, well and truly past my sell-by date, I left California for a job in a crumbling, ancient Irish asylum. I didn't mean to; I was sweetly conned into it by the tall, elderly, gangly chairman who closed the interview with a whiskey recommendation but omitted the word "asylum" from the job description. It was my first exposure to our future conflict of cultures; Americans who can't shut up and the Irish, who provide only the most necessary of information. It's a skill honed from 800 years of English oppression, or so I'm told.

I'd hoped for a job in the serene, picturesque English countryside. But my degree was under a ten-year layer of dust and I worried that I couldn't pass the English exam. Ireland's desperate need for speech therapists made my latent skills attractive. They needed a body and I had one. My dubious success at landing this job in Dublin can be solely attributed to the obsessive, bespectacled, ginger-haired, bipolar hitch-hiker that I'd picked up in Dingle the summer before.

I didn't mean to go to Dingle; I meant to go to Killarney. But I stopped on the way, spending the night in a Waterford bed and break-fast. After unpacking, I went looking for a meal. The local hotel was buzzing and I grabbed a seat at the bar. I got to chatting with the Irish gentleman next to me who, upon hearing my plans, suggested that I bypass that "tourist trap" Killarney and head straight for Dingle with its pubs for food, pubs for music, even pubs to repair your shoes. He was adamant. When it got late, I noticed the barman coming round asking the customers for their room numbers. Even though the hotel bar was still buzzing, it was apparently closed. I didn't know it but I was now drinking under the Residents' Rule.

When the barman moved toward me, my neighbor gave me a wink. I took that to mean that I should come up with a room number of my own to avoid expulsion. Totally convinced that the barman would check my response with an official guest list, show it to the all-night front desk clerk and back it up with on-site security, I panicked. Identifying my babbling as guilt, my companion reached over, rested his hand on my forearm and then seamlessly jabbed me in the ribs with his elbow. This caused me to choke on my honesty and blurt out "my" room number, a sloppy inversion of the one just given. Satisfied and checking nothing, the barman moved on.

When I left, at some god-awful hour of the morning, I thanked my companion and assured him that I would indeed head straight to Dingle. The barman directed me to a slim, side door that he unlocked and held for me as I poured myself into the moonlit night. Obviously, I wasn't a guest but I needn't have worried. I had provided only the most necessary of information; it's a skill.

I reached Dingle late in the evening of the following day. It had grown dark so I left my car in an open dirt field that seemed to be passing as a car park. I walked straight up the road to the first bed and breakfast with the light on and rang the bell. I was greeted by Mrs. Mac who shooed me in and sat me at the kitchen table. Mrs. Mac was wearing an off-white housecoat and a pink hair net that barely covered the curlers wound tightly around her head. A filter-less cigarette dangled from her lip as we sorted out the days and the keys. She balanced an unbelievable length of ash over the table as she took my name and address. Mrs. Mac was in a hurry. She needed to be up to the church to sort out the flowers for tomorrow. She stalled then and told me that I must be wanting tea and something to eat. She was adamant about my thirst and hunger and went away to put on the kettle. When she returned with the tea, she started rummaging around the kitchen, pulling open the doors of a tall, crammed cupboard and causing a loaf of bread to roll off the crowded shelves and onto the floor. Although I admired her steadiness at ash balancing, I did notice a good bit of it was dusted off the bread as she retrieved it from the floorboards. Wiping it on her housecoat, she put it on the table and cut off a chunk, leaving it on a side plate next to the semi-melted butter already on the table. As she prepared to leave, she pointed to my keyring, drawing my attention to the picture of a smiling Pope John Paul II. I was not to worry. Everyone in Dingle knew that her bed and breakfast was the home of the pope. If I lost the key, it would come right back to her.

I visited numerous pubs in Dingle that night. Great music and loads of conversation. Mrs. Mac said that I was the only guest in the house, but in the morning, the bespectacled, ginger-haired Conor appeared at the breakfast table. He was sardonic and droll and not the least bit short of an opinion on Yanks. All Yanks. Conor paid for his breakfast, he was not a guest, and then suggested that he spend the day with me in Dingle. I didn't see us as traveling companions but his persistence won out and we spent half the day meandering around the pubs and shops. Then Conor suggested that we drive out the road to the beehive huts. He was also looking for a lift home and took it upon himself to map out my afternoon drive. Sure, I was going that way anyway, he insisted, why wouldn't I give him a lift? We loaded up the rental car and headed out of town. As we rounded a corner, he spotted a young woman hitchhiking at the side of the road. He became agitated at seeing her and ordered me to stop. I pulled over, rolled down the window and offered her a lift. She seemed pleased until she saw Conor lean across me waving his hands through the window and claiming my generosity as his own. Her smile vanished. I couldn't quite read the expression on her face but to me, it looked like fear.

Her hesitation calmed once she realized that she would be safely isolated in the back seat and that Conor would only be speaking to her from a safe distance. We dropped her at a nearby train station; her relief at getting out of the car was palpable. Then Conor began to direct me to his little village in the outskirts of Kerry. He was very interested in my desire to work in Ireland and had loads of suggestions as to where to search and how to apply for jobs. He seemed to have lots of experience with speech therapists or therapists in general and his knowledge of the health care system kept me interested all the way to our destination, which happened to be a pub just outside the village. It was late afternoon when we walked in, but a bit of a crowd was already at the bar and sitting at the tables. It seemed as if every head turned and stared at us as we walked in. I tried to disregard it, but I couldn't help thinking that their overall expressions seemed reminiscent of the look on the hitchhiker's face. We sat at the bar, but the barman reminded Conor that he "wasn't welcome here." He laughed it off. I did the same. Conor ordered a soda because of his "medication"; I did the same.

Drinks finished, we exchanged addresses and phone numbers. Conor said he would research opportunities for me and send off everything he could find. He was a mysterious, cerebral character, full of chat, well-read and interested in everything. I rang his house before heading back to the States and his sister answered. She seemed to know all about the Yankee therapist. She was sorry to tell me that Conor wasn't available, that he'd had another episode. "You know how that goes," she said. But I didn't know so I said nothing.

When I returned to California, Conor was as good as his word. He sent letters, newspaper articles, adverts from hospitals and clinics; he posted the addresses of all the health boards who were hiring therapists. I used his research to negotiate an interview with the now defunct Eastern Health Board. The timing was perfect. My marriage was outsourced to another woman, my career was downsized into nothingness, but more importantly, my mother had passed away after a long illness. One night, when she was floating through a coma-fog, I held her hand as she moved in and out of awareness. In our last twilight conversation, she whispered, "All I wanted to do was go dancing. Was it too much to ask? To go dancing?" It broke my heart to hear that simple request. My dream was to live in another country. I felt that her message was clear and so I accepted the post of senior speech therapist for North County Dublin.

I was hesitant to leave the diverse area of Los Angeles for an entire country whose inhabitants were all the same color, all the same religion and who spoke the same language. I did not know Dublin nor did I know one person in it. My brother, my only living relative, was completely unimpressed with my big adventure. "They speak English and you can figure out the money. Where's the challenge in that?" he asked. But my elderly California neighbors, born and raised in Dublin, cautioned me on how to act in my new country. "Whatever you do, say nothing," advised Leo from Fairview, "say nothing and you'll get along just fine."

I understood. I would be that Yank that blended in, respected my new country, adopted its rules and adapted to its quirks. I would be Irish. I would say nothing.

I found a studio apartment, my bedsit, on Dublin's south side. Each month I paid my rent by putting £230 in a tube the size of a toilet paper roll. I took the tube, marked No. 292, to the shed in the backyard, the back garden, where there was a trap door in the middle of a dirt floor. I lifted the door, dropped in my tube, No. 292, and my rent money was sucked into space.

Later I asked my boss, Mary, if a receipt for the rent should be expected. She assured me that it should. She asked about my rent book. Rent book? I had no idea. My complete and total ignorance of a process in which I had been participating for months clouded her face with concern. "Exactly how do you go about paying your rent?" she asked.

I explained: money to tube, tube to back garden, back garden to shed, shed to trap door, trap door to infinity. "And why do you do that?" she asked. Her question seemed uncalled for to me. "Doesn't everyone in Ireland pay their rent by putting their money down a hole in the ground?" She raised her hands to her glasses and removed them, rubbing her eyes while shaking her head.

"Say nothing" was going to be harder than I thought.

I was to be the therapist at several clinics in North County Dublin but the majority of my time would be spent in Portrane. The word itself seemed to have an effect on everyone I met. Whenever I spoke with someone on the street or on the bus, they would hear my accent and ask if I was on holiday. "No," I said, "I'm going to work in Portrane." That's all I said, "Portrane," and the person would give me a stern, silent nod. They all seemed to know something, but they said nothing.

I learned that Portrane was synonymous with St. Ita's Hospital for the Mentally Handicapped and that my job was so harrowing it had gone unfilled for five years, evidently not the most necessary bit of information. Mary knew the realities of the job and asked for a six-month commitment to see if I could sort out the post and make it appealing to an Irish therapist. It was a fair request and suited me just fine. I wanted an adventure, I just didn't want too much of one.

My temporary accommodation, a lovely bed and breakfast in Drumcondra, was on the north side of the river Liffey. As lovely as it was,

I was encouraged to look for accommodation elsewhere. The North Side had a tough reputation, and even though the city buzzed with the anticipation of the Celtic Tiger, it would be a while before it pounced on that side of the river.

I had a week to sort out my transportation to Portrane. I went to the bus station in the center of Dublin. Portrane was somewhere directly north of my temporary residence in the B&B. At the counter, I gave my destination to the clerk who showed me the route by way of a massive county map that was taped up and spread across a dull brown wall. As he spoke, he saw my face glaze over at his instructions. "I know what you're thinking," he said, "because you're here and you want to go there (standing up and dragging his finger in a straight line across the map) you should be able to go from here to there." I nodded. "Now so," he said, "if you'd moved to a normal country, that might be the case. But you didn't move to a normal country, you moved to Ireland."

On my first day, I followed the bus clerk's directions and took the bus to the bus, to the train to the bus, and arrived at Portrane on a rare sunny day. The last bus dropped me at the top of a narrow tree-lined street. The avenue was trimmed from side to side with cottages: tiny, compact, brown and solemn. Their common walls leaned in from cottage to cottage and had done so since the late 1800s. I would come to learn that now, in the mid-1990s, the cottages were still in use and housed the nurses who worked in the hospital for eight hours on and eight hours off, as they had done for generations. The nurses, mostly tall burly men, were trained to handle the breakdowns and outbursts of the occupants of St. Ita's. As I later found out, most of the residents of Portrane were not "mentally handicapped", a term as outdated as the architecture. Whether learning disabled or emotionally disturbed, the men and women had been co-existing for decades. Whatever the cause of their initial admittance, by now, their behaviors had merged with those of the other residents. There was a reason why the long, multilayered red brick buildings stretched from the avenue to the sea on the closest thing the county had to an Irish isthmus - historically, it was to give calm to the Dubliners of the late 1800s that the residents were safely locked away with no way into the city.

I entered the only open door I could find. It hovered under tiers and tiers of dark red brick that led up from the door to a high clock tower reminiscent of the home of a Brontë heroine. Through the door was a dark brown alcove. I walked through it to a vestibule with a high curved archway. There I met Pat who was instructed to show me around. We did not shake hands but we did say, "Cheers." Before starting, he handed me a large silver ring with ten keys of various sizes dangling and clanging in their closeness. I thought of the clock tower, and while the size and shape of the keys were unfamiliar to me, I was quite sure that Jane Eyre would have kept a similar set in her apron pocket. They were long and silver, the kind with the three-part teeth that fit into ancient locks. Pat instructed me that when entering a "unit", I was to turn quickly and lock the door behind me. I did not ask why but I did wonder if I wanted to be locked in, on my own, on the other side of the doors with the ancient locks.

We walked toward the sea and the Children's Unit. This was the name it was given when the hospital opened years ago. Pat was fairly certain that, by now, the youngest person in St. Ita's was at least 16. I wondered why he didn't know for sure.

We entered the unit by a side door. Several residents were in the sitting room and a young man with Down syndrome was sitting cross-legged on the floor. The chairs were old and the carpet was worn. There were Venetian blinds on the tall skinny windows. The windows were open and a breeze came in from the bay, rattling the blinds and their many loose pieces. The paint was peeling off the walls. Toward the side of the room there was a chest-high barrier and behind it, two female nurses were bathing a young man lying on a long plastic table. I introduced myself and explained that I was the new speech therapist. At the sound of my voice, the young man turned his head to look at me. His mouth was open and it looked as if his tongue extended as far as his collarbone. The nurses looked down at the young man and said softly, "We don't think that there's much you can do for Michael" and I must shamefully admit that I was immediately relieved.

Pat and I moved about the room, meeting other nurses and residents of the ward. Once again we passed the young man with Down syndrome. His socks had been used to tie his feet together, immobilizing him. When I asked why the nurses looked quickly from one to the other and said that he was "self-harming." "With his feet?" I asked. From nowhere Pat appeared, cupping my elbow and moving me toward the exit. As we passed I saw Michael standing behind the barrier where he had been bathed. He was alone and dressed in a one-piece jumpsuit. I asked why he was separated from the others. The nurses explained that when left on his own, he would corner the other residents and lick the clothing off them. Parts of nappies had been found in his lungs. Once again I was quickly ushered out the door but the memory of his tongue stretching down to his clavicle is with me still.

Pat walked me up the long winding path to the bus stop just as the wind was beginning to whip up from the sea. I was chilled to the bone, but not sure if it was the wind or the tour that had sent my temperature plummeting. I got on the bus and sat across from two workers that I had seen earlier that day in the hospital canteen. Numb, I followed them off the bus to what I hoped was the train station.

Over and over I thought of my interview. What had I missed? Certainly no one had breathed the word "asylum" for surely an asylum it was. The thought that Mary hadn't been able to fill the job for five years came reeling back to me as I waited for the train to Dublin.

When the train arrived a well-dressed young man held the door of the carriage for myself and another woman. The carriage was empty except for the three of us. She took a seat in the front, I collapsed in a seat farther down the aisle near a window and the young man sat in the back. As the train began to move, I could only stare out the window. Transfixed by what I had seen in Portrane, the movement of the train had a somewhat hypnotic effect on me. "What have I done? What have I done?" wove in and out of my thoughts with the rhythm of the train. My wish for a foreign adventure had taken a very different turn.

Then, out of the corner of my eye, I noticed that the young man was moving up the aisle of the carriage. Wary of overreacting from my first day at Portrane, I got out my book and began to read. The train moved closer to the next station and the young man moved closer to my seat. As we approached the first stop, Malahide, the young man walked past me and took a seat several rows forward and closer to the exit. My tenseness subsided. The train slowed down, chugging toward this most beautiful seaside village, slower, slower - toward the stop. The young man stood up as if to leave the carriage, but while it was still moving he turned to face me. As I looked up from my book, he whisked away the jacket that was covering his crotch and ejaculated, climaxing precisely between the seats of the 4:15 to Dublin. And then, just as quickly, he put his jacket back over his crotch exiting the train and leaving me in a state of shock right outside the flower-adorned train station at Malahide.

From the Dublin station I rang my boss in Coolock who brought me into her office first thing the next morning. Mary was my age and had been in this one job all her life. She was short and squat with curly gray hair, wire-rimmed glasses and a lovely soft accent from the Ring of Kerry. Her body was riddled with arthritis and she could barely hold a pencil her fingers were so gnarled from the disease. She's the person I remember most from my interview because when I shook her hand the feeling of her twisted fingers against mine made certain that I held eye contact with her for longer than the others. To say she was "grounded" was an understatement.

The tea and biscuits were ready when I arrived and she poured while asking me to go through the entire story; I was to leave out nothing. While I'm certain she was worried for my welfare, I think she was more concerned that I might quit. As my story moved from the tour to the nurses to the barrier to the tongue to the socks to the bus and onto the train, she nodded and clucked along with me. But when I got to the part about the passenger climaxing just as the train entered the station, she could only look at me and sigh, "Well, well," she said, "given that the Irish are always late you have to admire his timing."

Chapter 2 - The Holy Hour

I admit to some momentary panic. But I rationalized that nothing had really happened so, no harm, no foul? By the time I left Portrane I would have been exposed to more penises than I would care to count. But the next day when I got off the bus two stops too early to deliver a lecture at Grangegorman, Ireland's largest psychiatric facility, I burst into tears and cried, walking in the rain, all the way to St. Brendan's.

St. Brendan's was synonymous with Grangegorman just as Portrane was synonymous with St. Ita's. This explained the consistently concerned looks I would get whenever I said I was working in Portrane or Grangegorman. It automatically meant that I was employed, in some fashion, in one of Ireland's largest mental institutions. This Irish phenomenon of multiple names for one place existed in areas other than mental hospitals and could cause chaos if you didn't know the local history. I was living was just down the road from a pub called The 51. When asked where I was living, I would explain, "On Haddington Road, just down from The 51."

I was instantly corrected: "So by O'Flaherty's, so," they would say.

"No," I'd repeat, "just down from The 51." It turns out that years and years ago The 51 was known as O'Flaherty's and the locals continued to call it by that name. I clarified by changing direction; "Haddington Road, just up from The Beggar's Bush and down from Smyth's." This seemed to do the trick. Directions by pub were the first form of an Irish GPS.

When I finally stopped crying and got to St. Brendan's, a very kind nurse spotted my distress and ushered me into a small room beside the office. Once again, out came the tea and biscuits. I sat across from another friendly woman who appeared to be making tuna sandwiches and stacking them somewhat awkwardly on a small plate. She chatted away while I drank my tea, encouraging me to eat something to calm my nerves and offering me the plate. Just then, the nurse reappeared in the tearoom, facing me but standing just behind the sandwich lady. As the plate was handed over, the nurse began to shake her head, wave her hands in the air and exaggeratedly mouth the words, "No, no, she's mad."

I replaced the sandwich, with thanks. Eventually I learned that avoiding the sandwich lady was out of concern for hygiene and not for behavior. But by now I wasn't sure what to expect. This wouldn't be the last time that the lines were blurred between patient and staff, but it was the first of many times when the female nursing staff came to my rescue.

Regardless of this rocky start, I never gave a thought to leaving. My agreement to stay for six months and sort out this post was daunting but challenging.

"Six months?" my Irish friend said, "It'll be gone before you're married."

Because I came from business, Mary asked me to sort out the hierarchy of the hospital while identifying what speech and language issues might realistically be addressed. To this end I met another Pat. He seemed to have more of an administrative focus toward the hospital residents. Historically, Portrane had maintained one enormous patient population. For decades, people with learning disabilities had co-existed with those identified as having a psychiatric illness. To meet the behavioral needs of so many of these patients, the nursing staff was composed of mostly men, often big men, who were trained as psychiatric nurses. My job, in addition to providing speech and language therapy, was to supplement staff training. I was to provide the skills that would support a "people-centered" approach, using language and empathy when working with the patients who had a learning disability. This change of approach was not all that well received. Many of the nurses had worked there for decades and knew the patients well. The addition of an American therapist to teach a "new" system was hardly met with overt enthusiasm. My naiveté ranged from pathetic to thick. I was accused of taking a job away from an Irish therapist.

"But no Irish therapist will take this job," I explained.

Or "We were fine before you came and we'll be fine after you're gone."

"But I've only just got here," I pleaded. It didn't help.

At the end of the day, as we walked toward the bus stop, Pat pointed out parts of the huge expanse of buildings identifying the various areas where I would find patients to meet and interview. I thanked him for his time as I stepped up and into the bus. I pointed to one of the outlying buildings and asked, "Is that where I'll find the files so I can plan my sessions?"

"I'm sure it must be," he said with a whimsical smile and he stepped back to let the bus doors close.

Then one Sunday afternoon, in a busy Baggot Street pub, I fell in love with a music loving, poetry writing, Guinness guzzling, giant man from Donegal. I meant to keep my pledge of losing the lonely, empty nights and the long California workdays and to have anonymous, raucous fun during my six months in Dublin. I found him dazzling.

We met just before the pub closed for the Sunday Holy Hour. This meant that from 2-4 in the afternoon, the pubs closed and no drink was served. If you were in the pub, the front door was locked and the window blinds drawn. The drink, however, continued. After a while, I got to know the knocks on the window that could open the door or the back doors that were always left open. Holy Hour could become pretty lively on a Sunday afternoon. And never mind that 2-4 was more than one holy hour. That was in keeping with other Irish anomalies like having Christmas midnight mass at 9 pm. (Mary explained that if midnight mass was at midnight, too many parishioners would show up jarred. To avoid the disruption, midnight mass was moved forward to 9 and the drinking could be done after.) This logic made its way to other Irish systems such as "people were to remain in the public care for a *maximum* of 12 years or 14 years *at the most*." On this particular Holy Hour, I was locked in at O'Donoghue's pub. It was my first.

O'Donoghue's was packed but I had a seat at the bar. There was music in the corner, the Guinness was flowing, the voices were booming, so the craic, the ambience, was mighty. I was sitting next to Frank, from Donegal, who had the biggest hands I had ever seen and the most musical accent I had ever heard. I could have listened to him talk all night. I did manage to ask him why the afternoon closing was called the Holy Hour. He became slightly perturbed and explained by saying, "Because your lot are supposed to be home, cooking the Sunday roast. But what's the point, when you're all in here and there's no dinner on the table?" I took this to be a somewhat negative slant on Irish feminism but it didn't deter my good time. I was reminded of my neighbor Leo telling me that when I got to Ireland, I should remember that ladies never drank pints, but instead, should only drink a half pint, or in Ireland, a "glass" of beer. Not too long ago women weren't even *allowed* to order a pint nor was it acceptable to come into the bar. Ladies were to sit in the lounge where the seats were padded and the drink cost more. Leo always said that it just wasn't right to see a woman sitting at the bar behind a pint of stout. I was sitting behind a pint at the moment when Frank ordered one more for each of us. Leo would be appalled.

The music on this Sunday afternoon was amazing. The seating area by the window at O'Donoghue's was crowded with musicians who seemed to sense where the melody was going and instinctively follow it. As I turned to talk with Frank, some man jumped from the floor to the bar and began to step dance at a level that was even with my gaze and my Guinness. I was mesmerized. With incredible speed and rhythm, he moved up and down the bar clicking his dancing feet in and around the pints. He finished with a flourish, leaping off the bar, landing directly in front of the musicians and taking a deep bow to receive our hoots of appreciation. By then I still had one and a half pints in front of me. The barman came over, lifted the full pint, put it directly in front of my face and began to scold me, "Look here now," he said, "this is a living thing. It needs oxygen to survive and you're after killing it." Then he threw out the pint and replaced it with a full one. "I'm giving you one more chance, now drink!" he said, and I did.

After several more pints, Frank and I moved on to two more pubs and a Chinese Takeaway. The phrase "I could murder a Chinese" came into my vernacular, not as a racist comment but as anything to do with intense hunger. One could also murder a kebab and or a curry. We sat outside on the steps of the flat and finished our meal. We didn't discuss meeting up again but it was understood that we would. The basement of Haddington Road had a coin phone just as you entered the below street level bedsits. I gave this number to Frank. This was the only contact number that I had at the moment. I found the lack of landlines and answering machines pretty hard to handle. If I was lucky, and a phone call came for me, someone might leave a message taped to the wall. But I was instructed by my fellow bedsitters that if it was important, "they" would call back. I learned to live with this philosophy and found it to be true. "Irish Time" is its own reality. Frank took the number and disappeared into the darkness.

This lack of contact was also present at work. I had yet to get an office with a telephone so I sought out the first Pat to ask if I might get a pager, or in Portrane terms, a "bleep." In addition to Portrane, I was working in clinics in Swords and Coolock and in the training center on the Dublin-Belfast Road, as well as setting up programs in several of the national schools. This appeared to be an unusual request because *only doctors* had bleeps. I was hard-pressed to see how a pager could be a status symbol but evidently it had some sort of hidden meaning. I campaigned for my bleep by using the difficulties of being in five different locations while trying to set up appointments with clients and staff. It took a while but eventually Pat left a pager in my hospital mailbox.

I took the pager to "reception" in the St. Ita's entryway. Behind the reception counter was the hospital switchboard, the epicenter of everything that happened in the hospital. This area was called the switch and the person operating it was also known as The Switch. At any given moment there were several male clerks behind the counter in reception. The switchboard was a one-person operation so I never knew who was the official Switch. They seemed to take turns whenever a call came in. I showed the pager to The Switch on duty and attempted to give him the number. If I got a call, he was to bleep me. I would have to find an office, unlock the door, find the phone, call the switch and get the message. The Switch looked at the pager and shook his head. "You're not a doctor," he said.

"Yes, but I need the pager for messages."

"You're not a doctor," he repeated.

"I'm not sure I understand," I said, "I'm working in five different places. I need to know if there are messages for me. Obviously it's approved by Patient Services. Pat gave me the pager."

"Still," he said, "you're not a doctor." But at least he took down the number.

As I walked away from The Switch, from down the dark hallway, I heard someone call my name. "Christeeeeen," sang this deep voice from a shape wobbling just under the distant archway. "Christeeeeen," it came again and I turned to face the source. The shape ambled forward as the sound projected toward me. I started to walk backwards, away from the voice and toward the floorboards under the skylight. It barely illuminated a small square of space directly across from reception but at least I could make out the shape lumbering in my direction. I waited for my eyes to focus and then I recognized one of the patients in Portrane.

"Hello, Raymond," I said in my best Client Centered Speech Therapist voice, "Are you well?"

"Christeeeeen," he said as he came closer. Raymond looked about seven feet tall as he slowly ambled toward me, still in the dark and passing under the very low archway. The image was enough to cause me concern.

"Nice to see you, Raymond," I said, "But I'm away," and I turned to walk toward the front door.

"Christeeeeen," came the voice again and as I looked up, the male clerks from behind the reception counter were lined up watching Raymond approach me. I kept walking past the switch and toward the big, front double doors but Raymond came closer. I tried to ignore him, tucking my briefcase under my arm and reaching forward to lift the front door latch. Raymond came up behind me, clasping my shoulders and wrapping his upper body over the top of my head then lowered his head to be parallel with mine.

"Hands down, Raymond," I said in my quivering non-client centered voice. He continued to enfold me as the clerks only watched. "Hands down *now*, Raymond," I said trying not to let my voice crack as I looked past his head, through his bent elbow and toward the switch looking for help.

"Christeeeeen," he murmured quietly into the side of my head. It was then that I heard a woman's voice resonate from the far end of the corridor.

"Raymond," she commanded, "leave Christine alone." And immediately Raymond dropped his arms and turned away, shuffling down the dark hallway and stopping where she waited. The men at the switch turned away but the lone female nurse, Deirdre, kept her eyes on me as she stood waiting for Raymond. When he stopped in front of her, she gingerly hooked her arm through his and I heard her utter the kindest of reprimands, "Raymond" she whispered, "that's inappropriate." I paused briefly at the switch, but I said nothing.

Chapter 3 - The King of the Faeries

By now I was getting fairly well settled in my new digs on Haddington Road. It was on the south side of Dublin in an area often referred to by its postal code, Dublin 4. My bedsit was in the basement, the first of three and on the other side of the telephone alcove, three more bedsits took up space. I had met Tess, who lived across from me and Paddy who lived in the flat at the end of the dark hallway. Tess was a hefty young woman who worked as a bookkeeper. She was somewhere in her thirties, with a great sense of humor and a somewhat feckless attitude toward her bookkeeper life. She kept very late nights and more than once she forgot her house key and would buzz my door to be let in. My bedsit life was completely enhanced and dramatized by having the top buzzer on the outside door. Eventually I realized that drink might glaze over a person's vision but feeling one's way to the top buzzer would always sort you out. My bell was quite handy for someone who could lean but not look. Tess might forget the outdoor key but she always had the key to her flat. This didn't help much as she lived on the other side of the alcove. I marveled at the system she had developed over her years of late night bookkeeping. On these nights/mornings when I let her into the building, she would approach the alcove and give herself a leg up into the small opening. From there, she hoisted herself up, folded her body into thirds and nestled it directly into the alcove, wrapping her body around the coin telephone. For a few seconds, she seemed to form a human mollusk complete with dial-up midriff. When the time was right she would "pop" herself out and into the other hallway. Her late, late nights didn't seem to affect her professional life but her private life was devoted to the management of a local rugby club. If I ever got an actual written message from our group coin phone, Tess would have been the one to leave it.

My other known housemate, Paddy, worked the night shift for an Irish newspaper. He was older, maybe in his late 50s or early 60s, with white hair and wire-rimmed glasses. He had a bit of a paunch and usually wore a white shirt with dark braces, a tweed coat and a woolen cap. His picture could have been on the front of any Irish product sold in America. I would often hear him come home at various hours of the night. He was quiet and subdued. His white-white skin was covered with loads of tiny broken blood vessels; most likely the sign of a career late-shift newspaperman. He was friendly but he was a long way from loquacious. Paddy seldom gave off much of the Irish chat but we became connected housemates for the years that we were there. Mrs. Enright came on Tuesdays to clean his flat. She was quite the proper looking older woman with her brown hair pulled back tight, dark-rimmed glasses, and no matter what the weather, she always wore a winter coat with a scarf tucked into her collar. I never saw the inside of Paddy's flat so given that he had a weekly cleaner, I suspected that he had the deluxe bedsit of the building. I could practically reach from one end of my flat to the other. Cleaning it didn't take much of an effort but maybe housekeeping wasn't in the remit of a night sub-editor. If Paddy happened to be recovering from an extra late night, it was left to me to let Mrs. Enright in as well.

I felt quite lucky to find a place to live in Dublin 4, one of the more prestigious postal codes in Dublin. When people thought I wasn't listening, I often heard the comment, "Of course The American would live in Dublin 4," but in fairness, I had no knowledge of the neighborhood or the postal code. I ended up in Dublin 4 by sheer luck or faery dust. By the time I left Dublin for the States, there were toadstools blooming through the lino-over-dirt bathroom floor so I can't say that a postal code is the end-all of fancy living. But the location suited me just fine. One Saturday morning I came out of the building to find the road blocked off with banners and bands and outdoor cooking. I had no idea that the home of the Irish rugby team was the nearby stadium, Lansdowne Road. This Irish form of Mardi Gras happened whenever the rugby team played at home and my little bedsit was right in the middle of everything. It was perfect.

Moving into my own flat was a welcome relief but it took much, much longer than I anticipated. The extended stay in the Drumcondra B&B was causing a definite drain on my limited funds. To economize I began to frequent the takeaway restaurant, Abrakababra not Abrakadabra. Pronouncing the "b" instead of the "d" was a trick question for those of us who weren't locals. There was a shop just by the bus stop and I would get a takeaway there whenever I felt like murdering a kebab. My favorite, the lamb doner kebab, was an edible physical commitment. I had to sneak it into my upstairs room and layer the very brightly colored yellow printed bedspread with mounds of napkins to keep the sauces from permeating the linen. They oozed out of the pita and all over my face and hands. It was mushy but cost-effective. I ate it while listening to a production on the national radio station that had serialized a book by Brendan Behan, one of Ireland's most famous writers. "Brendan Behan's New York" saw me through nights of solitude and pita bread. At the end of the serial, I went into the library at the Dublin Ilac Center to get of copy of his book. When I asked for "Brendan Behan's New York", the young woman at the desk had no idea who he was and directed me to the travel section.

Dublin was expensive, and even as a senior speech therapist, my income was less than substantial. After a very convoluted process I managed to qualify for a credit card from my local bank. Credit cards were not the norm and very few people used them. At the time, the people

I knew only spent what they had. If there was no money, then you stayed home. The concept of credit was non-existent; it was a "pay as you go" way to live. This system was in place whenever you were out drinking with friends. I found it fascinating how everyone remembered who owed for the next round, it was like clockwork; you knew and everyone else knew when it was your turn. If you did forget, a friendly nod might be sent in your direction. It also meant that if you were out with six people then you were going to be drinking at least six drinks. Turns were not to be missed. But if you started out with one or two friends and then found yourself in a crowd, you had the option of saying, "We'll stay on our own." It could feel like a slight social rebuke, but it actually meant that you were responsible only for your own drinks. This was a seriously honored custom because it meant that funds were low and since it was said in code, it avoided any embarrassment. Not "staying on your own" could make for a very early evening. By now my funds were running pretty low so thankfully my credit card was approved. One afternoon it was hand-delivered to my B&B in a company car, driven by a bank manager and accompanied by two guards. At first, my landlady was terrified and then she was impressed. When I got home from work she asked me how I deserved such treatment. I found it hard to believe that all new credit cards were delivered in this manner but I didn't ask, and instead, I said nothing.

On the weekends I kept looking for a flat but the process was a nightmare. I would find a notice in the paper, figure out the four buses that it would take to get across town, go across town, and when I found the flat there would be a note on the door saying "Flat Let." Gone. Hopeless. More than once I sat down on the curb and burst into tears. Other than being confronted by a masturbator on a public train, it was the only other time that I balanced on the edge of hysteria. And then, on a cold, wet, freezing, spring day, I found a flat solely through a spontaneous interaction with an Irish faery.

I met the King of the Faeries while standing on the curb of Lower Dorset Street. It was a rainy, windy Saturday morning and I was wearing my usual spring wardrobe of an unattractive, two-toned raincoat with a hood that covered my head and totally blocked my peripheral vision. I could not judge the Dublin traffic coming from the unnatural right and this immobilized me. I was certain that the large hood that covered my head would be my undoing; that it would prevent me from seeing the Irish traffic and in the end I would die on a Dublin street having been annihilated by my choice of wardrobe.

From somewhere a man walked up behind me and in a lovely Irish accent sang, "Come with me darlin', it's safe to cross now." Then he gently supported my elbow and steered me over to and up on the opposing footpath. He held my arm until we got to the other side and I thanked him for his help. When he heard my American accent he reached into his pocket and said he would honor my visit to Dublin with a commemorative 50p piece that he gently folded into my hand. "But I'm not a visitor," I said, "I live here."

"Well now, that's another story," he said. "Let's have a pint." He turned me around and guided me directly into a darkly lit pub called The Auld Brogue.

This was Sean. He nodded hello to several people in the pub and we sat on the banquette just in front of the window that looked onto the street. I was very aware that instead of searching for a place to live, I was sitting in a pub on an early Saturday morning drinking Guinness with a total stranger. But sure, I wasn't here to live some California norm. Sean got us two pints and explained to me that he was just back from Cork, attending to some "business." He loosely implied or I strongly imagined that there was some connection to the IRA. I was intrigued beyond belief. He expected to be called back to Cork in the near future because there "are some bad characters" out there. When I told him that the Irish people seem to be full of stories, he explained by saying, "We're crazy, but we're nice." As to his work down in Cork, "We bow to no man."

Sean ordered two more pints. He commented on my dark eyes (I am half Portuguese as well as Irish) and how unusual it was to see warm brown eyes around Dublin. But Sean has other dark eyes in mind. As he ran his fingers through his somewhat long silvery hair, he started to tell the story of meeting a mother and daughter when he was only 12 years old. They were Indian, the daughter was somewhere in her twenties. Her name was Sabrina and he was enraptured with her. When he looked into her eyes he saw a dark and narrow tunnel that went on forever just like this and he pointed to the dark, dark bottom of his pint of Guinness. In his mind, he had always held a picture of the profile of the perfect woman. When he met Sabrina, he realized that the profile was hers. Giovanni, her father, took her back to India and for years, she kept in touch with Sean. But that link was broken many years ago. Sabrina was the woman of his dreams.

Sean removed his wire-rimmed glasses and wiped away the rain as he paused to gaze over the top of the banquette and out the window where we were sitting. I decided to stay with him and wait for the next story. He seemed lost in a memory that, given his appearance, must have gone back fifty years. I offered to get two more pints but he insisted on paying. "When you have no money, you have no money. When you have some money, you have a lot." I nodded in agreement having absolutely no idea of what he meant. I retrieved the pints while reminding myself that I had escaped to Ireland for a reason and I was still waiting to see what that reason might be. Sean went on to talk about his younger Dublin days when he stole Cadbury wrappers from the chocolate factory, loaded ships in the harbor and fenced sugar from the holds of the very same ships that he was loading. I bummed my second cigarette off him and we finished our pints, with me pulling the bits of tobacco from my lip. We agreed to meet again next week and before we left I asked the bartender to take our picture, and she did.

I met him on the street the following week. He was waiting on the corner dressed in a coat and tie, a blue pullover sweater with an emblem on the right breast and he carried a raincoat in the crook of his arm. He brought me filtered cigarettes, Silk Cut Blues, and we went into the Auld Brogue. I was bemoaning my lack of success at finding a place to live. He told me that I should look on the south side. "I see you living on Haddington Road," he said, "look there."

The next time I saw him was on Dorset Street, walking his bike along the footpath. It seemed to be a coincidence that we met up but as soon as he saw me he popped a small bottle of Bushmill's into my handbag to help me with my never-ending cold. I assumed that we would head up to his local, the Auld Brogue, but he took hold of my arm and turned me towards town. "We won't go in," he said, "there's a bad character in there." Instead, we walked down to O'Connell Street and into Mooney's. "You can't miss this pub," he said nodding toward the statue at the bend of the road, "Parnell is pointing right to it." We went in and he ordered a pint. For medicinal reasons, I had a hot whiskey. I asked about the "bad character" in the Auld Brogue but Sean was not forthcoming and I didn't ask any further. He did tell me that I may not see him for a while as he had "some business" to finish in Cork. It was his duty, he said, because the worst thing you could ever do is abandon a friend. Then from his inside pocket, he pulled out a map of Dublin and showed me the south side. He drew a circle around the area of Haddington Road and reminded me that he saw me living there.

We collected his bike and left the pub agreeing to meet up on the next Thursday night. He walked me to the bus stop but we let the first one go by. "There'll be another one," he said and we walked a little bit further to the next stop. It was pouring down rain by then so I kissed him goodbye and thanked him for his help. The bus came and just before I got on I confirmed our meeting time for the next week. He nodded but something was different. I got on the bus and turned to wave at him but he had already turned to walk up the road. As the bus passed I watched him, hoping to wave again but he kept walking, his head bent low.

That Saturday I took his map and went to explore the south side. While wandering around I found a rental agent on Dawson Street who was open for business. He immediately made a phone call and arranged for me to meet Eoin (OH won) Bowen, the owner of an apartment building on Haddington Road. I didn't hesitate. Once Eoin Bowen agreed to a six-month lease, I took the bedsit that very day.

The next Thursday I was in Mooney's fifteen minutes early. Sean wasn't there and he didn't come. I waited until 8:15 and then I began to walk up the road to the bus stop. But his words, "Never abandon a friend," rang in my ears and I went back to the pub to wait for one more hour. He never came.

On Saturday I went back to the Auld Brogue. I could only assume that the business with the "bad character" was finished by now and I was desperate to tell Sean that he was right, that I would soon be living on the south side just as he had pictured. I went into the pub and I recognized some of the people from weeks before. Luckily the bartender was the same woman who had taken our picture when we first met in this pub, his local. I made my way to the bar and got her attention. I reminded her that we had met several weeks ago and that she had taken my picture with an older gentleman. Yes, she remembered the picture but no, she did not remember the gentleman. "His name is Sean," I said, "this is his local." She turned to me and leaned across the bar, "I certainly remember taking the picture," she said, "but I've never seen that man before in my life."

And that was it. He was gone. And I moved into No. 292 Haddington Road.

Chapter 4 - Adaptation

My personal motivation for coming to Ireland was to have the "craic" and all the options of craziness that came with it. My professional remit, to help Mary define my post at St. Ita's, also seemed fairly straightforward. But I was clearly mistaken if I thought that I was ready to put either plan into action. I hadn't expected to become involved with the residents of Portrane but they were slowly weaving their way into my new Irish existence. My personal life plan, to do whatever came my way without too much thought, or guilt, seemed easier to implement. After all, I would be fleeing the island in half a year's time, taking my American anonymity with me. But I was foolishly underestimating the Irish skill of seeing all and saying nothing. The capital city, home of one-fourth of all the citizens of the country, would somehow "have time" for me.

My adventure was confirmed with the signing of a six-month lease on the subterranean bedsit. Eoin Bowen assured me that he only ever leased his flats for a year, but in my case, he would make an exception. On my first home-based Saturday I walked from the flat to the tourist office in town. I wanted to make a list of every Irish event that I could attend by September. I was starting now, supposedly this was spring, but the gigantic balls of ice that pummeled my calves as I walked down O'Connell Street obscured the fact that winter was technically over. The ugly two-toned raincoat (with hood) had yet to kill me but even in its new role as my "wardrobe staple" it was too short to protect me from the rain that blew sideways and pelted me with frozen ice. I ducked into the tourist office as soon as possible and made a list of all the events that I might attend between that Saturday and my flight home to the States. That list included Puck Fair, the Dublin Zoo, Kilmainham Goal (Jail), the Galway Arts Festival, the Galway Races and other race meets at Listowel, Fairy House and Leopardstown. I wasn't much of a gambler but growing up in a small California town I had a friend whose Irish mother worked at a local department store. Each day after tea in the store cafeteria she would write down a bet on a tiny piece of paper, fold it up and leave it under her teacup. The next day, her winnings would magically appear. I found that fascinating and a little sinister but gambling is second nature to an Irish existence. I put this on my list of things to do.

After sorting out my social calendar, I walked down to Guiney's on Talbot Street to sort out the interior design of the single room that would be my home for the next six months. Guiney's was two floors of linens, towels, bed sheets and everything in between. It was a north side, cost-effective, low-income resource for those of us with permanent jobs but little income. I wanted to dress up the flat, but in fairness, there wasn't much to enhance at No. 292. Once inside the door of the flat, the toilet, sink and shower were in a very small room to the right. The shower was so narrow that I had to step out of it to stretch the towel across my back. One forward step into the flat led to the sitting, sleeping, eating room. Against the wall on the left was a short, single bed. Straight ahead was a gas fireplace with a mantel, a grate and some sort of fake stone surrounding its opening. To the right were a table and two chairs. One more half step to the right led into the kitchen with a cooker (stove) and sink. The brightest thing in the place was the red toggle switch on the wall that turned the electricity off and on. There was no kitchen electricity on demand. I opted for red as my highlighting color: red bowls, red measuring cups, red hand towels and red handled utensils. These knives and forks could also be purchased at Guiney's and they came with a handy circular mounting stand from which all the utensils dangled. They were helpful because drawers and cupboards were virtually non-existent so every inch of counter space was used. Every home I visited during that time had dangling utensils. I also bought a mirror to hang over the fireplace. Guiney's was the source of all my bedsit occupier needs.

Having dolled up the place as much as possible, I learned to manage its quirks. I turned off the red toggle switch so that my electricity bill wouldn't be inflated. I stopped brushing my teeth in the bathroom sink. I had mentioned the odd taste of the water to my co-worker who explained that the water for the bathroom did not come from the pipes but from an open cistern on the roof of the building. This meant that it was open to flying creatures, leaping creatures and airborne debris. And of course, the fireplace terrified me. It was gas and heated the room with an open flame. At night the basement flat was freezing but I was too scared to sleep with the gas left on. For weeks I slept bundled up in the two-tone insulated coat (with hood) to avoid hypothermia, but after a while, I gave up. If I died, I imagined that Eoin Bowen would simply move my body to the back garden, leave me to decompose near that strange pneumatic-rent-absorbing-tube, and then put the flat up for a full year's lease while keeping my deposit. Being anonymous had its drawbacks.

I was still traveling by public transportation but I was starting to get the hang of the bus to train to bus schedule. I managed to eke out my bus fare and buy a copy of *The Irish Times* for less than my morning allotment of £1.00. There were several buses that could get me to the train station and all of them were dependent upon the time that I left the south side. In Dublin, buses waited for no one and I learned to get to the stop by jaywalking with the best of the local Dubliners, an art form unto itself. I prided myself on being able to dance across four lanes of city traffic during both morning and evening rush hours. It was an acquired skill and not for the faint-hearted. I managed the Dublin city bus schedules and the more strict-by-the-rules attitude of the city drivers, but out in the country, only a half hour out of town, the bus drivers had a different mandate. Once they knew you, they would stop anywhere to pick you up. In Portrane, there was one elderly lady who took the bus but consistently confused her appointments in the village. The bus driver would just turn around and take her home. He would also take her back if she forgot to turn off the cooker. Perhaps her toggle switch wasn't red. The rest of us went along for the ride. This could explain the times that I came out of the train station and waited and waited but no bus arrived. One sunny day I began to walk to work but then I saw the ambulance from St. Ita's meandering along the main road on its way toward the avenue. I flagged it down and the driver stopped. "Can I get a lift?" I asked. "Lift" being the operative word. (Asking for a "ride" had implicit sexual overtones.)

The driver rolled down the window and warned me, "You can get in if you can stand the smell," he said. He wasn't kidding. I tucked myself into a dry corner where the window was slightly open. Evidently the "ambulance" was more of a pick-up and delivery service for the day patients at Portrane, some of whom had to wait until reaching the hospital before their personal needs could be met.

Members of the staff would meet the ambulance as it weaved through the many low-lying buildings and dropped people off at the various "therapies." There was a Day Center, Farmyard Therapy, Horticulture, Knitting and the Schoolroom. I didn't have direct contact with too many of the day patients but I got to know them as they began to recognize me. If I stopped at Horticulture I would often see Dessie who seemed to have the run of the hospital. He was everywhere. Portrane was laid out like the Pentagon with a central area that branched out into many different hallways. I was continually lost and confused but by following the staff I managed to learn the way to the lunchroom. Dessie was always there, mingling with the staff that was queuing for food. Dessie was from Cork. He was tall and pudgy with a very youthful face. He only ever said one thing, "What age am I? What age am I?"

I learned early on that the only acceptable response was "I don't know, Dessie. What age are you?"

And he would sing back to you in his Cork accent, "I'm fawrtee two, I'm fawrtee two" and then he'd go on his way. Later, when Dessie had a birthday, we tried to tell him he that now he was forty-three but the emotional calamity that followed just wasn't worth it. He remained forty-two for the entire time that I worked at Portrane.

Walking from Horticulture to the school, I crossed a wide patch of grassy land with a lone shade tree standing between the buildings. It separated the different therapies, giving the residents a place to wander when they went out for a smoke. From across the grass, I would often see Rachel, an older woman with a learning disability who most likely also had epilepsy. She always wore a bicycle helmet as did a good many of the residents around Portrane. She would wave her arms whenever she saw me across the grass and scream, "Hello, hello, Christine."

"Hello, Rachel. How are you?" I would yell back and she would correct me, every time.

"I'm Gene Kelly," she would say. Every time. I often wondered, of all the people that we might fantasize to be, how did this middle-aged woman living in North County Dublin manage to come up with Gene Kelly?

From the therapies, I would walk to the Day Center and check in with Cormac, the charge nurse. The Day Center was more of an open-ended "therapy" where people mingled throughout the day. They could come and go to other therapies but many of them just stayed in the large oval room with big windows and overstuffed couches and chairs. The head nurse, Cormac, had grown up in one of the cottages alongside the hospital. His father had also been a psychiatric nurse in Portrane. As a child, Cormac used to peek through the surrounding wire fence and watch the very same residents that now, 30 years later, were under his care. In the Day Center, I got to know Kevin and his older brother, Anthony, who worked in the main hospital building. Anthony had a job in The Stores where the supplies were kept. This appeared to be one of the best jobs around. Anthony moved freely about the building, visiting people in their offices and on the wards. He loved driving the small forklift needed to move the heavier objects down on the loading dock. Anthony walked with a slight limp due to his wooden leg. When looking down the long, dark corridors, Anthony was always recognizable by his quick walk and the way his artificial leg would sort of swing out and away from his body as he ambled down the hallway. He modeled a kind of macho behavior that he must have thought went with his position in The Stores. Whenever I saw him he was wearing a white shirt, the sleeves rolled up to his elbows and the front unbuttoned two-thirds of the way down his chest exposing a minimal amount of chest hair. The shirt was tucked into tight black jeans and he accessorized with two or three gold chains. He had a bit of a swagger when he walked and he took his job seriously. He was a small man, five foot one or two, slightly built and he kept his hair savagely slicked down on each side. His job gave him the confidence to flirt with every female that he met. He had loads of personality but you had to mind, in this process of flirting, that you didn't stay talking with him for too long. If you did, he would eventually offer to show you his wooden leg and begin to loosen his trousers. Fiddling with those buttons was the cue to find someplace else to be. His brother Kevin suffered more of an intellectual disability but he still had the family personality. Kevin seemed to know everyone on the grounds and that helped him as he wandered around always on the lookout for cigarettes. Kevin appeared to have very poor vision; his eyes were unaligned, one pointed in various and varying directions from the other. I asked about his vision but I was told that it was perfect. I always wondered how they managed to communicate the instructions of the eye test in order to get an accurate result. Kevin was also very social and he managed to get through his day with a few phrases that he put to good use. His receptive skills were definitely better than his expressive ones. He was fascinated by my wire-rimmed glasses and would take them off my face and wear them around for a while. If he saw me with cigarettes, I always gave him one. If he needed it, he would break off the filter and smoke it right away. If he had scored an extra one, he would break off the filter and stick it behind his ear for later. In contrast to his brother Anthony, he always wore a shirt and tie and braces but the braces would often come undone. When I saw that one was loose, I convinced him to stand still for just a minute while I fixed it. "Ah loves ya," he would say, "Ah loves ya." I often found Kevin in the Day Center where the self-appointed leader of the group was a resident named Joseph. He sat in the same place, every day, and seldom got up to move around. I never really got to know Joseph. But every time I came into the Day Center, he would bless me, and without moving from the overstuffed sofa, he would begin to say the entire mass in Latin.

Because my post had been vacant for so long, the staff wasn't quite sure what to do with a speech therapist and I was confused as well. I might get a referral to help someone with their speech, but 30 or 40 years in an asylum with minimal social interaction, various muscular disabilities and hearing problems, didn't bode well for a positive outcome. One of my first referrals was to help an older resident named Orla with her speech. She didn't often talk and when she did, they found it difficult to understand her. Orla was tall and willowy with lots of long black hair. Her features were angular and well defined. When

I met Orla it was obvious that her limited speech came mostly from popping her lips and gums. "Could we get her some teeth?" I asked the referring nurse.

"Would that help?" she asked in return. I assured her that having teeth would definitely be an asset, in theory, anyway.

In search of dentures I chanced to meet a visiting dentist who came to the hospital from time to time. He sat in a bit of a ramshackle office off one of the corridors, with a desk and a gurney or a "couch." His door was ajar and he was sitting up on the couch with his legs stretched out while smoking cigarettes wrapped in brown cigarette paper. He continued to smoke and drop his ashes on the couch as I asked about Orla. In a very abbreviated fashion, he questioned me about her needs. I admit that I was fairly distracted by his smoking but I was transfixed by his hair; it perched at a decidedly right angle to his forehead. He didn't appear to know Orla which bothered me as he seemed quite intent on pulling out whatever teeth she had left. To be fair, he knew the patient population far better than I. Extraction was possibly the only option left at this stage. It took months to get her fitted with dentures and in the end, she wouldn't wear them. She was never very motivated to talk or to chew, for that matter. After meeting Billy, I gave up on dental referrals altogether. He was wheelchair bound but he took the ambulance down to a training center at Lissenhall, just outside of Swords, every day. He had loads of language and a great disposition. He laughed all the time but speaking was difficult. His upper teeth protruded in a very uneven, slanted and exaggerated manner. He could barely get his lips around his teeth to speak and he also found it difficult to chew. Watching him at lunch took a lot of effort on both our parts. When I suggested dentures to his case manager, I was seriously disappointed when she asked Billy to "pop-out" his teeth. Those were his dentures.

These were the first of many attempted changes that never success-fully materialized. I gave up on teeth but I pursued the issue of hearing and dragged people into town for hearing tests. Many of them finally got hearing aids and then traded them for Woodbine cigarettes. I'm fairly certain that just getting them out of Portrane and taking the bus to Dublin was the real pinnacle of my success.

My next referral was to meet a resident named Nolan, although the nurses who referred him never mentioned a speech problem. I was severely cautioned NOT to drop by his room during Coronation Street (a very popular British soap opera), as Nolan could lose his evidently notorious temper. I made a mental note to check the TV listings. Nolan was apparently very independent. He cycled all around the hospital grounds while taking care of his localized window cleaning business. He would go down the avenue where the nurses lived in the little pushed together houses and clean the windows on the cottages. He even had a bank account with enough savings to buy himself a new bike to help with the business. He sounded pretty good to me and I commented that he would be the first available man that I had met in Ireland who had a steady job and money in the bank. I definitely want-ed to meet him. As an entrepreneur, Nolan had cornered the market of his startup venture long ago. His business plan, as the story goes, was to give the nurses an estimate. But when one of his very first customers rejected his pitch, he cycled back later and broke the dirty and now cracked cottage window. His future market was secured. Nolan did not come to speech therapy.

I had yet to figure out what my role was to be in Portrane. I was to-tally on my own. Over time I happened upon several co-workers who were also setting up caseloads and providing a service to help various residents. It was just by luck and rumor that we found out about the existence of one another. Early on I met a young woman named Aisling (ASH ling) who worked with Cormac in the Day Center. Aisling had been trained in LAMH (LAHV), the Irish form of sign language for people with a learning disability. She was not a nurse and somehow that put her outside the hierarchy of the hospital staff and into a different caste. She was forever taking courses and had trained in aromatherapy and sensory integration. Like me, she made her own caseload and focused on those people who could best benefit from her skills. One afternoon I asked to observe her doing some sensory work with Irene, one of the residents who had difficulty with self-abuse. Aisling's objective was to help her stay calm and relaxed for a certain period of time and provide her with some peace. She had managed to secure a room up on the top floor of the hospital. Irene was sitting on a chair in the middle of the dark room. Aisling kept the lights off but there were skylights up above and the gray Dublin weather cast a silvery glow over the large space. Irene's hands were resting on the arms of the chair and the restraints that were used to keep her from self-harming during the day were now gently positioned to hold her arms in place at her side. When I arrived the therapy session had begun so I took a place at the back of the room and stayed by the door. Irene was quiet and calm, she was not displaying her usual aggressive behavior and she was breathing deeply and rhythmically. Aisling's demeanor was professional and direct, she took her patients' needs to heart and worked diligently to support them. Irene had her head down and seemed to be very relaxed, close to sleep. Aisling moved away from her and came to the doorway where I was waiting. I was amazed at the change in Irene's behavior. In fairness, I found her actions to be very upsetting. I was not at all comfortable witnessing her self-harming but here she looked so incredibly calm. I asked Aisling if she thought Irene could maintain her calmness without the restraints. I stayed at the back of the room while I watched Aisling walk slowly and quietly across the huge dark space and move to stand beside Irene while speaking to her in a low subdued voice. Irene didn't move. Her deep breathing continued. From where I stood I could only see the back of Irene, her head bent down and her shoulders slumped forward. She seemed to be totally at peace. Aisling stroked her right arm and slowly removed the restraint. In a flash Irene's hand flew up and across the top of her head, grasping a clump of her own hair and pulling it out at the roots. I couldn't believe the speed at which she moved. Aisling calmed her in one motion and managed to replace her arm in the restraint. I was amazed and horrified at the same time. I began to question the reality of long-term success when battling a history of institutionalization. Instead, I gave more thought to the short-term success of providing calm and quiet, or in my case, returning a bit of social interaction where it had been taken away.

I started to foster relationships with the many residents that I would see on my days at St. Ita's. Even though I knew it was not very clinically supportive, I felt I could at least add one more social contact into their lives. Slowly, very slowly, I identified the people that I thought I could help. These were the people that became part of my routine and who made my time there so rich and rewarding. I was beginning to think that six months wasn't going to be enough.

Chapter 5 - Shrinking Violet

By now my days were sorted but my nights were long. In Dublin, the evening doesn't get started until 10 and as an employed Yank, I was used to being in bed by then. Not to mention the overwhelming and intimidating aspect of being a single, older woman walking into the pub and knowing no one. I resolved to acclimate to my new time zone and its pub life but I found it difficult to override my previous life-style. One lonely night I went up the road and gave O'Flaherty's a try. Eventually, I got into a conversation with a congenial group of younger people. We were having the craic when it came close to 11 and the barman lifted his voice to say, "Last call for drink." At the time, the pubs closed at 11:00 in the winter and 11:30 in the summer. The trick was to order two pints at "last call" and have them in front of you at closing time. There was an unwritten agreement that allowed you to finish your drink in your own time. No more drink was served, as was the law, but no one was rushed if there was drink on the bar. Many's the time I would hear the barman sing, "Ladies and gents, drink up, it's closing" and not a soul would move. The staff would sweep the floor and stack the chairs all around you but no one would leave their drink unfinished. Some pubs would run the risk and continue to serve. If by some stroke of bad luck, the guards came into the pub they would penalize the owner and take the names of all the customers. There was no need to show any identification to the guards; they just took your name, whatever name you gave them.

When O'Flaherty's called for closing time one of the men in the group next to me let me know that they were going dancing and would I like to come along? Nightclubs operated under different regulations and could stay open until late. I thanked him but excused myself by letting him know that I had work in the morning. Evidently this was mildly insulting. "Sure," he said, "We all have jobs, too!"

I said "Thanks, but no" and walked back to No. 292. As soon as I entered the dark little flat I began to second-guess my decision. After all, most of us didn't start work until 9:30. That gave you time to party and still get plenty of sleep. I was going to have to develop a new attitude if I expected to have the adventure that was first on my list of things to do.

The pub life was still pretty scary for me and I spent a lot of nights at home in the flat. I decided that I could afford to rent a television, a telly, for a few pounds a month. Televisions were expensive and loads of people rented rather than put out a lot of money to buy. I took the bus to a little rental shop in Ranelagh (RA nuh la) where I selected a basic set and arranged for delivery. Anyone with a television must purchase a TV license to partially fund the national broadcasting service. I asked the owner of the shop about the license as he wrote down my address and took my deposit. He didn't answer me but I noticed that a slight grin began to eke out across his face. As a trained, tax-paying American, I asked him if his order book was cross-referenced with the government and could I expect to hear from them about the license? This question almost brought on full-blown laughter obviously at my expense. And then I got it. I was being logical but I wasn't being Irish. I took my receipt, left the shop and said nothing.

Affordable gyms were rare in Dublin in the mid-nineties so I developed a regimen of walking from the flat to the GPO, the General Post Office, on O'Connell Street at least three times a week. I clocked this distance to be one-half mile. I would make sure that I had at least three pieces of mail to be posted giving me the motivation to get one mile of exercise three times a week. My other form of exercise was to slowly jog from No. 292, along the Grand Canal, up to the betting shop at Harold's Cross and then back again. When it wasn't raining this form of exercise was my preference. But unknown and unseen to me were the midges that flourish around stagnant water. This was an accurate description of the water in the Grand Canal. Midges are teeny, tiny black flies that thrive on calm, cloudy, moist days and that's pretty much the standard weather report for Dublin. I was proud of myself for developing this exercise course and I would head out at dusk whenever I wasn't headed for the GPO. As it happens, dusk is the favorite time of midges. On my last jogging exercise that spring, I headed out for Harold's Cross. I was on my way back when a swarm of midges swirled their way up from the canal and around the locks where I had slowed down to make my way around the bridge. Something caught in my throat and I stopped in a fit of coughing that totally enveloped my lungs. I leaned, hacking, at the top of the gate of the lock, while bits of midges propelled themselves from my throat. From then on I stuck to posting letters and gave up on the Grand Canal.

One Saturday, in my ongoing effort to fill up my weekends, I walked into town toward my destination of the Dublin Zoo. I got as far as Phibsborough when I stopped to ask for directions. I was told to 'keep walking," that the zoo was only "45 minutes away." I stopped again. "Keep walking, the zoo is only 45 minutes away." I stopped again and got the same again. I kept walking. I began to think that 45 minutes was one of those ongoing Irish pub expressions like "We'll only go in for one" which I eventually learned was also an impossible objective. I didn't mean to give up on the Dublin Zoo but it got late and dark and then it started to rain like mad. I was lost in Phibsborough and soaked to the skin. When I finally pulled back the hood of the two-toned jacket I found myself at a roundabout with a pub directly in front of me. An oasis from the rain, I acknowledged the omen and walked straight in.

The pub was crowded and warm with a peat fire burning brightly in the fireplace. I put the dripping two-tone insulated jacket on a hook and found a seat at the bar. I was one barstool away from my favorite spot, the one next to the wall. An older man intently doing the cross-word already occupied that seat. I ordered a hot whiskey and after hearing my accent we started a conversation. As it happened, he was from Los Angeles, had retired to Dublin nine years ago and he hadn't "warmed up yet." But he assured me that having now purchased an electric blanket his life was taking a turn for the better.

He was quite chatty and proprietary toward me as I was apparently in his local. He let me know early on that he spends 8 to 12 hours a day in this pub. He was also drinking hot whiskey and he would dip his fingers into the hot liquid, pinch the fruit and eat the lemon off the rind. Mary, who was working the bar this night, was his favorite bartender. He loves her because she never lets his glass get empty. He followed this with the news that he had survived cirrhosis of the liver 3 times, had 8 teeth left in his mouth and had been married 5 times and divorced 3. While I was trying to get my head around this equation he proclaimed that by the third marriage he had finally fallen in love. Before I could find out what happened to wives number 4 and 5 he reminded me that every night he met his friend in this very pub and in this very spot. I missed this gigantic clue and kept talking. As I blath-ered on his friend, another older gentleman, came into the bar and stood directly behind me. I was mid-sentence when the LA Irishman put his right hand under my seat, lifted it and tipped me up and off the barstool. His friend immediately sat down in my place. I regained my balance, retrieved my coat and headed back to the flat.

From Phibsborough I managed to find my way back to O'Connell Street and locate the stop for the number 10 bus to Baggot Street. The harsh rain had abated but the drizzle carried on. I was waiting at the bus stop alongside an older, rounded, little lady wearing a tattered raincoat. Her hair was tied back with a blue cotton bandana and she carried a basket with groceries. She looked up and began to speak to me in a thick Dublin accent. "You're a lady you are," she said to me, "You're a lady and I'm all alone."

"I'm alone, too," I assured her as one bus went by.

"Go way," she said. "You're young and a lady. You could move with the best of them." Her accent was so strong that I could barely understand her.

"No," I said, "I know that feeling. I'm alone, too." She shook her head and went on to say that she could take the rain and the cold but "tis the loneliness" that truly pains her. She told me then that I would find happiness in the rest of my life; she said that she can "feel" it. Just then the number 10 bus pulled up at the stop a few feet beyond us. I told her "thanks and goodbye" and ran to catch the bus and as I ran she yelled toward my back, "You go, God bless you. Happiness is yours." I paid my fare, found a seat by the window and hoped to God she was right.

While I loved being called "...young and a lady..." it really was unnerving to be my age and single at this time in Dublin. I was an anomaly. Women in my age group were married and at home, happy or not. If they were out, they were out with other women who were also their age and married. At times my presence in the pub could have a noticeable effect; I wasn't really that far away from the lady at the bus stop. Friends in my age group eluded me. Every once in a while I went out with Claire, a much younger speech therapist. Neither of us habitually smoked but on our occasional Fridays out we would get one pack of Benson Hedges cigarettes, sit in the pub and smoke the whole lot. I really looked forward to those Friday nights. Left on my own, I spent my nights alone just like I did in California. This was unacceptable.

Finally, on just another lonely Friday night in No. 292, I stood in front of the fireplace, looked into the mirror from Guiney's on Talbot Street and gave myself a pep talk. I was not going to replicate my boring life in Pasadena. I was in Dublin, Ireland for God's sake where the party starts at 10. So I put on some makeup and my favorite red jacket and off I went to a pub by the flat. I wasn't in there for long when a younger man started to "chat me up." I remember thinking that this was going to be easier than I thought and I was delighted that, for an older woman, I was still fairly attractive. We talked for a few minutes and then he asked me if I was going to buy him a drink. I wasn't quite sure if I should respond to such a direct request so I sidestepped it by asking about the bar, "Is this a pretty old Dublin pub?" I asked.

He answered, "Old? You mean like you?" I left without buying him that drink.

This public pub humiliation had quite an effect on me but God loves a tryer so I didn't give up. I decided to temporarily avoid the pubs and instead walked down Baggot Street to the Horseshoe Bar in the Shelbourne Hotel. I've loved the Horseshoe Bar since Maggie Smith, in *The Lonely Passion of Miss Judith Hearne*, tried to impress Bob Hoskins by blowing all her money on a few nights in the best hotel in Dublin. At the time, I mentioned this movie to everyone that spoke to me as some sort of stupid social conversation starter. But not one person had heard of it including George, the barman. At least he felt an obligation to humor the tourist, thank God. For years George remembered that I drank single malt scotch with *two* cubes of ice. He was my saving grace. The good thing about the Horseshoe Bar was that it was entirely populated with customers my age and older. I always sat on the very last seat at the far end of the horseshoe planted firmly against the wall. From this vantage point, I got to know Eamonn and Brendan and Denis. It was a little upmarket for a local but I could always join the chat in the Shelbourne.

With my new pub courage, I got up enough nerve to go back into O'Donoghue's where I had spent my crazy Sunday afternoon Holy Hour. There was always a buzz and plenty of music and loads of tourists so I was pretty sure I wasn't going to be the token older lady. In fairness, my brown Portuguese eyes did well in O'Donoghue's. My pub fear began to dissipate once I learned that to earn your status as a local all you really had to do was show up. That was the secret. Anyone's peculiarity wears off after numerous nights of whiskey and music. After work I began to take my mail, my post, into O'Donoghue's and sit in the back to write checks and read the paper. People just got used to seeing me, which met my objective. This also turned out to be one of Holy Hour Frank's Dublin locals, so we managed to run into each other on a somewhat irregular basis.

Even though Frank had the number from the coin phone in the flat, we hadn't been able to get together with any consistency. He worked construction so he started early and finished early. When the job was done, he would stay out as late as possible. If I ran into him in O'Donoghue's our activities would depend on the time of day that we met up. If it was early in the afternoon, we might get a pint and do the crossword in *The Irish Times*. He finished it, every time. On the weekend I might follow him to the betting shop to put some money on a horse. There was a rhythm to betting on the horses when we were in Dublin. We met in the pub and reviewed the notes of the race. Frank knew the jockeys and their history and he knew the skill of the horses on the turf. He checked the weather report and he would fold the rain or the mud into their speed and his statistics. After an in-depth analysis, we would cover our drinks with a beer mat, go next door to the betting office, fill out the tiny betting slip and place the bet. Then we would go back to the bar, watch the race on the telly and then go back to the betting office and collect the winnings. This could go on for hours. I was fascinated.

Frank was one of the smartest people that I had ever met. With Irish secondary education still not free, Frank was awarded a training scholarship and left Ireland, on his own, to complete his education in England. To support himself he got a job as the tea boy on a construction site. This lead to actual paid construction work and his education fell by the wayside. He seemed to have an artist's soul even though he tried to keep it hidden under a substantial head of Guinness. He wrote me poetry and taught me about The Troubles. He was political, informed, opinionated and he was huge. It was the first and only time in my dating career that I got to feel "petite."

Frank doted on his son and was always in contact with the mother of the child. All the time that I knew him, that is what he called her. In parts of Ireland, child and son are a set of concepts that are interchangeable. When a woman gave birth, people asked, "Did she have a boy or a one?" No need to spend a lot of time guessing the hierarchy there. "Boy" would definitely have more status than a "one." It didn't say much for us "ones."

I was beginning to have a pretty good time in my off hours due to my Horseshoe Bar contacts and my horse racing Frank. I think he may have been a bit of a hedonist but in the context of nighttime Dublin, I found it hard to tell. He certainly paid no attention to the rules and would give you "stick" if you tried to follow them. He often rang the flat late into the evening to ask me to come out for a drink. I usually declined. By that time of the evening he would have had plenty of drink on him and be ready for an intense debate if I said "No." There was really no discussion and I would have to just say "sorry" and hang up the phone. This happened more often when the weather was bad and the construction work was slow. Sometimes he would call the hospital and ask me to leave work so we could hang out at an "early bar." I managed to meet him once at Slattery's on Capel Street. I couldn't believe the number of people drinking there so early in the morning. Not just construction workers but solicitors and barristers and nurses from the night shift.

There was one afternoon when Frank rang me at the hospital to see if I could leave early so that we could have the afternoon in Dublin. He was in Swords, just down the road, and he would drive to St. Ita's and collect me. I changed my schedule and told Frank that I would meet him just down the avenue by the grove of trees on the right-hand side. Technically I was mitching from work and I wanted to avoid being seen. I managed to get out a side door and walk to the grove before Frank got up to the hospital roundabout. He drove a dilapidated old off-white Vauxhall so I knew I could spot him coming up the avenue and step out just in time. I got to the trees and I waited, stepping out just every so often to see if he was coming. I would have to move quickly. The passenger door was permanently stuck and couldn't be opened from the outside. I planned to wait for him to turn around so that it would be on my side and he could pop the door, grab my briefcase and let me in. I saw the Vauxhall coming up the road and stepped out slightly to see him. As he got closer I could tell that someone was in the car with him. Someone very, very large completely filled up the passenger side. Frank drove slowly, scanning the grove as he looked for me. The passenger window was rolled down and in my place, I recognized Raymond, my patient from St. Ita's. Frank didn't see me but Raymond did and as they passed by I could hear him wail, "Christeeeeen" as I quickly ducked back into the grove.

Chapter 6 - *You'll Never Walk Alone*

I was now working between several locations: Portrane; the health center clinics in Coolock and Swords, and two of North Dublin's national schools. When I worked in Coolock, it was in a health care center not far from The Northside Shopping Center. The bus dropped me off there and I would stop at the bakery and get a "flies graveyard" to eat for my break. This was some kind of pastry with mince filling; mince as in "mince pie", not "mince" which is another name for ground meat. At the clinic, there were two porters, a man and a woman. The porters minded the waiting room, answered the phone if needed and emptied the "bins" twice a day, like clockwork. This was one of those permanent and pensionable jobs that helped to sustain the service-based economy. There was also a receptionist who made appointments and answered the phones except when the clinic closed for lunch from one to two. There was no answering system and no way to leave a message. The phone would just ring and ring. When I asked Mary what people would do if they were desperate and needed to get in touch with someone at the clinic, I was told, "They'll call back." And just like the coin phone callers in No. 292, they did.

Working with the team in Coolock meant the treat of an occasional pub lunch. This was notable for the absence of Dessie in Portrane and his need for reassurance that he was still "fawrty two." We would go to The Goblet or the Sheaf of Wheat. There was always an extensive carvery in the pub; turkey or ham freshly sliced and half a dozen side

56

salads. The most popular and cost-effective lunch was soup and brown bread; more often than not the soup was potato leek. With my limited kitchen facilities in the bedsit, I would go for the complete meal although the choice of side salad was a different concept for me. The salads were always mushrooms in mayonnaise, potato salad, and pasta with mayonnaise, everything in mayonnaise. I asked Mary how everyone managed to drink Guinness, eat mayonnaise and still not gain weight. She suggested that there was an Irish gene that allowed for survival if only on a diet of stout and whipped egg whites.

In the hospital, I went to the dining hall but if I didn't see someone that I knew, I took my lunch back to my office in the Old Nurses' Home. I spent a good bit of time trying to shift that adjective. Many years ago, this part of the hospital was an extension built to provide living space for the nurses. Since that time a new home had been built so "The Old Nurses' Home" stuck. As far as I knew, all but one of the offices down the dark, dark hallway was empty. The only other occupied space was the first one, by the toilet. That was the base for the ambulance drivers when they weren't out collecting patients. I could hear their voices above the noise of the telly, but I never saw them as I walked down the long corridor.

People were starting to get used to seeing me and I managed to set up some alliances with two of the doctors and several of the teachers. All of these people were women and they all seemed to know the patients well and were concerned about their growth and their support. The teachers were a high-energy group and they based their curriculum on a Montessori approach. The only problem I had was that several of them were named after the Holy Mother, as was the case in all of Ireland at the time, but the variations on the name drove me demented. There were Marys, of course, then there were Maries and then there were Maries but pronounced "Mahry" and Moira and Maura and Maire and Mairead. This was not the case with all the Margarets, Catherines and Kathleens but there were plenty of those, as well.

Several of the women residents seemed to be in my age group. In most cases, they had been in Portrane, or in the health care system, for decades. I tried to imagine what it would have been like to be in St. Ita's as a 16-year-old who shamed the family with an unwanted pregnancy or was blocking the way of a family inheritance. My own brother labeled my adventures as "harebrained." What would have happened to me, thirty years ago as one of two children, single, with no parents and an unusually creative and wandering streak? Delving into some of the family histories would reveal various reasons for admittance to Portrane, and in lots of cases, the person who had admitted their family member was now dead. Except for only one of my patients, the people that I worked with had no advocate other than the nurses, the doctors, the teachers, and now, me.

My "American-ness" attracted attention on several levels. I was one of the very, very few women who wore makeup, and the patients, especially the women, were curious about the color on my face. The residents often had keener visual skills than auditory skills and they noticed lots of things that seemed unworthy of attention. In the Children's Unit, there was a new resident named Francie. Francie was a very young teenager with short, dark, ginger hair. He had a very slight build and was non-verbal. He communicated by screaming and waving his hands. He could often be found kneeling on the ground, banging his head violently onto the floor. The rumor was that he had been this way for all of his life. I sometimes wore a white shirt with various neckties when I went to work in the hospital. One tie in particular had a red, modern, abstract design and right in the middle were two obscure shapes that could be perceived as eyes. I was wearing this tie one afternoon when I went down to meet Francie in the ward. When I entered, Francie turned to see me but instead of making eye contact with me, he made eye contact with my tie. He walked up to it, not to me, and he leaned forward pressing his eyes against the tie and he stayed there, quietly attached to my chest.

Just around the same time that I met Francie, I received a call on my pager from a nurse named Deirdre. By now I had been working alone in the hospital for many weeks. Deirdre introduced herself and asked me if it was true, that I was actually a new member of the staff. I assured her that it was. Deirdre was one of three behavioral therapists who were also working in the hospital. They were a bit of a vanguard in that the three of them had started out as psychiatric nurses but had taken advanced coursework to expand their roles. They had moved into an office down the hallway and unknown to me had been working there for many months. No one had told them that I was there. No one had told me that they were there. So we created our own team of the three behavioral therapists, Deirdre, Nora, Nicola and me and they soon became a strong source of support. I shared my list of potential patients and between the three of them, they seemed to know all the patients and all the staff in the hospital. We agreed to start with Francie and we developed a plan to help him use sign language in an attempt to communicate.

Deirdre, Nicola and Nora had worked in Portrane for several years and were well informed as to the ethos of the hospital. I used them as my barometer for hospital behavior with regard to both the patients and the staff. They had experienced the attitude of the nurses who were understandably defensive toward the change of culture from a strictly psychiatric approach to one that included skills based in intellectual disability. I was never clear about the cause for this change in policy but my guess was that the intrusion of the European Union had something to do with it. I understood that the administration needed to demonstrate that there was staff support for those residents labeled, not identified, as learning disabled. But Aisling, the health care worker, sign language teacher and aromatherapist pushed me into reality. She sensed my frustration when I looked for support for some changes in the program. "You don't understand, Christine, they need you to be here," she said, "but they don't want you to do anything."

St. Ita's was the final stop for any patient in the country who couldn't function in any other facility. People came to Portrane with various and complicated diagnoses and they left just as erratically, at all hours of the day and night. We tried to explain to the administration that after years of living in the same dormitory or sleeping in the next bed, the residents had become attached to each other. Waking up in the morning and finding your roommate missing would be disconcerting to any person and patients should be forewarned about an ensuing change. These people had been together for years and years. Change was not part of their routine. While it wasn't discussed, it was assumed that same sex relationships had occurred over the years. I asked the staff about one woman who seemed to be very flirtatious with the other patients. I was concerned for her safety should her flirtations cause a reaction. I was told that there was no cause for concern. "She's a good girl. She doesn't think about sex."

One morning I responded to a referral by making a spontaneous visit to one of the wards. Because the nurses worked one day on and one day off I had to juggle my days to meet up with the nurse who had the information. On this day I managed to find him and get his attention for a few minutes in the ward. He was a very tall, muscular man and I remember that when we met I had to tilt my head and raise my chin in order to meet his gaze as we spoke. He had stopped in the middle of the ward to talk with me and several residents also stopped and formed a circle around us. As I began to speak with him about the referral, a resident named Vinnie moved quickly around the outside of the circle but stopped to stand behind me. I moved around the circle to another spot. He followed me. The nurse told me, with a smile, "Don't worry, he's harmless. He just likes to punch new people in the back." I was fairly certain that the nurse was just giving me "stick" but just in case I lifted my backpack over my shoulder keeping it between Vinnie and myself. It became a dance. I moved around the circle, Vinnie followed. Then the nurse volunteered that Vinnie was overly anxious because his ward partner of many years had vanished several nights ago in one of the hospital's post twilight transferring procedures. When I turned to face Vinnie, he stood still, staring at me. His body remained rigid as he slowly brought his hands up to his face. Then just as slowly he dragged his fingernails down his cheeks causing the blood to flow in rivulets down his face. As I watched him, my horror became obvious. The nurse looked down at me and said sardonically, "You seem to have a problem with blood." I tried to keep my voice calm as I assured him that blood didn't bother me but seeing it flow as the result of self-harming, did.

I walked back to The Old Nurses' Home and knocked on the office door of the behavioral therapists. Luckily they were all in. In a very stressed voice, I rattled off my story about the nurse and Vinnie. They looked from one to the other and then Deirdre said, "Sure, I don't know what to do with Vinnie. He's a difficult case. He pulls out your hair and then flosses his teeth with it."

Nora looked from me to her, a slight grin crossing her face. "Has he nice teeth?" she asked.

"Oh he does, he does indeed," Deirdre confirmed. I leaned heavily against the doorjamb. I admit that it was funny, but I closed the door and said nothing.

Chapter 7 - Wait til I Tell You

The male residents at Portrane maintained a look somewhere out of the nineteen fifties or sixties. I guess that might be due to the time that they were admitted to the hospital. The men always had a coat, usually a tie, often a hat and the occasional vest or waistcoat. They would have been called "dapper" in another incarnation. At first, I found it difficult to distinguish some of the patients from the staff or the visitors. This may be hard to believe, but Ireland is the Land of Chat and being relegated to Portrane didn't take away their ability to charm.

I got to know Archie while waiting for the bus to Swords. The bus stop was right in front of the hospital and Archie seemed to be on the same schedule as myself. He was a lovely soft-spoken man, very verbal and quite adept at flirting with the ladies. He was tall and thin, always appropriately dressed, his pragmatic skills were fine, his eye contact was good and he demonstrated suitable give and take in the conversation. As the speech therapist, he met the criteria for normalcy. Then one afternoon just as the bus was arriving, Archie suggested that we get married and asked if I would accept a ring. Only then did I realize that he wasn't someone's visiting uncle but was, in fact, a long-term resident. I managed to sidestep the proposal. I wasn't sure how a resident might react to being rejected for marriage.

Until then, I hadn't realized that many of the patients had the freedom to leave the hospital and take the bus into Swords. That was how Raymond ended up getting that lift with Frank. For a while, I managed to avoid Archie at the bus stop but then I ran into him in the accounting office chatting up the clerk. He leaned into me, tipped his hat and cocked his head to one side and asked, "So when would we be getting married, then?"

"I don't know, Archie," I said, "after all, where would we live?"

He leaned down just a bit further and said, as if it was the most logical of thoughts, "Why, in a mo-by-ul home in Rush." Archie had a plan.

I sometimes found the line between sane and not so sane to be quite blurred during my time in Ireland. There was a high tolerance for "peculiar" and that suited me just fine. Often, when the bus came down through O'Connell Street, the main street of Dublin, I saw a lovely older woman, dressed in white, with long, flowing silver hair, singing while moving rhythmically along the divider of the widest road in Ireland. She would sway down the verge, twirling, with her arms outstretched and waving smoothly through the air. When the bus made a stop I could hear her loudly singing something operatic. As she turned I was fascinated by the bright red lipstick that made her lips pop out of the all-white picture of her performance. When she moved through the crowd, no one noticed, looked or commented. They just moved out of her way and went on about their business. Then one day at Bewley's Cafe on Grafton Street, I found myself sitting next to her for coffee. She was there, chatting with a friend, red lipstick intact. Not a bother on her. Who would ever know the inspiration for her melodic, operatic, twilight songfest? To this day, I'm not the only one who remembers her swaying along the median of one of the widest streets of Europe. But it's not much of a muchness, as we say in Dublin. No harm, no foul.

In Portrane I was creating a caseload of clients that I hoped to help on some level although that was continuously changing. I met Delia whom I liked very much. She was in her late twenties and had been in Portrane for more than ten years. I found her to be quite "normal" in my limited Portrane experience. Unless people looked or behaved in a very drastic or severe fashion, and many of them did, I was never really sure of their diagnosis. I had learned from Deirdre that it didn't really matter. Everyone in Portrane had been institutionalized for at least ten years and some for as many as thirty or forty years. We were working with the results of their everyday living and not some label.

Delia became a favorite of mine and I set about trying to find a way to support her. When I was working in the hospital, she would find me and walk with me as I went to meet other patients. At times, she would fill me in on what she knew about them and she knew a lot about a lot of things. She was highly verbal, very opinionated and totally in sync with the day-to-day goings on in the hospital. She was a "sturdy" young woman who was susceptible to mood swings and she was well able to speak up for herself. As an outspoken young woman, her behavior was often an anathema to the mostly male nursing staff. She was not the quiet docile patient that met their comfort zone, she knew how to push their buttons but I got on with her very well. By her own admission, Delia had been subjected to electric shock therapy, years ago, in another hospital, when she was much younger. Since she was only 29 at the time, that was a frightening thought. She would wrap her arms around herself and re-enact the quivering feeling of the time. I had been cautioned not to take the residents too seriously when they shared this type of information but I am hard pressed to think that Delia created this scenario. The more I got to know her, the more I realized that she was past due for finding a good listener and the chance to vent her life stories.

Delia became my right-hand woman and the self-appointed assistant to the speech therapy department. When we walked into a ward, the nurses would look at her suspiciously but she would point at me and say, "I'm with her." She was high energy and highly emotional and to be honest, I drove her crazy. If I was in a particularly jovial mood, my loud laugh would do her head in. She tried to shame me into not laughing but it never worked. "I'm in a good mood," I would say. "Can't you stand it?"

"Well, I'm here," she said, "I've not got much of a choice, have I?" Delia had this very direct way of talking and walking and these two skills seemed to work in a mutual motor pattern. She bounced up and down when she walked and talked. I suggested to her that we could go farther and faster if we spent less time going up and down and more time going forward. Then I bounced in rhythm with her. "You're mad, Chris," she said to me.

"Then I'm in the right place," I told her.

One afternoon we made our way down to the Children's Unit so that I could meet Hugo who had recently been admitted to Portrane from a long-term placement at Madonna House. He had just turned 21 and he was physically too big to be lifted by their staff. St. Ita's was his last and only option. Hugo had cerebral palsy, spina bifida, a severe learning disability and God knows what else. His body was bent and twisted, his eyes did not appear to focus and his hands and fingers were extended, spastic and stiff. But somehow, when I met Hugo, even though I don't think he could see well, I could tell that he responded to sounds and voices. His hearing appeared to be very acute. He laughed all the time especially when he heard me laughing. I didn't like seeing him tucked away down in the Children's Unit but I couldn't explore other options without an updated personal file. I felt that people might be reacting to Hugo's appearance and possibly overlooking skills that were present for learning, If I wanted to explore other possibilities for Hugo, then he would have to be tested but no one seemed to know how to get that started.

In Portrane, this request for testing was unusual given that at the time St. Ita's was the last stop for the residents. Even if some potential was revealed, not a lot would change. Fortunately, the newness of my placement and its accompanying total ignorance made me oblivious to this fact and I went ahead with my request. I had to fill out loads of forms and write a very detailed report on what I thought were Hugo's strengths and weaknesses. If accepted, a psychologist would be sent to test him.

Whenever the weather was nice the nurses would take the residents from the Children's Unit out to sit on the huge lawn that paralleled the hospital buildings and divided it from this amazing beach. The isthmus of Portrane meant that it backed up against a most beautiful body of water with a wide berth of white, white sand. We would spread blankets on the ground and free Hugo from his wheelchair, leaving him to roll on the blanket and get some sun. The other residents were engaged in some kind of sport or they roamed the grassy area under the watchful eyes of the nurses. I began to create Hugo's file here. I pitched a lawn chair at the end of the blanket with Hugo at my feet and began with the required interview even though he couldn't answer. It was a formality but he seemed to enjoy the attention. I was wearing a skirt and boots at the time and Hugo was rolling back and forth with his head tilted back. I accused him of trying to look up my skirt and I moved the chair slightly away from the blanket. The teasing made him laugh, he thought that was hilarious. I began to write again when I heard Marie yelling from across the grass. "Mind yourself, Chris!" I looked over at her but I didn't really understand what she was saying. She said it again, only louder, "MIND YOURSELF, CHRIS!" And just then someone came up from behind me and began to slowly wrap their thickly mitted fingers around my throat. I jumped straight out of the lawn chair and over Hugo. I wasn't harmed but I did ask the nursing staff to be more direct in the future; I requested "Run for your life, Chris" rather than the more benign Irish expression of "Mind yourself." Unfortunately, this wouldn't be the only time that a patient decided that they had heard enough of my American accent, loud laugh or both.

Little by little, we were all getting used to each other. The male nurses began to tolerate me and I started to develop some really nice working relationships with the teachers and the behavioral therapists. The patients got used to me as well and they would actually participate in the incremental conversations that I socially forced upon them. Several of the female residents sought me out just because I was new, spoke differently and wore eyeliner. I met Kitty who was the fashion plate of the hospital. She was bright eyed and feisty, with shocks of white blondie hair, cut stylishly short and she was totally tuned in to whatever styles were in at the time. Kitty had grown up in a tough part of Dublin called Dolphin's Barn. She had been diagnosed as deaf with a secondary diagnosis of epilepsy. Dublin in the nineteen sixties was a difficult time for people with disabilities such as Kitty's. To this day I believe there may not have been anything severely intellectually wrong with Kitty, but her deaf speech combined with her ongoing seizures could certainly give the impression of "craziness." She could speak, so she must have had some language at an early age. But by now, she had all the effect of someone considered "slow." Anyone hearing her speak and witnessing a grand mal seizure would not have been able to offer Kitty many options. She was very, very social and would always introduce herself using her complete name. She would never just say "I'm Kitty" but would always say "I'm Kitty O'Doherty." But due to her deafness, it became "I hiity o dah ty." In the beginning, she said it every time I saw her.

Kitty was one of the first residents to move to a halfway house on the grounds of the hospital. She thrived there with her own room and the freedom to move around the grounds. She also had a job in the house that gave her a sense of purpose. The nurses didn't seem to have too much time for Kitty, she was fairly self-reliant and not in need of much assistance. That was difficult for me because she was one of my favorite clients and I felt there was some potential for improving her skills. Not long after meeting Kitty, a nurse who worked with her agreed to meet with me and give me some background on Kitty's disability. We met in the library of the Nurses' Home The nurse was quick to tell me how Kitty had destroyed this very library one weekday afternoon. Shaking her head, she was at odds to explain what had set Kitty off, given that she had been a model patient on the trip they had just taken to Paris. It was hospital policy to occasionally take the residents on trips. They received a stipend each week and this was put aside for them for such an occasion. They usually went to Lourdes or Medjugorje, it was Catholic Ireland after all, but this time it was France for the lucky few who could handle themselves on such an adventure. The nurse went on to say how much Kitty had loved Paris. She went on the Metro, shopped at the Galleria and tried all the food. Not two days after being back, Kitty destroyed the library. The nurse could not understand it. And I couldn't understand her.

I asked the nurse to imagine living in St. Ita's for the past 25 years, all the while loving music and dance and fashion, and then, someone takes you to out of Portrane and over to France. For the first time, you visit Paris! You see it, feel it, experience it. You can't know how long it will last but you want it to last forever. And then, with no understanding of time or distance, you are whisked back here, to a dark, dreary island, to a hospital on an isthmus by the cold dark sea. I asked her, "Wouldn't you want to tear up the library?"

In fairness, she thought for a moment and then she looked at me, "You know," she said, "I believe I would." Tearing up the library was one of the sanest things that I had heard so far during my time in St. Ita's. I decided to make a plan for Kitty.

While Kitty and Delia kept me aware of the more unofficial things going on in St. Ita's, I got most of my up to date information from Annie. Annie was short with long dark hair that she tied back in a ponytail. She often wore red plastic-rimmed sunglasses. She always wore loads of clothing no matter what the weather. She always wore a coat over her jacket with a scarf, or maybe two wrapped loosely around her throat. There was costume jewelry and plastic jewelry on every part of her body; she still wore pop-beads around her wrists and she always carried a handbag. I would guess Annie to be about fifty, but to be fair, I could never really suss the age of anyone in the hospital. If I asked the staff, the residents always turned out to be much older than I suspected. The staff tried to convince me that this was due to a life with no stress. Then one day I heard Mia Farrow interviewed on RTE. She was in Dublin to promote a film and the interviewer was praising her appearance saying that she never seemed to grow older. "Didn't you know," she said to the interviewer, "crazy people never show their age." That became my standard as well as my aspiration.

Annie was always in the entrance vestibule when I got to work in the morning. If something had happened the day or the night before, she would repeatedly tap me on the arm and get me to look at her while she acted it out. This was always in front of the clerks at reception so they could fill me in if I didn't completely get the message. Annie didn't speak and I was told that she couldn't hear. I was never really sure how that diagnosis was established because she seemed pretty connected to me. Or as Delia pointed out, "Chris, if they think she can't hear then why does she always walk around with a transistor radio against her ear?" Delia had a point about the hearing but speaking was another matter. In the past, Annie had done a lot of self-harming. She most definitely had inserted many sharp objects into her body and she would show you the protrusion of the needles and pins that extended around the area of her larynx. I never heard her vocalize a sound but she could certainly get her message across. Annie became the mainstay for filling me in on the many things that happened in the hospital. I was developing my own St. Ita's network and it was beginning to intrigue me with its possibilities.

The weather had turned fine so Frank went back to work. I hadn't realized that the construction site had been closed for a holiday and that was why he was around Dublin so often. It had been great fun following him around the pubs, the betting office and the late night chippers. I got to know Dublin under his tutelage. When he went back to work he sent me a note at Haddington Road calling it "Hiways & Byways." It read:

"Hello, Chris. Well, as my holidays are finally drawing to an end, I never thought I could travel so little and have such a wonderful lovely time. I just hope life will continue for us like a soft breeze, gently blowing across meadows of purple flowers gathering little speed and ceasing where we rest. Let it last forever! Love, Frank"

Ireland is all about the chat! I went to the clinic in Coolock to tell Mary that I wanted to extend my six-month commitment. She was delighted to have me keep this post that no one else would take and had been empty for so long. I told her that I was willing to stay and just see what happens. "Of course you are," she said, "because you think you're living in a movie script." And she wasn't far from wrong.

Chapter 8 - On Yer Bike

After my ominous first day of work at St. Ita's, Mary met me for a debriefing once a week in Coolock. She did not want me spending too much time on my own without being able to "unload" the intense feelings that accumulated from days and days of dealing with patients and trying to work with an unyielding administration. She was a caring listener. She knew the system so well that she could put my observations into perspective and keep me from overreacting. It was a wise move and it saved my sanity over the years that I worked there. I told her everything up to and beyond St. Ita's. She was my barometer for social behavior and Irish men. Eamonn, one of the friends that I had met in the Horseshoe Bar, was going to Cork for a business trip and invited me for the weekend. He assured me that I would have my own room and we would meet up for meals. I asked Mary if this was feasible. In California, it would be naïve to think that the invitation was sincere. She was as shocked as I was doubtful and then she was emphatic, "If he said that there would be separate rooms then he will honor that commitment." I went and he did.

For months and months, Eamonn and I roamed around the city. I accompanied him to business dinners that were often in the best Dublin restaurants. I met loads of people through him, many of them associated with academic programs sponsored by the European Union. The EU was engulfed in a richly positive business environment at the time and people from many countries were meeting up in Dublin to propose ideas for the future. Eamonn was instrumental in facilitating a lot of these meetings and I was delighted to be included. It was fascinating to meet with scientists from Switzerland and foresters from Norway.

Then one Thursday night we were to meet for dinner and I was delayed and thought I would be late. I didn't have a number for Eamonn so I began to go through the Golden Pages to find him. I had an idea of his address and was able to match that to the number that was listed. But I didn't call. Next to his number was his name and next to that was a woman's name. It looked suspicious. I managed to get to Haddington Road in time to meet him and off we went to dinner and a business meeting. After the dinner, Eamonn drove me home to No. 292. Before I got out of the car, I asked him if I had located the right phone number for him and if so, who was the woman listed at his address? His answer showed him to be the consummate grown-up. "C'mon, Chris," he said. "You knew I was married." I was gobsmacked. It never occurred to me that he was married. Never. How could he be so available? It was my first introduction to No Divorce Ireland and the various types of relationships that men and women would devise to live in marriages that were no longer viable. Evidently, as long as the sin of divorce was avoided, other life choices were deemed acceptable. In addition to sin, finances also played a big part in determining a couple's change of lifestyle. The exorbitant property prices that were to come with the Celtic Tiger had yet to hit Dublin. So leaving or selling the family home was seldom a good financial choice. Besides, if you left the family home and set up accommodation on your own, that could be seen as abandoning the property and your financial interest might be forfeited. This caused many couples to stay together exacerbating an already fractious relationship. I briefly dated a barrister who did let me know that he was married but separated. Neither he nor his wife would leave the family home so they decided to divide it, and they did, by building a wall directly down the center of the two-story attached house. They were, literally, separated. Even the leader of the country, the Taóiseach (TEE shock) Bertie Ahern, was separated and living with his partner, Celia Larkin. She attended most political and social events; her name was embossed in gold on the government invitations. Her presence invoked the widespread use of the term "partner" and this title was picked up and used by all couples living together without the benefit of marriage. "Partner" eventually overtook the labels of "husband" and "wife" throughout the country. It became so common that when a gay friend of mine visited from San Francisco this constant reference to the term "partner" overwhelmed him with what he viewed as an amazingly liberal Irish attitude toward homosexuality. He even thought that the Taóiseach was gay.

I learned to rethink my attitude toward marriage in my newly adopted country. Obviously things were done differently here and not just because of the fear of sin. Divorce was prohibited by the Irish constitution. That was the law. A referendum to change the constitution and allow divorce was scheduled for November 1995. I had already registered to vote. Until then, I would say nothing.

One Friday in April, Mary rang me in Portrane to tell me to take an early bus home. She advised me to get to Dublin before the buses stopped running I assumed a strike, but no, it was football. Ireland was playing in the World Cup. I didn't get the connection but I let her know that I didn't follow football and I wouldn't mind staying at work and missing the match. She assured me that if I didn't get to Dublin before the kick off, I would be stranded in Portrane on a Friday afternoon. Not only would the buses stop, but the trains and the taxis as well. I thought she was mad but I learned never to question Mary. I got the bus into town just as the match was starting and she was right, the buses stopped, all of them. Wherever. Instead of going across the river, my bus parked on

O'Connell Street and I followed the crowd into the Gresham Hotel. The only available seat was on the floor where I found a space and sat there, mesmerized by my first exposure to The World Cup.

In Ireland, sport is massive. Throughout the country, Gaelic football and hurling are supported and encouraged by the GAA, the Gaelic Athletic Association. The GAA is one well-oiled machine and it creates and supports these two sports from birth to death across the country. Girls play too and a good camogie player is also highly respected. No matter where you go in Ireland, even in the smallest of villages, you will see a pitch for the GAA. But football (soccer) is English, and even though most Irish sport lovers would support a soccer team, the GAA is sacred. In the World Cup, it's country against country. So the pretense of a dislike for the English sport is disregarded every four years. I learned about the GAA from my time spent living in the bed and breakfast in Drumcondra. I had nothing to do and no one to talk to when I first arrived, so on Sundays, I would cross the road and go to the matches in Croke Park. Sometimes it was Gaelic football and sometimes it was hurling. I watched for a while, totally confused, and then I'd scout a group of older men and sidle up next to them. They usually pretended that I wasn't there but my curiosity was stronger than my fear of rejection. As the match went on I asked them about the rule or the penalty or why someone received a yellow card. I could tell when I was testing their patience so I learned to get my answers before they were totally exasperated. Over the weeks that I was stuck all alone in Drumcondra, I learned the basics of the GAA and the seriousness of sport in Ireland.

Ireland didn't make it through that World Cup but the exciting atmosphere in Dublin lasted for the many weeks of the event. For me, it became a lesson in geography and I decided that it was football, not politics, that linked countries together, with the exception of the United States. Even the roughest of football supporters knew the locations of the smallest of countries. In addition to football, the Catholic missionary system also linked Ireland to the rest of the world. In Portrane, Doctor Mary chastised me for not knowing the countries of Africa. She not only criticized me but my entire nationality as well. She put "me back in my box" with her accurate assumption that I was ill-informed, but then I realized that Irish families still "donated" a child to the Catholic cause and they often ended up working in some far away country in Africa. Cards and packages sent to previously unknown places helped to support the Irish who in turn supported the people in the various countries of Africa. In my own Irish American family, my uncle, the first-born son, as well as my father, had been assigned to the priesthood so I understood the concept. I passed on the Catholic approach and opted for the World Cup attitude to worldwide learning, as soon as someone could explain the concept of "off sides."

The World Cup wasn't the only big event to hit Dublin that April. Ireland was the host for the Eurovision Song Contest. An Irish American friend and I decided on that particular Saturday night we would go on the "tear." This meant an unapologetic-purposely-alcohol-fueled night on the town. We hit the ATM and began walking to Baggot Street. We were ready to party. Laughing hilariously, we walked into the pub and stopped. It was packed but dead quiet, so we got quiet too. Everyone seemed to be looking straight at us as we walked in the door but then we realized that they were focusing on the telly up on the wall, directly over our heads. We slinked to the bar and ordered drinks. When we could get the barman's attention for a few minutes, we asked him what was going on. "Eurovision," he told us. We still didn't get it. "Each year," he said, "All the countries submit an original song and perform it for the Eurovision members. Then we vote on the best song." We stared at him.

"That's it?" my friend asked. "A song? Everyone in the pub is listening to songs? And in languages that you can't understand?" We had obviously missed the point while irritating the barman. He walked away, leaving us to deal with our ignorance of musical things European. We asked around and found out that Ireland had won the Eurovision Song Contest for the last two years and had a good chance to win it again. It was the lyrical equivalent of the World Cup and carried with it a huge amount of national pride. Winning the competition could create a new hit song and make international stars of the performers. Think ABBA. We could hardly go on the tear when the entire pub was fixated on listening to songs from Cyprus, Iceland and Lithuania. That night Ireland won for the third year in a row and introduced the world to Riverdance. By then we had found a pub without a telly, resumed our night out and missed the whole thing.

The possibility of getting stuck in Portrane for the World Cup began to fester in my mind and I started to think of buying a car. Now that I had committed to Mary for a longer stay I knew I couldn't depend on my bus to train to bus to ambulance commute. In Ireland, at that time, most everyone drove older cars in various forms of disrepair. I started to look around for a used motor, as cars were called, regressing with other common expressions as "Let's go to the pictures" and "I heard it on the wireless," still used around Dublin. The movie script that was playing in my head and so aptly identified by Mary, was circa 1943.

Cars were expensive and there was no shame in driving a "banger." In fairness, when you saw someone driving a car with a brand new registration, you could often hear the driver quietly referred to as an eejit. Spending money on a new car was seen to be more foolish than enviable. It was a great attitude coming from status conscious LA. I only knew that I didn't want a red car or a car with a hatchback. I ended up with a Volkswagen Golf, red, with a hatchback and I loved it.

My California driver's license got me a "temporary" Irish license that I used for the next 10 years. Insurance was pricey but cheaper if you were married or had a partner. I was all over the place in that car. Down to Cork and out to Kerry. One Saturday I gave Frank a lift home to Donegal. The Peace Process was on at the time but Frank, a staunch supporter of the Republican cause, still insisted that we drive the long way, bypassing any possible Unionist lookouts. He took me all the way from Dublin to Donegal through nothing but backcountry roads. Along the way, he showed me the many tall outposts that would have housed the armed sentries of the British Army. They were there still, high platforms overlooking the road and surrounded by barbed wire. He knew all the locations.

We drove to Rossnowlagh where there was a beach that was so long and so wide that I drove the Golf out onto the sand and along the sea for a twilight tour. Then we stopped in Donegal Town and had a drink in a house with a pub cum sitting room before going to dance in a cowboy bar. Donegal is a one-off for quirkiness and beauty.

I loved having the car and not having to depend on public transport. I could get from Haddington Road to St. Ita's in half an hour. That was a huge improvement. I set about looking for someone to take care of the maintenance of the car and a garage in Lissenhall was recommended to me. I knew the area. My friend Una was a training manager in the center in Lissenhall that was just south of Portrane, down the motorway toward Swords. Several of my patients from Portrane would go to her during the week for work, filling envelopes or assembling items for small companies in the area. Supposedly there was a good mechanic directly behind the training center, housed in the row of mostly empty buildings. One day while working at Lissenhall, I located the shop and found the mechanic. He turned out to be one of the nurses from Portrane who just happened to be very good with cars. The garage was open every other day, whenever the nurse wasn't working at St. Ita's.

He took care of all the nurses' cars and, just like Nolan who washed the nurses' windows, he controlled the entire niche market. All the nurses went to him as they could easily schedule their car repairs on their every other day work schedule and he was canny enough not to risk looking for business outside of Portrane. He had set up the garage years ago by "squatting" and he knew well enough to keep the business among colleagues. I was flattered that I was now included in the Portrane ring and trusted enough to do business with a wink and a nod.

One morning on my way to the clinic in Swords, I found a note on the windscreen of the Golf. It was written, in pencil, on a piece of notepaper and said, "For information regarding the damage to this car, ring the Gardai." It included a name and a phone number. Sitting on the bonnet next to the note was my side mirror. I put the mirror in the car and headed off to work. At the clinic, I rang the guards and spoke to the officer. He asked me to come into the station, now, to talk about the damage. I explained that I was working so he asked me to come in later that evening. After work, I left the Golf at No. 292 and walked down the road to the station. I was taken to an office where the guard explained that other cars on the street were also damaged and they were in the process of finding the perpetrator. He asked me to get an estimate to repair the mirror.

Two days later I was at home, ill, when the doorbell rang at No. 292. Because of my subterranean view of the car park, I didn't have to go to the door. Instead, I went to the window and pulled the curtain to the side. Parked at the side of the road was a police car with an officer waiting at the wheel, and out front was another officer, waiting at the door. I cranked open the side window and stuck out my head, "Can I help you?" The guard greeted me and then reminded me that we had met two days earlier about the damage to my car. He wondered if I had the estimate? If so, he would collect if from me now. As it was the middle of the day, I let him know that I was home ill and hadn't had time to get to the repair bid but I would let him know as soon as I had the paperwork. He got into the car and they drove away. I couldn't believe that there was enough time in the day to drive a police car to my bedsit with two officers just to collect a piece of paper that wasn't even available. When I did get the estimate, £140, I dropped it off at the local station.

A week later I received a telephone call on the coin phone at the flat. It was 10:30 at night and the officer said that he had my money and asked if I could come down to the station.

"Now?" I asked.

"Too late?" he asked.

"Yes," I said. "I'm ready for bed."

He suggested that I come the following night, around 7:30. After work I parked the Golf and walked down to the station as before. I checked in at the desk and an officer took me into the station and down a long narrow corridor that turned sharply to the right. Then we entered a very small room that to me looked like it might be used for interrogation. I was told to sit in a hard, grey, metal chair and the guard stood behind the grey, metal desk. He explained that "we think we know who did the damage" and then he reached into his pocket and pulled out an enormous wad of money. He slowly peeled off £140 and put the money on the table. I looked at him. "You *think* you know who did it?" He smiled, leaned forward and pushed the money toward me. "Should I sign something?" But he just pushed the money closer and then stood up straight. So I stood up, too, took the money, and said nothing.

Chapter 9 - God Loves a Tryer!

At St. Ita's the little red Golf quickly became identifiable by the residents who worked with me. Once they saw the car parked out by the front door, they would meet me there or come looking for me, Kevin for cigarettes, Delia for gossip. Kitty might try to persuade me to go back with her to look at a new hat or scarf. But Annie was always there to give me the latest news. She would wait for me by the reception counter under the large skylight that even in summer barely eked out enough light to brighten the ancient archway and illuminate the creaky steps to the upstairs toilet. This was the guest area of St. Ita's. Visitors were meant to be greeted by the clerks in reception and then sign in as guests. Across the wide hall, to the right of reception and just under the archway was the visitor's toilet. There were four short steps that led you directly to a door that opened inward. Only once did I attempt to use this toilet but upon opening the door found it to be dark and discolored. It was difficult to tell if it needed a good cleaning or was just a victim of decades of wear and tear. The floor, the sink, the toilet and the walls were all various shades of brown, which didn't help in the perception of its tidiness. In desperation I used it once, paying close attention to the sign on the wall that read, "Please leave the toilet as you found it."

On this particular Friday morning, Annie met me in front at reception and held onto my arm to get my attention. When she was sure that she had it, she brought her other hand out of her pocket. Curling her three fingers under and extending her index finger at a right angle to her thumb she created the shape of a gun and began to fire it all around the foyer. I looked toward reception to see if anyone was watching, I needed help to fill in the blanks of this pantomime. "Wait, wait," I said as I folded my hand around her extended digit and lowered it down to her side. I held on to her and slowly shuffled her with me toward The Switch who, as usual, was watching everything from behind the counter. Even though she never spoke Annie was well able to communicate all the goings on at Portrane, but guns? I had my doubts. "What is she saying? Is it true?" I asked. Annie stared at him dutifully waiting for his corroboration.

"Is what true?" Ken, the clerk at the switch, asked me back. I took a deep breath once again seeking an immediate straight answer.

"It looks like Annie is saying that someone in the hospital had a gun. Is it true?" Annie was still letting me keep her in my grasp. She appeared to be chuffed that she had spilled a hospital secret and had me as a willing audience. Ken shrugged and explained, "The hospital always pays out on a Friday so a lot of cash comes into the office on Thursdays. Every once in a while we get robbed." When asked why the location or the date wasn't changed to avoid this, he shrugged again and went back to the switch. Annie had been intently watching him and she certainly appeared to be listening because when he finished speaking, she clasped her open hand to her chest, proclaiming that she had been right. A big grin spread across her face as we walked away. Annie, of course, was silent and so was I. We both said nothing and after that, I never doubted Annie again.

The behavioral therapists, Deirdre, Nora and Nicola and I set about putting some therapy plans into place. The original Pat was assigned to help our group but he seemed mildly suspicious of our teaming. I assume that's why the four of us co-existed for three months without being told of each other's existence. I never understood why but it seemed to have something to do with the hierarchy of the nursing staff. Everyone in the higher offices of hospital administration had been a nurse at some point, they were all men, and there was some hidden fear of the rest of us getting together and starting something. But we did it anyway. We began with Francie, who was the youngest resident in the ward. It seemed simple but the task that we set for Francie was to teach him and the nursing staff to use the LAMH sign to signal the need for the toilet. We felt it would be best to start with something that would not only benefit Francie but would save time for the nursing staff and gain their cooperation. It sounded like a basic simple task, but in fact, we were trying to toilet train a sixteen-year-old. Common sense might tell you that if it could have been done it would have been done long ago but once again, "God loves a tryer." If Francie could get to the bathroom in time, it meant less nursing time devoted to his hygiene, freeing up more time for the nurses and their other duties. In this way, we could justify the imposition of our plan to the nursing staff and their schedules. We had to teach everything at least twice due to the day on/day off timing of the nurses so we doubled up on training time. The staff agreed to participate and we set about using the sign and placing pictures of the sign around the bathrooms in the ward. The remit of the behavioral therapists was to address the challenging behavior of the residents but we expanded it to address the issues of self-harming and the assimilation of typical developmental behaviors. If we could reduce Francie's stress and keep him comfortable our hope was that we could then add signs, grow his communication skills and accomplish the long-term goal of stopping the continuous banging of his head on the hospital floor.

Even though he was twenty-one, Hugo was also down in the Children's Unit. I had received approval for his testing and was now waiting for a psychologist to be sent from the health board. I had high hopes for getting him some extra help. When Hugo was down in the Children's Unit he was often out of his wheelchair, propelling himself along the hallways. The nursing staff had set him up with something like an elongated skateboard and placed him on the ground with the skateboard under his tummy. Hugo could push off with his toes and glide along the floor. He had some use of his hands and arms helping him to maneuver through the corridors. The Children's Unit was a maze of hallways with a lunchroom at one end and living quarters sprouting off in various directions. I would often be down there with Delia or Deirdre and something they said would make me laugh. The loud laugh that Delia kept asking me to squelch became an auditory beacon for Hugo. Wherever he was in the unit, Hugo could find me, his hearing was that good. I would no sooner laugh than I would hear Hugo coming around the corner. But it wasn't the skateboard that I could hear, it was Hugo calling my name. Not "Chris," that was too much of a challenge, but "Hsssssss, Hsssssss," would greet me as he slid across the floor and over to my feet.

I made the rounds of the other wards to follow up on referrals but by now, no matter where I stopped, the residents would be up for the chat. A new face in the crowd made them exceedingly curious. In the knitting therapy, there was Ruthie who always seemed to be happy to see me. The nurse called her "self-absorbed" and cautioned me that she would be jealous if I walked out of the room and spoke to someone else. I had to concern myself with causing *her* behavior to become disruptive if *my* behavior wasn't as she expected. Tara was in Fidelma Finn's Therapy. She consistently wore a plaster (a Band-Aid) but it moved to various parts of her body. And I met Majella who always made a comment when she saw me. She spoke in short, abbreviated sentences and would come with questions like, "What are you doing here?" or "Where did you get that?" Her responses were mostly mumbles and grunts if she bothered to respond at all. She was an interesting woman with large dark eyes and short, jaggedly cut black hair with fringe that reached down to her lashes. She walked hunched over with her head down but she didn't seem to miss much. She sometimes got a look in her eye that I couldn't decipher. Whenever she saw me she would take my right wrist and lift my hand up to be level with her face, look me in the eye and lick my palm. The first time she did it I stood transfixed. I looked around for guidance but the nurses just shrugged their shoulders. Whenever these instances happened to me, and there were loads of them, I said nothing. These were people with challenging behavior and I simply didn't have the experience to deal with what might come next. So if it seemed harmless, I would wait it out and then go and wash my hands. In all aspects of my new Irish life, in the pub or in Portrane, I walked a fine line of never really knowing what to do. And Raymond was still around, of course, but he was now used to seeing me in a sweet, predatory sort of way. Whenever he walked past me, he would pet me, like a dog, on the top of my head. Where's the harm in that?

I was becoming accustomed to the residents and their individual behaviors and I was getting better at recognizing what might set them off. When visiting the ward with the more challenging residents, the ring of pronged keys that I had received on my first day was always in my hand. I had become accustomed to the rhythm of quickly unlocking the door, getting into the ward, and turning, just as quickly, to lock the door behind me. It was a rhythm that was soon to become natural as well as functional.

The teachers had come to me with a plan for Kitty. Once a month they organized a day of horseback riding north of the hospital at New-bridge House. The residents could use their stipend to help pay for the day out just as they did for the trips to Lourdes or Paris. Newbridge House had the advantage of also having a tearoom so everyone would go for tea at the end of the day where acceptable behavior in public was practiced. The long-term goal for some of the residents of Portrane was a placement out in the community and these activities were part of their social training. For Kitty, the nurses wondered if developing some signs might assist them in communicating the riding instructions. This meant that I had to go horseback riding too so that I would know the vocabulary needed for the instruction. Fortunately, it was a beautiful day in Dublin and we filled up the minivan with four nurses, six residents and me. I sat in the middle next to Kitty and since the seats were taken, Majella sat next to me on the floor. The residents were smoking but Majella had a habit of putting the warm ashes in her mouth causing her to gag. As we were getting into the van she had a coughing fit and Sheelagh, one of the teachers, scolded her with the warning that she wouldn't be allowed on the trip if she acted up. Majella agreed but just as we started off she had a spasm. Sheelagh grabbed a plastic bag and reaching from the front seat to the back, held the bag in front of Majella who spit out the ashes and the tobacco. Handing it back to Sheelagh, Majella slumped down onto the floor and nudged herself into a tiny space, in-between the cushions and the door of the van.

From my seat in the back, I began to tell the nurses about my first day at work and the Malahide railway masturbator. Marie turned around from the front seat to hear my story. She listened attentively and then asked me to describe him and I did. Before I could finish she interrupted me by accurately filling in the blanks. She knew his look, the color of his hair and how he dressed. It had to be the same person. Supposedly he had also harassed her on the train by following her to the toilet and peeking at her through an opening in the door. I couldn't believe it. According to Marie, he was "known" to the guards. In the Irish vernacular, this meant he had a police record of some sort. He hadn't been stopped, obviously, as he seemed to be in the process of polishing his routine. The train was his preferred venue. My skin had gotten much thicker by now and while I was astonished that she knew him, I also found it to be amusing in an ironic sort of way. I was mid-laugh when

Marie, still watching me from the front seat yelled that now-known-ominous-phrase-of warning, "Mind yourself, Chris, mind yourself." I quickly looked to my left where I saw Majella standing up in the van and coming at me, her hands outstretched, reaching for my throat. Kitty got into the fray and managed to keep her from grabbing me while, at the same time, Marie stretched from the front of the seat of the van, grabbing her and getting her to sit back down. I was disappointed having believed that Majella and I had been friends. I was still naïve on so many levels that I had to let my asylum learning curve continue. After that day, Majella never licked my palm again.

We finally made it to the horseback-riding arena and Kitty did exceptionally well. She displayed a completely natural sense of rhythm and managed to easily get herself around the inside arena. She seemed to get a good bit of information from watching the teaching demonstrations and off she would go. I sometimes thought that the staff reacted to her more in terms of her perceived intellectual disability rather than her obvious hearing loss. She continuously picked up information from her surroundings, a good demonstration of her ability. I didn't think she needed any signs for horseback riding. She was a natural. This may have been linked somehow to her love of music and dancing. Evidently she was quite the performer when the opportunity came around.

Kitty and I had spent some time together and by now she had started to vocalize. In the tearoom at Newbridge House, she ordered a "cup of tea" and I heard her say "nice" when asked if she liked it. I commented on this to Sheelagh who told me that Kitty had begun to vocalize immediately after our first one to one therapy session. She had also heard her say, "Well done," and in the kitchen, she had asked Joanne for "food." These were very small steps, but just like Hugo, I was seeing some response to something I was doing, even if it was just a friendly interaction. I was happy enough with that but Joanne commented that she thought my relationship with Kitty was questionable. She'd seen

Kitty touching me and hinted that she might have lesbian tendencies. I was reminded of the other comments about a female resident, "She's a good girl, she doesn't think about sex" and I wondered how Kitty had missed getting this stereotypical label. I was unconcerned about Kitty and her sexual orientation. It seemed like just another sign of normalcy to me, like tearing up the library. I asked Joanne if she thought that Kitty would throw me to the floor and "have her way with me?" I meant it as a joke but she actually gave it some thought before saying, "No, I doubt it." In this instance, it was best to say nothing.

Now, when I leave St. Ita's, I have a cadre of well-wishers. On a Friday I say, "Have a nice weekend" and the nurses reply, "Touch wood, please God." I feel a certain amount of spiritual pressure from this comment as in if I don't have a good weekend does that make me a bad person in the eyes of God? I loaded my therapy materials into the Golf and I could see Kitty from across the yard. I waved goodbye to her and she blew me a kiss. I drove down the avenue while keeping a keen eye on the grove. The hospital manager warned me that a patient had taken up residence there and was pitching stones at passing cars. I circled the roundabout at the top of the avenue and headed down toward the main road. I managed to avoid a cracked windscreen but I couldn't avoid Dessie, still "fawrty two," whose tall puffy form seemed to mag-ically appear from behind the row of trees. I slowed down to wave goodbye but instead of waving his hand he reached into his trousers and waved his penis. By now I was a veteran of Portrane genitalia. I drove on toward Dublin and the pub, Dessie could wait until Monday.

Chapter 10 - That's Gonna Leave a Mark

I squelched the image of the exposed Dessie emerging from the forest and motored on toward town. There was just enough time to miss the traffic and stop in Swords to do the messages (errands). Swords is a bedroom community of Dublin, just north of the city and south of Portrane. It could be labeled as an Irish suburb. People there had detached houses and children and jobs in town. It was different enough from being in Dublin and way too settled to appeal to me. Frank had a house there that he had built on a little piece of land. I never saw it but his long-term goal was that it would end up as a great investment when Dublin began to prosper and spread north.

I found a parking place and went into the local butcher shop for mince. The butcher gave me the ground meat wrapped in paper. I offered to pay but he silently shook his head at my offering of money. I remained, hand outstretched, totally confused. Then he stopped shaking his head and instead lifted his chin pointing it in a westerly direction. I followed his chin toward what looked like a small kiosk backed up against the sidewall of the shop. At the far end of the butcher shop was a glassed-in hut that housed a woman sitting behind what looked like a small, old-time cash register. I could only quickly glance at her because my gaze was suddenly transfixed by the large, brightly colored picture of the Sacred Heart of Jesus centered on the wall directly behind and above her. It wasn't the benign, calming image of the Son of God, but instead showed the glowing heart, surrounded by thorns and dripping with blood. I couldn't get my head around that picture while standing in a butcher shop. I turned back toward the speechless butcher whose still bobbing chin reaffirmed that the woman in the kiosk was indeed my next stop. I glided through the sawdust on the floor (this was to soak up the blood should any escape from the back room) and took my place in the queue. Much like the porters in the health center, this was the creation of a job to keep people in the workforce. My job was "permanent and pensionable." This was the code for me not having to worry about anything in the future. I could qualify for a mortgage, take my paid holidays and short of being caught robbing the payroll in St. Ita's, on a Thursday night, I would have a job for life. And as I now knew, even that didn't seem like much of a risk. I wondered if the woman sitting in the kiosk felt the same? I knew she would get her morning and afternoon tea breaks and that she could keep up with the Swords gossip. But would that be enough for thirty years of employment? I'm guessing that the Sacred Heart of Jesus helped her to accept her fate.

I parked the Golf at No. 292 and took in the mince and collected my mail. There was finally quite a bit of it stacked by the phone. For weeks no post had been delivered. I was beside myself with no contact from home. I lived for letters and cards and even the bills that kept me connected to my other life. As he was leaving for work, I asked my neighbor Paddy about the mail, wondering if he had noticed the same lack of delivery. He wasn't concerned. He simply explained that the postman had most likely been on holiday and there was no one to take his route. "And the post?" I asked. Paddy sighed at my ignorance.

"Your post is there," he said, very succinctly and slightly exasperated as he pointed to the stack by the coin telephone. The post could wait, the holiday could not. So much for "Neither snow nor rain... nor gloom of night..." Holidays were sacred in Ireland.

I piled up all my post and headed for O'Donoghue's. I had developed a habit of taking my magazines and my checkbook to the backroom where I did my "bits and pieces" over a pint of Guinness. On this particular Friday I managed to get to O'Donoghue's early in the afternoon and walked into an almost empty bar. I was no sooner in the door when Carlos, of Irish and Spanish descent, announced to everyone in the bar, "Jaysus darlin', that's grand. You got my message!" I froze. Was he talking to me? I looked around and yes, he was definitely talking to me. Now I had spent a good deal of time trying to avoid Carlos and his advances. In our first conversation, he had found out that I was Irish and Portuguese. In 100% Irish Ireland he felt that our relatively similar ethnic origins were a reason for us to get together. Carlos was tall and slim with black curly hair and dark Spanish eyes that he felt he had in common with me. He always seemed to wear a white dress shirt, open at the neck while hiding a t-shirt that was imprinted with some sort of picture or slogan. Meeting him meant that you had to be ready to side-step his flirtations while trying to read his underwear. He was loud and demonstrative and not at all like the average punter. I wasn't the only one who found him hard to take so I didn't usually have to fend him off on my own. But this afternoon, I didn't know anyone else in the bar. I stayed in the doorway and then looking at the barman I proclaimed to him and to anyone else who could hear me that, "I didn't get any message from you," while emphasizing, "I *never* gave you my phone number." It sounds archaic but my reputation as the unmarried, on her own, American Woman was still up for grabs. The bandying about of pure pub gossip could get me the title of "the town bike," - any man could take me for a ride.

"But sure," he said with a great big grin and widening his already open arms exposing the "Guinness is Good for You" undershirt, "I asked you to meet me at 4:45 and here you are, 4:45 on the dot!" I tilted my head toward the clock above the door and sure enough, it was exactly 4:45. When I looked back toward the bar, all the men were staring at me. They believed that Carlos was telling the truth and that I was just girlishly embarrassed at being caught out in our little tryst. I found that men always sided with men in these pub conversations. I had been seen with Frank several times in the pub but this still wasn't enough to avoid gossip in Ireland of the nineties. I briskly bypassed Carlos and hid from him in the back room on a bench seat with a tiny round table. The sexism in the pub was running neck in neck with the obnoxiousness of Carlos's personality. That aspect of pub behavior knew no age limitations. Carlos wasn't liked all that well but even he could get points for the implied seduction of The New Girl. Carlos kept up this pretense for months but it stopped bothering me when I realized his status in the pub. Eventually he offended a well-known, well-paying male customer and that got him barred from O'Donoghue's forever. By then my troubles with him were finished.

With my post answered I left the pub by the creaky, skinny back door and moved down the dark and stout stained laneway to Baggot Street and the Horseshoe Bar. Brendan was there and we decided to leave the Shelbourne and go on a Friday night tear. We walked down to Mulligan's on Poolbeg Street where the Guinness was supposed to be the best in town. Mulligan's has been on Poolbeg Street since 1854. It's dark and dank and the ceilings are low. We entered the pub through the lounge and found two places by the door. The pub was decorated with faded paintings hung with yellowed twine that came behind the artwork and ended up in a triangle attaching them to the wall. Mulligan's had a long history of serving the neighboring journalists and editors. By our seats, thumbtacked to the wall was a handwritten price list of the available beers, spirits, and the mixers of tonic, soda, red and white lemonade. I thought the costs were odd; a whiskey being something like £3.37. I suggested to Brendan that the prices be rounded off so we could avoid getting back so much small change and he was instantly incensed! "I already pay enough for my drink. Why would I want to pay one penny more?" I realized then that drink was sacrosanct, a weekly item for the budget, just like heat and the rent.

We went from Mulligan's to Kitty O'Shea's to the Beggar's Bush and then finished our tear in a gigantic circle by heading back to Baggot Street and Joy's (subterranean) Nightclub. Joy's could be found by a flashing neon light that was just higher than the tarmac, level with its customer's knees. To enter Joy's, you went down a metal stairway of about six steps to be greeted by a bouncer at the door. Joy's was the place for older people, separated people and married people who wanted to be separated. In a nightclub, you could party til 3 am or longer. Given our ages, the bouncer didn't need to check for ID's but as a "late bar" Joy's clientele would have already been on the town for many, many hours. He was there to make sure that the older people could still hold their drink. He didn't often have much to do; this crowd would have built up a good level of resistance by now. But there were always loads of taxis outside Joy's to whisk away the customers who just might make a scene or forget "their place." The bar was limited to pints of beer or wine by the bottle at some extraordinary cost. There were throbbing disco lights and a DJ and everyone was encouraged to regress to the sixties. I never heard a second name mentioned in Joy's. Everyone remained on a first name basis and this could be maintained even if a liaison was created and completed outside of the hours of Joy's. In "no divorce Ireland," people sought out new relationships and intimacies with an agreement of discretion. When we left Joy's, Brendan took the Nitelink and I walked safely home, at three in the morning, to No. 292.

I had just gotten into my bedsit and turned on the single overhead light decorated with a Guiney's pink paper lampshade when I heard a slight commotion out on the street. I peeked through the curtains where I could see a group of people who seemed to be just standing around. There was a murmur of voices that sounded very like a group discussion but it was dark and intimidating and it didn't concern me. In fairness, I didn't give it too much thought. Drink was ever present but

I never saw anyone violently argue or fight in the pub or on the street. Frank could get quite argumentative when he drank, but because of his size, he never encountered any trouble. I listened at the window for a moment and then closed the curtains. When it got quiet, I looked out again and the people were gone. But there did seem to be someone still outside and awkwardly sprawled along the footpath. This time I did go out and found poor Paddy face down and stretched diagonally from the footpath to the edge of the car park. He was moving slightly and he seemed to be trying to get up. I helped him to his knees and eventually he stood. His face was scratched and bloody, his palms were bleeding and his glasses were crinkled across his nose. He was hatless but I found his cap as we made our way down the few steps to the front door and I brought him into my flat. Once inside I got him to sit in one of the two kitchen chairs while I got him ice water and a face cloth to daub at his wounds. He was groggy but still so polite. He kept saying that I had the soft touch of a kind nurse. I was just getting him tidied up when someone rang the doorbell to No. 292. I hesitated. People often mistakenly rang my bell because it was the first of the three. Ordinarily I would open the window, not the door, to find out who they were seeking. But at four in the morning, I wondered if the people who had been surrounding Paddy had come back to him for some reason. It rang again and this time I pulled back the curtain without opening the window to see who was standing at the door. To my surprise, there were two paramedics waiting under the front door light. I opened the window and they asked if I had an injured man inside. Strangely enough, I did and I went to let them in. Evidently one of the people who had seen Paddy on the street had called 999 to report his accident. The paramedics came in and quickly began to assess Paddy for whatever damage had been done. They were kind and complimentary to me, commending me on being brave enough to deal with the blood spill without wearing any gloves in this era of HIV. Coming from San

Francisco that put me off for just one short moment. If anything, my older, roundy, fellow flat dweller would be on the "low risk" list. They bundled up Paddy and took him away to check him out at the hospital. I saw him the next afternoon going into his flat and he didn't seem any the worse for wear but then he always sort of shuffled through the building. He tipped his recovered cap and thanked me for helping him as he quietly closed the door to the room at the end of the hallway. I learned later that things were bad at the newspaper where he worked and Paddy was in danger of losing his job. I found this out in a brief chat with Mrs. Enright who also showed up, surprisingly, late on this Saturday afternoon. This was out of character for the cleaning lady who always came on Tuesday. I met her in the entryway and we spoke quietly for a few more minutes. I filled her in on the previous night's events and as we spoke it became obvious that she knew Paddy very well. We said our goodbyes and I watched her walk down the hall to Paddy's front door where she silently took out her key and let herself in. It was then that "the penny dropped." Mrs. Enright, with her tight dark bun and her warm winter coat, wasn't Paddy's cleaning lady at all - she was his lover! I said "nothing" but Jaysus, Eoin Bowen would be shocked!

Chapter 11 - Some Tulip

On Monday morning when I drove up the avenue, passing the grove of trees that lined the way to St. Ita's, the vision of Dessie slinking out of the shrubbery and waving "goodbye" from his lap instantly popped into my mind. How could it not? I assumed that I would have to report something to somebody but I wasn't sure what to say or to whom I should say it. I had been in Portrane for months by now and seen my share of hairy bums, with patients trying to pull up their ill-fitting clothes or trying to make a semi-quick get-away from taking a strategically misplaced pee. And to be fair, zippers could be difficult or just forgotten, so the threat of an inadvertent partial exposure was ever-present. I had prioritized my battles for Kitty, Delia and Hugo and by now, reacting to the unintentional flasher was not very high on my list. But in Dessie's case, I had to give him credit for his timing and execution. He had lain in wait for the little red Golf and stepped out from the trees with the ease of a man who had done it before, somewhat reminiscent of the Great Railway Masturbator. I felt that I had to say something. We were, after all, coaching people to adapt to living in the community, so Dessie's behavior and my follow-through needed to be folded into a learning experience, not just for Dessie but for me as well.

I started at the Horticulture Therapy room where, other than the staff lunchroom, I often saw Dessie. Horticulture Therapy was a large, open space with many low tables covered with loads of little plants growing in tiny plastic containers. The room opened out into a greenhouse of sorts, which was more of a lean-to, covered in plastic sheeting. No matter what the weather outside, the inside air was always wet with a feeling of dampness that coated your skin. In this "therapy" as with many of the others, the nurses were indefatigable in their support of the patients. They exhibited non-stop encouragement for digging and planting and pounding dirt. Their use of language, both social and instructional, was a great model for their budding gardeners who just might find employment somewhere outside of St. Ita's. In Horticulture, the nurses really believed that growing and planting and minding the shoots would provide some support or structure for their patients. In other therapies, jigsaws or puzzles could be elevated to an art form. The staff knew that they had a job for life and the patients felt that they had been committed for life. Over time, how could those two life sentences not affect some very different people in a very similar way? The change of European Union regulations had caused talk of a plan to begin moving our residents out into the community. This was invigorating to some, but to others, it meant a radical shift in the "Portrane- a job for life" mentality. My job was to help with this change. This made me the enemy to some, a nuisance to others and a willing partner to certain core staff who had developed their own schemes to move us forward.

Horticulture was a very popular therapy in St. Ita's. The staff did their best to keep the residents focused and productive but it was a difficult task with the temptation of being outside and having lots of space to move about. It was here that I found Dessie, standing off and away from the plants but keeping his eye on the door. As soon as he saw me he lowered his head and slinked away, moving toward the back of the greenhouse. He kept taking quick glances over his shoulder, watching me as I went looking for the charge nurse. When I found her, I told the story about the car, the grove and the exposure but my resolve was dampened by my lack of conviction. I really liked Dessie and considered him harmless but the nurse knew far better than I the direction of Dessie's future placement. She was adamant that if nothing else there was a lesson to be learned here for "cause and effect." While she listened to me she looked around for Dessie, catching his eye from over the potted plants. As he watched me whispering to her, he lumbered through the hothouse, to the greenhouse, always looking back. I'm sure Dessie had no idea of his size in proportion to his environment. It was as if he thought we couldn't see him behind the rows of 6-inch sprouts. Poor Dessie. It must feel terrible to be caught out in this way. There he was thinking that he had made a clean getaway. With only the exchange of glances, he even started to look guilty. His shoulders curled over, he bent at the waist and tucked his chin into his chest. The nurse brought Dessie over and asked him some very specific yes or no questions and Dessie admitted to doing the deed. He kept glancing at me out of the corner of his eye while she scolded him. I had sold him out. I didn't relish the picture of one more resident going for my throat but I didn't have to worry. Dessie received his discipline but from then on, whenever I saw him in the lunchroom, he never again asked me, "What age am I?"

This was the same week that the health board had managed to find a psychologist to come up to Portrane and test Hugo. I had seen some really nice spontaneous and accurate responses from him so I was excited to start looking for an outside placement just to see what more stimulation, in any form, might do. Hugo's listening skills were his strength. He demonstrated that he could "tune in" to what was going on by a head turn, sometimes an upper body movement and the occasional automatic response of "Oh my!" It didn't seem like much to the staff but his recent transfer to Portrane was enough to alter his expectancy system (in a good way) so that he began to pay attention to the differences in his new surroundings. Hugo's disability didn't allow for horseback riding or trips to Lourdes but his exuberant response to a new voice or the sound of my laughter just left me feeling that not all efforts to reach him had been exhausted. He deserved to have some options just like the other residents. I had been searching for placements for him with no support from the hospital administration. I felt that they might be letting his physical impairment, his poor vision and his intellectual disability, define him. I went everywhere and asked for anything. I finally found a day placement in Coolock on the health center grounds where Mary had her office. There was a nurse there, Marie, who ran a progressive, communication-based group with different patients coming and going on different days. It was fabulous. She came up to see Hugo and willingly opened up a spot for him. But before he could move, I had to get him tested and then I had to get permission. A hospital supervisor gave me free rein to pursue my plan for Hugo but his attitude was reminiscent of Aisling's earlier caution, "They need you to be here, but they don't want you to do anything."

I received a bleep that the examiner was waiting for me in the hospital entryway. I rang the Children's Unit and asked if they could transport Hugo in his wheelchair to meet me at the front office. I went to the entryway where I met the psychologist who was lean and tall and young. We went into a little side office off the hallway where we had a chance to talk. I reviewed the referring information on Hugo's history, as far as I knew it. In fairness, Hugo's overall appearance could be fairly off-putting if you weren't prepared for it. His involuntary motor movements had him wriggling in his wheelchair and he found it difficult to keep his head and neck movements stable. His hands and arms would float and flap of their own accord and his eyes seemed to work independently of each other. I explained as much as I could as the examiner removed the testing materials from his briefcase. A slight pang of hesitation hit me as I watched flip charts for multiple choice and objects for verbal description take their place on the table. I tried to remind him of Hugo's disabilities. He was, after all, a young man who had spent all of his life in long-term mental institutions. I tried to suggest that in Hugo's case, some form of nontraditional testing might be called for, perhaps an observational overview? I wasn't looking for numbers on a chart. All I had requested, at the very most, was a letter to support my outside efforts for Hugo.

Hugo was wheeled into the little office and he was delighted with the change of venue and the extra attention. I got a resounding "Hssssss" when I greeted him and introduced him to the examiner who did try to shake his hand. I explained the situation to Hugo and wheeled him up to the little table. We attempted some small talk while the testing booklet was opened and placed above a row of brand new pencils. The first question, "Hugo, what are the colors in the Irish flag?" made my heart plummet. Evidently, in addition to being lean and tall and young, the examiner was also newly qualified. I could tell that there was no way that we were going to have the option of a nontraditional route. He repeated the question.

"Hsssssss" replied Hugo.

I interjected, "Hugo would need to understand 'flag' before he could answer what colors were in it. Could we try something else?" We couldn't. We struggled through the first page of questions until I convinced him that this was not a good use of his time. I rang the Children's Unit and they came to retrieve Hugo. We were both flustered with the end result of our efforts and I couldn't understand how all my preparations for the day had fallen on deaf ears. It became painfully obvious that when it came to Hugo I was on my own. But I had no intention of giving up. I would go to Coolock and try to persuade Mary to pull some strings.

On the days that I was at Portrane, I used to walk around the grounds or go into the various therapies looking for my clients. One afternoon just before lunch, Kitty found me outside the front office. Her language had been coming on so she both spoke and mimed her wish for me to follow her back to her house on the grounds of the hospital. We walked past the main hospital and along the old, high, rusted wire fence that cordoned off other areas of the old buildings. We saw another resident, Camilla, who was bent over while pushing her body tightly against the fence. As we walked past her, I could see that she was leaning on it to steady herself. I thought she needed help but as I got closer I could see that she was using a long old wooden stick to stab and collect the cigarette butts that had landed on the other side. Kitty quickly pulled on my arm to keep me moving. She shook her head and used very animated facial gestures to indicate her disgust with what we had seen. Her observations and evaluations of acceptable behaviors continued to impress me. She didn't appear to want me to make any time for Camilla; Kitty had plans for this part of our afternoon.

We got to her house just as the nurses were preparing the lunch. Several of the housemates were working in the kitchen. They were peeling potatoes, setting the table and making the tea. It was a cooperative effort. Kitty's house was somewhat of an experiment on the part of the hospital to help bridge a move to the community. Kitty had her own bedroom but she shared the house with several other residents as well as a member of staff. As we came into the kitchen, I gathered from the comments made by the nurses that Kitty was late and had purposely avoided the job that she had been assigned for that afternoon. If Kitty didn't hear them she certainly appeared to grasp their meaning. She frowned, crinkled up her eyes and waved them away in a very royal fashion. Kitty's behaviors continued to foster my curiosity to know her history. I would love to have known Kitty's background and family life. By now she had been in St. Ita's for almost thirty years. How did she acquire her love of travel, her eye for design and her fearless curiosity for the outside world? She took me up the stairs to her room where she had cut out several pictures from magazines and taped them to the door of the wardrobe. Irish bedrooms did not have built-in closets but wardrobes, big separate pieces of furniture with doors that opened out. Kitty had filled her wardrobe to bursting with dresses and jumpers and hats. She pulled out the newest pieces and then held them up against the pictures she had taped to the wardrobe door. How was she able to locate something that would so closely resemble the item that she desired? The more I got to know Kitty, the more impressed I became with her abilities. She was able to plan and budget for what she wanted. She had a sense of how to act appropriately and she was observant and aware of her surroundings. What would her life have been like if she had been diagnosed at an earlier age, in a later decade and been given the training to help bypass her disability? The nurses called us for lunch, and even though she didn't want to go downstairs, I insisted that we meet the others.

When we went down to the kitchen, the nurses started giving out to Kitty about her lack of work and she gave back as good as she got. They had a bit of a row and Kitty stomped off to the sitting room. I followed her there and watched her plop down on one of the old blue overstuffed two-seater sofas. She folded her arms and proceeded to sulk. Nestled together on the other sofa were Annie and Maurice. Maurice (MOR us) was a portly but spry gentleman who looked to be somewhere in his fifties, but of course, it was impossible to know for certain. Maurice always wore a spring sport coat, often a pastel color, with a brightly colored tie. How he could locate a blue plaid sport coat in the St. Ita's laundry room was beyond me. Maurice may have had family looking out for him and perhaps that was why he always looked so well put together. He was quite a character, very jovial and friendly. For some reason he always made Annie laugh which was twice as funny since we all thought she was deaf. Maurice had long, streaky white and dark gray hair that he topped off with a strikingly rectangular grey and white toupee. The hairpiece sort of sat across his head instead of on it. He must have had this one particular hairpiece all of his adult life. The nurses gave me great "stick" because it took me a while to realize that it wasn't his hair. In my defense, it hardly seemed likely that someone living in an asylum on an isthmus in Dublin would be admitted with his toupee in tow. But after giving it some consideration, I thought, why not? Maurice is living a real life in St. Ita's. If the strange, self-absorbed, chain-smoking dentist could have his ill-fitting hairpiece, then why not Maurice? Maurice quickly became one of my favorite people. He always had a smile and a laugh, sometimes for me and often at me.

Kitty continued to sulk in the sitting room and I couldn't understand what had happened to change her mood. She had been in such good form that I couldn't deduce what had made her so agitated. When I went out into the kitchen and asked the nurses they explained that Kitty consistently refused to eat in the dining room with the residents and insisted on eating in the kitchen with staff. This was an ongoing battle. As it got to be one o'clock, people began to come down the stairs or in from the therapies to meet up for their lunch in the dining room. I stood in front of Kitty who hadn't budged from the blue sofa and I spoke while I acted out moving from there to the dining room. She emphatically rejected this idea. Then with no prompting from me, she got up, moved to the hallway and stood just outside the door of the dining room. There, she would imitate the residents having their lunch by acting out their behaviors and their table manners. When I realized that she was actually ridiculing the other residents, I shuffled her away from the doorway so that they wouldn't see her mimicking them. I needn't have worried. Everyone was into "their feed" and their attention was focused totally on the meal. Kitty and I walked down the hallway to the kitchen where the nurses made a plate and a place for her. When I asked why having her eat with them was a problem, they explained that avoiding the dining room and the other residents showed that Kitty was "acting above her station." She was due for a move and in her new home, the option of eating with staff would not be an option for her. I understood that this seemed like a behavioral issue to them, but to me, Kitty continued to impress me with her efforts to create her surroundings in a way that suited the picture that she wanted for her life.

We finished our meal in the kitchen and after tea, all of us helped to tidy up. The residents brought in their plates from the dining room and those who had helped to cook the meal left for their therapies while the others stayed on to help. There was a work roster so everyone knew what their job was to be for the week. With so many people helping it went quickly. I did notice that certain cups and utensils were placed in specific "presses" or cabinets. I would come to know where to look for the staff teacups in all of the many departments or therapies in the hospital. It was a simple matter of hygiene that had to be taken to heart. Residents could have all manner of health issues and it just made sense to be cautious.

My personal level of cautiousness had been enhanced earlier in the week when I had gone up to see a new patient in one of the locked wards. When I got there, I knocked on the door and then let myself in with my dangling ring of keys. I cracked open the door and just took a peek inside to sort out the loud voices coming from across the room. I saw a young man on all fours, sort of hopping around the floor at a surprisingly fast pace. He moved spritely from the desk to the chair to the doorway and back again. There were two male nurses standing at the edges of the room and the young man appeared to crawl up quickly toward them and then just as quickly back away. This was a scene that was totally unknown to me. I slipped into the office but this time I broke the rules by standing in front of the door and not locking it behind me. Something told me to be ready for a quick exit. I introduced myself and without waiting for a response I immediately suggested that I come back at another time. The nurses wouldn't hear of it. "The time is perfect. Come in." I moved slightly forward into the room.

"I was asked to meet the new patient," I said. Keeping my eye on the young man, I kept one foot stable and moved the other slightly sideways toward a table and the rolling desk chair that was resting in front of it. "What's the reason for the referral?" I asked in a quivering, non-professional voice. The young man had temporarily stopped crawling around to eye the new person in the room, me.

"Don't worry," one of the tall, male psychiatric nurses said to me, "he just likes to bite people that he doesn't know, especially women." At that moment, the young man took off again but in the opposite direction of where I was standing. I took the opportunity to reach over and move the rolling desk chair directly in front of my legs. I dragged it with me as I slowly moved back toward the door. I knew the nurses were "taking the piss," and that they just wanted to see my reaction, but piss or no piss, I was on my way out.

"Right," I said, "that's me gone" and I disappeared behind the door locking it as fast as I could. I headed back to the Old Nurses' Home where I asked Deirdre about the new patient. She didn't suggest speech therapy but she did feel that he was prone to violent behavior and that just to be safe I should continue with my sequence of hepatitis B injections. "What injections?" I asked. As it turned out, all members of staff were put on a program for hepatitis immunization. I knew that the nurses had teased me about the biting but Deirdre assured me that it happened fairly often. I immediately called Mary in Coolock and my injections started the following week.

After that office visit, using the appropriate teacups in Kitty's house didn't seem like much of a muchness to me. Having already experienced two harmless but intimidating attempts at strangulation I was hardly going to ignore the possibility of hepatitis. There were things that you simply had to do to stay healthy and safe. But if you weren't a nurse, you had to sort them out for yourself. We finished tidying up the kitchen and the nurses reminded the residents of where they were to be for their afternoon sessions. I said goodbye to all the new people I had met with a special goodbye to Maurice. As he went out the door laughing, he turned to say, "Goodbye, Christina, you're some tulip." I was delighted with my new conquest. I turned back to the nurses, grinning with pleasure at winning over a new resident. They all burst out laughing at my smug demeanor. "What's so funny?" I asked.

"He called you "some tulip," they explained.

"I know," I said defensively, "I think that's sweet." They laughed even harder.

"Sweet? He just said you were mad!" I should have said nothing.

Chapter 12 - Touch Wood, Please God

I knew something was up when I saw all the tall, very green potted plants lining the entryway from The Switch to the visitor's toilet. Our usually unfettered décor was adorned with enough greenery to rival the entire Horticultural Therapy department. As it happened, we were due for a visit from the health board and this was our effort to create a good impression, rows of potted plants. Over the years when I saw the plants trotted out and primed for show, I knew that we were due for a visit from someone important for something important and that's about as much information as we ever received. In this instance, the administration was rolling out its plan to add to our team. For me, it was a welcome announcement. No longer would I be the sole proprietor of the only office on the always-dark hallway of the second floor of the Old Nurses' Home. True, the ambulance drivers had a room just at the head of the stairs but the only sign of life coming from that room was the sound of the always-on telly. I assumed that the ambulance drivers came out to do their rounds of collecting the residents and then reappeared later to take them home. In-between they vanished behind that closed door. I could occasionally find the behavioral therapists down the hallway but they were most often working on the wards.

The Old Nurses' Home was an established part of the hospital although, at the time, not much of it was in use. The plan was to move the new team members into offices across and down the hall from mine, but until they were officially on-site, it remained a dark and dank

Dickensian place to work. One rainy Monday morning I walked up the old wooden steps to the top of the stairs rounding the corner by the office of the ambulance drivers. Their room was curiously silent. Looking down the long, long hallway it seemed uncommonly bleak, most likely because the rain and the clouds were now blocking any possible morning light that might break through the high narrow windows. I started to walk down the corridor to my office when suddenly my boots gave out from under me. I fell backward, and with a loud thump, plopped down on the newly polished wooden floor landing directly on top of my briefcase. As it happened, in addition to enhancing the downstairs entryway, the Old Nurses' Home had also been given a much-needed once-over in preparation for the arrival of the new team members. The combination of the shiny waxed floor, my leather heels and the leather briefcase had me slipping and sliding in a repetitive half circle each time I tried to get up off the floor. My thump of a landing was loud enough to catch the attention of someone down the hallway and I heard the familiar sound of "Christeeeeen." I twisted my upper body toward the voice. All the way down at the far end of the hallway I could make out the huge figure of Raymond. I fixated on his motionless silhouette and then it started to move, slowly and awkwardly in my direction. "Christeeeeen!" he called. "This is it," I thought, I'm sure to be raped or killed on the floor of the Old Nurses' Home. No one will find my body until the ambulance drivers' return and I was pretty sure the sight of my mutilated form wouldn't have much of an effect on any of them.

I panicked. What in good heavens was Raymond doing in the Old Nurses' Home? Why was he lingering down at the far dark end of the hallway so early in the morning? I scrambled to get to my feet but my heels kept slipping on the polished wood. I was terrified. I watched the dark shape of Raymond getting closer and closer as he sang my name, "Christeeeeen, Christeeeeen." I tried desperately to get to a standing position by pushing myself up with the palm of my hand but it only caused my feet to pop out from under me. Raymond came closer and closer. I sat there, quiet and still, closing my eyes and covering my ears. I began to chant in a voice that I prayed would mimic the stern nurse who had saved me from Raymond at the switch, "Leave me be, Raymond, leave me be." As he came closer I could feel my bum, now resting on top of my briefcase, roll and undulate as the weight of his approaching steps caused the old wooden floor to slowly ripple in my direction. I sensed him coming up behind me and in the middle of my chanting, I felt his two hands penetrate the space between my rib cage and my armpits. My breathing stopped. Then in one quick move, he lifted me up off the floor, suspended me in space and plopped me on my feet. I was still wobbling on my heels when he patted me on the head, whispered "Christeeeeen" and shuffled over to and down the stairs. I had passed some strange Portrane initiation. I never worried about Raymond again.

Now that I had an office and a phone I was operating at a distinct advantage when compared to my dependence on the clerks at the switch. They still refused to send me my messages but at least I could let people know when I was in my office and be there to receive a call. With the office and a phone, I was able to do some research on a placement for Hugo, and with Mary's help, we confirmed a spot for him in the clinic in Coolock, and the supervisor, Marie, agreed to keep it open until we had a decision from the hospital. This was unbelievably lucky. I had time for Marie; I had visited her social group sessions and found her to be open-minded and forward-thinking, two qualities required for what I was trying to accomplish.

I went to a supervisor and made my proposal of a weekly day out for Hugo. By now I had good information on Hugo and could document his behaviors and his interactions that might, over time, lead to improving his communication skills, or at the very least, help him to get a closer link to his environment. Hugo was still relatively new to Portrane and having just turned twenty-one he was running out of options and looking toward a limited future. Any of the other programs that I had found would not consider him due to his age. Having met Hugo, Marie could see what I saw and we both felt that a day out once a week would help to clarify the skills that Hugo had and help us to focus on enhancing them. I made the pitch but it was going to need some intense support.

Without a background in intellectual disabilities, it would be easy to overlook any underlying potential in Hugo's demeanor. His combination of cerebral palsy, spina bifida and mental handicap didn't offer up much of a positive prognosis. But his acute listening skills helped him to connect to his environment. It would be one thing if he had these skills and didn't use them, but he did use them, every day. He recognized sounds and voices, and if we didn't try, we would never know if we could build on this skill to improve his everyday life. As far as I could tell, his earlier placements were fairly limited. The main reasons for his transfer to Portrane were his age and his size. At twenty-one, I thought he deserved a chance and thankfully Marie and Mary felt the same.

It became a logistics nightmare. Hugo would need transportation. Portrane couldn't release an ambulance once a week to take him the ten miles to Coolock and collect him later. A taxi was suggested or possibly a combination of both. This brought up the subject of funding for the transportation. At the time, all the residents of St. Ita's were given a stipend by the government. Each person had an individual fund and this money was used to help pay for their outings, swimming, horseback riding, a trip to Lourdes, or it could be used for their luxuries as Kitty did with her fashion updates. But I pleaded, Hugo had benefited from none of these things and he never would. Was his stipend a possible resource? Could we locate his family and make a proposal to them? These questions were never answered but interestingly after asking them a group of managers convened and agreed to a six-week trial placement for Hugo. I was delighted. He was to start the following month.

My office became something of a meeting place for my clients. If they saw the red Golf in the car park, then they knew I would show up in the office sometime during the day. Kevin would come for cigarettes and Annie would come for gossip. Delia came just to hang out. On this particular Monday Delia was beside herself to let me know that I had flowers waiting for me down at the switch. Nothing would do other than we had to go right away and collect them from the nurses' station. When we got downstairs we found a single, tiny potted flower with a paper American flag stuck in beside it. Aisling had left it as a surprise for the Fourth of July. I had totally forgotten the date but Delia was pretty excited about her first American holiday. I managed to find Aisling sitting with Pat and Cormac in the canteen. I went through the cafeteria line and found a seat at her table. I started to thank her for her kindness to a Yank away from home when I became totally transfixed by what she had selected for a meal. As I sat across from the slim and petite form of Aisling, I watched as she took a large piece of thick, white bread from the plate and slathered it with butter. On her tray was a deep porcelain bowl chock full of golden fried chips. She selected numerous crispy sliced, fried potatoes and then lined them up, side-by-side, along the thick white bread. She deftly folded it in half and raised it to her lips. It was then that she met my glance and registered my look of horror at what she was about to ingest. "What?" she asked, "You've never had a chip butty? Delicious." And she consumed every last bit of the thick white bread and the entire bowl of chips. I was reminded about Mary's belief that somewhere on the Irish chain of DNA was a gene for processing chips and stout that had morphed during the famine and to this day kept the citizens fed, happy and thin.

The word at the lunch table was that our department would be expanding by way of two psychologists. We were about to look like a real team. This might mean that the plans for several of the other residents could soon be put into play. In addition to my plan for Hugo, the nursing staff was very impressed with Anthony. He was doing well at his job in "the stores" of the hospital and he was sincerely motivated to try and live outside of Portrane. The plan was to move him to a supervised community placement away from Portrane in the south side of Dublin. His younger brother, Kevin, would most likely stay with us in Portrane, getting cigarettes from the staff and coming to me to fix his suspenders. There was also talk of Kitty moving up north to a community placement in the seaside town of Skerries and Delia was on the list to share a little house in Garrylough Mill several hours away in Wexford. Delia was beside herself with anticipation of this move. She became obsessed with doing everything that was expected of her and behaving in a way that would gain everyone's approval. She wasn't quite thirty years old and the idea of being in her own home, with her own bedroom and some freedom was almost more than she could handle.

In a move that was uncharacteristically Irish, the new team members appeared as expected and showed up on time, moving into offices that actually had furniture. We began to meet on a regular basis and my decision to stay in Portrane started to feel like it had some structure. Imogen and Niall were the new psychologists and they joined the three behavioral therapists and myself. We were told that Imogen was the senior psychologist but somehow everyone deferred to Niall. This didn't surprise me in the male-dominated world of Portrane. While there were several female doctors who came and went, there were no women in any of the management positions of the hospital. One of the female consulting doctors was Dr. Connor. I got on well with her and she would graciously help me with anything to do with hearing or speech. She must have been in her fifties by then and she had spent a good deal of time with the residents of Portrane. She knew them well and she wasn't the least bit hesitant to try something new. When we met for lunch in the hospital canteen and she would fill me in on the plans for the moves and state of the hospital in general. She often mentioned her son, Conor, who had just completed his education and was getting ready to leave the country. After several lunches, I finally got up the courage to ask her why she would name her son Conor Connor. "I worked all my life to be a doctor," she said, "do you think I would give over my last name to a man and lose the recognition that I worked so hard to achieve?" I was embarrassed and impressed at the same time. Here was a woman who had achieved her goal while maintaining her independence and her relationship. From Dr. Connor, I learned that in Ireland women often kept their own names. How they never managed to break the glass ceiling in Portrane was beyond me. After I got to know so many of them, I became fairly certain that it was only because they didn't want to.

No longer on my own, meeting up with other professionals was having a very positive effect on my Dublin experience. In Portrane, the psychologists were now my connection to management. I didn't have to depend on or wait for any of the Pat's. This proved to be exceedingly helpful given that the Pat's never left their surname on a message nor would The Switch tell me which Pat was asking to see me. This plethora of Pat's was not in my imagination. In Portrane, we had many residents named Pat or a derivative thereof and in town, there was my neighbor Paddy and my new friend Pat the Yank. Interestingly, they all seemed to be in the same age group. One of The Pats told me that he was to be christened Desmond, but as it happened, he shared his baptism day with all the new babies in the parish, March 17. The bishop simply announced, "All the boys baptized on this date will be known as Patrick." Desmond no more.

My co-workers began to include me in their lives and the lives of their friends. As my social circle expanded, there was one observation that kept leaping out at me no matter where I was in Ireland. At first, I thought it was my imagination but as I got to know more people I noticed that so many of them were missing the same tooth; right-hand side, third from the front. Loads of them. Dentists in Dublin were a rare breed and very expensive. So rather than invest in a bridge or a crown, the offending tooth was summarily yanked out. While socialized medicine might help with a fever or a pregnancy, dentistry was still not a part of it. As soon as the dentists were trained, they moved to a country that would use and could afford their services. This was not a surprise to me and in preparation for my move I had several crowns completed and fillings repaired before I left the States. After all, the only time I was offered any local dental advice was when Deirdre confided that Vinnie would pull out your hair and then floss his teeth with it.

But now I knew that I was going to stay in my new country so I had to find a dentist to at least clean my teeth. This still baffled some of my older friends but a new team member put me onto a dentist that was in Parnell Square, exactly on my way home. I made an appointment and found my way up the stairs to his office. He was a sort of "beaky" man with wild, curly, gray hair and silver wire-rimmed glasses. He introduced himself, showed me to the dentist chair and clipped the paper bib around my neck. We had a brief discussion of my request and he explained that the cleaning equipment was broken and he would have to clean my teeth "by hand." I wasn't really sure what "the equipment" was and I didn't ask. He propped open my mouth and inserted multiple cotton tubes around my molars. He began to ask me questions, which of course, I couldn't answer as he poked and prodded my teeth and gums. I had been in Dublin for a while now without the benefit of a dentist and I began to worry that something bad might have happened. He jabbed me one more time and then lifted his head out from under my nose and called out to all of the people in the office, "Pat, Martyn, Kathleen, Maeve, can I have a word? You need to see this." Then he coached his staff into a half circle around the tilted chair and they surrounded my angled body. Before I knew it ten pairs of eyes were peering into my face and down my throat. I wanted to explain the California Philosophy of Preventative Dental Care but I couldn't, I could say nothing. Then he cupped my chin, tilted it toward the light and my dental abnormality became clear as my worries vanished... "Take a good look," he proclaimed. "This is an American mouth."

Chapter 13 - An Actor's Life for Me

Summer had come to Dublin, and to be fair, the weather wasn't bad. But it wasn't as good as the summer of 1983, a comparison that my boss Mary brought up ad nauseam. She would sit back in her office chair, a slight smile eking across her apple-cheeked face and then lapse into a trance-like state remembering the record-breaking heat and the crowded beaches. Of course, I wasn't there but I was pretty certain that she was working off of some old, inflated adolescent memory. I mean, jeez, we were just talking about the weather. I had yet to learn what could happen to your state of mind when it is deprived of sunlight for weeks or sometimes months in succession. Layer those gray skies onto the constant rain and it can take quite a toll on your psyche. Just like the Eskimos have numerous words for snow, the Irish are continually putting the same bad weather into relatable categories. It has to be really bad to be "bad." Too many bad days and you risked losing your perspective. I grumbled about the rain to a gentleman standing with me at the bus stop and he chided me for my lack of fortitude. "Rain?" he questioned. "You think this is rain? Sure this is only a 'soft' day." Soft day or not, I was getting pretty wet but I said nothing. Eventually I learned that a "soft" day was no comparison to the category of rain that was "pissing down." He was right to put me back in my box.

When the weather is warm the entire country pours out onto the fabulous Irish beaches. There is an incredible stretch of beach behind St. Ita's that curves in a half moon all along the back of the hospital.

But no one I knew would go to the beach in Portrane. I supposed that it suffered from some stigma due to its proximity to the hospital and its inhabitants.

Whenever the days were warm and sunny the entire labor force benefitted from an understood dispensation from work. We were no exception. On the really nice days, we would meet with the residents outside but we never took them as far as the beach. Instead, we would put blankets out on the huge stretch of grass that paralleled the old brick buildings, and the staff and residents alike would bask in the sun whenever they could. I never ventured as far as the beach either. It held a bit of mystery to me ever since the freezing spring morning that I arrived at work to find Annie waiting for me in the entryway. She was doing her best to pantomime some event of the previous week but I just wasn't grasping her message. I turned to the clerks at The Switch. They seemed well able to interpret her gestures and movements, but at times, it also felt as if they might be censoring her stories due to her American audience. People assumed that Annie was deaf but she always appeared to be listening and following when the nurses gave their interpretation of her story. At times she would interrupt them by shaking her head in an agitated fashion, grabbing my arm and turning me back to face her. Then she would reenact her story and wait for the nurses to give me the correction. As it happened on this morning, Annie communicated that someone had gone out alone in the early evening, walked out onto the beach and drowned after immersing themselves into the cold, cold water. I was horrified that one of the patients had left a ward and made their way, all alone, to the beach. The staff seemed intent on keeping the details quiet but eventually the truth came out. It wasn't a patient but a nurse who had intentionally walked into the sea. I would come to realize that for many people, there was a fragile balance to living and working in Portrane and soon I, too, would have to learn to live within that same delicate balance.

But for now the warm summer weather endured and Dublin was awash with drink and music. Even though it was against the law to drink on the street, the footpaths in front of the pubs were six, seven, eight people deep with all of them holding a pint in one hand and a cigarette in the other. It was hard to maneuver the little red Golf down Baggot Street with so many people crowding the road. I loved it! The party went on and on 'til closing with everyone staying outside for as long as they could stand it. A small fortune could be spent on drink while staying outside for the chat and the craic and the weather. I had created my own barometer to measure the change of seasons in Dublin. When the weather was just beginning to get nice there was an increase of sick on the footpath. When it actually got hot, the sick moved closer to the cash machine.

The music that summer was everywhere and anywhere. To a Dubliner, that may have been normal. But to me, it was an onslaught of sound that was captivating and intriguing. The spontaneous sessions in the various pubs would ignite in a corner or start up in a back room. And just like the dancer who leapt onto the bar in O'Donoghue's, you never knew when it might happen. The musicians could start with a fiddle, a tin whistle and a bódhran (drum) and then shift to a guitar, a flute and some uillean pipes. Then more musicians would join in replacing the guitar, the tin whistle and adding an extra fiddle or two. And the singing, the most beautiful voices could come out of those pub sessions. You could be in the middle of a conversation when a song would begin from anyone in the pub. A musician or a barman or a patron would raise their voice to say, "Lads, Lads" and gesture that your talking should stop. And it did. It became dead quiet until the song was finished.

Frank was an absolute lover of music. He could suss out a session anywhere in the greater Dublin area and we would sit and drink and listen for hours. He especially loved traditional music but he was open to all kinds. I had an audiocassette with "Desperado" by Linda Ronstadt that became a favorite of his. We played it whenever we were out in the Golf. If we happened to meet up at the flat after work he would take a rest by covering the tiny single bed in Haddington Road with his huge Donegal frame, close his eyes and listen, over and over, to my soundtrack from *Out of Africa*. Music was always in him. He loved it all.

One Friday night Frank managed to sneak us into the Olympia Theatre to see Sharon Shannon. He knew someone at the door and we ran up the stairs to the balcony. People were standing up and dancing in their seats, in the aisle, everywhere. It was chock-a-block. The music went on forever and just when we thought it was finished, Christy Moore came out from the side curtain and the crowd went mad. He stayed to perform for the rest of the session and Frank was beside himself. As much time as I had spent with him, I still found it hard to reconcile this gigantic Donegal construction worker with his love of music and his innate ability to write me beautiful letters that were just short of poetry. Little by little he was shattering the stereotype I had of him, my giant builder with the big hands and the lyrical soul. But I wasn't the only one who reacted to his appearance. I could read the looks that people gave him when he navigated his way around the bodies in the pub or when they passed us together on the street. Those looks became even more intense if Frank had some drink on him. Men would just stand aside when they saw this great unwieldy figure and heard that deep northern accent. The more time that we spent together the more that stereotype began to melt. I often wondered what his life would have been like if he had been able to complete his education in London. I found it heartbreaking to think of him making such serious life choices at such a young age. He knew that I was living out one of my dreams in the little flat in Haddington Road. But I found it hard to get him to disclose any dreams that may have still been lingering on for him. We were truly a conflict of cultures, Frank and me. I had the luxury and the opportunity to fanaticize about a dream and then make that dream come true. In fairness, it hadn't included a 19th-century asylum on the north side of Dublin, but most of my picture was in view, including Frank. But he had been forced to live in the real world, starting at a very young age. Frank had given up his dream of an education but I truly believed that he must still have a dream or a two tucked away. It took a long time to get him to talk but he eventually confessed that he would love to see the horse racing at Cheltenham in March. He seemed almost embarrassed to admit that his big dream could come true with a ferry trip across the sea to England. But the Cheltenham meet was the place to be for Irish punters. His love of horses and racing and having the craic would be at their pinnacle at Cheltenham. It reminded me of my mother's simple wish to "go dancing." I made up my mind that I would help him with that wish if he decided that he wanted to make it come true.

I was getting to know both the south and the north sides of Dublin. There was a distinct difference between the two and it could be sensed as soon as one crossed the Liffey. It was especially obvious when there was a match at Croke Park. The fans of the visiting teams would congregate on O'Connell Street and fill up all the hotels and pubs with their team colors. Behind O'Connell Street, there were certain areas of the north side that were to be avoided, although I often found myself driving on Sheriff Street or Sean McDermott Street before I knew it. I was told to put my handbag in the boot and never to open the sunroof. Gurriers had been known to break the window to get the handbag or jump up on the car, reach through the sunroof and pull the gold chain from around your neck. The fear was firmly implanted. I did as I was told, but I never had a problem.

The north side could be an advantageous place to find a flat or a house to rent. It would be much less expensive to live there than to put £230 down a hole in the dirt for a subterranean bedsit. But the advantages, closer to work and cheaper rent, could never overshadow the perks of Dublin 4. Once I had moved in and revealed my address I took some criticism for my choice of neighborhoods. People still commented that "It figures the Yank would live in Dublin 4." I could hardly tell them that I ended up there because the King of the Faeries had helped me across Dorset Street in a rainstorm. Dublin 4 meant nothing to me. In Arnott's, I bought a lovely black winter hat with a wide brim that folded back at the top. "That looks like Dublin 4," someone disparagingly said to me. I complained of this to my friend Catherine who lived on the north side when we met at her house for tea. No sooner had I started my moan when all the lights went out and we were enveloped in total darkness.

"Quick, quick," she said, "Do you have 50p?" Not knowing the layout of the house I fumbled around the sitting room to find my handbag. When I found it I located my coin purse that luckily had one 50p piece. I grabbed the coin and cautiously moved toward the sound of her voice where I found her outstretched hand. I gave her the coin and then I heard it plop into something that sounded like a tin container. In a few seconds the lights came back on. I couldn't believe it. Electricity by coin-operated-meter. Evidently this was the system in "the old days" but most houses had been upgraded years ago. I hoped we had enough credit to make the tea and keep warm. I couldn't imagine how much electricity we would get for 50p. I thought about my roundabout choice of a snobbish neighborhood that included being mocked for a new black hat. I decided that even though I paid my rent by putting my money down a hole in the ground, I still preferred the south side.

My social life had improved somewhat if only that people were talking to me more now that they assumed that I wasn't going away. Like Raymond, they must have decided that tolerating me would be the best approach. But still, the friends that I had made were all quite a bit younger and I knew that I wasn't likely to meet many women my age out and about in the pub. They were home where they were expected to be. Even though he didn't know it, I even had ten years on Frank. So I decided to look for an evening class that might keep me occupied and possibly introduce me to some people that were out of St. Ita's and into my age group. I settled on a once a week drama class through the Gaiety School of Acting. I had started as a drama major in college and I worked in television so it seemed like a logical choice. I was wrong. With the one exception of the instructor, everyone was still at least 20 years younger. Still, the teacher was a fascinating woman with a background in Irish theater and her first session of warm-up exercises was so much fun that even though it taxed my budget I chose to stay.

It's safe to say that in my desperation to weave something out of my older woman isolation and the intense emotions I was experiencing in Portrane, I was highly motivated to risk whatever emotional investment the instructor might ask of me. When she painted the background of the characters that we were to portray, I found myself not only drawing on my history but on the brief histories that I learned from the women in St. Ita's. It wasn't just an acting class; I knew that it was my own mental health that was about to come into play.

At the beginning of each class we did a warm-up exercise and then a session of improvisation. We broke into groups of four or five and she gave us the scene and the parts that would support it. I found it slightly frustrating in that no matter what the role, whenever there was an older part, my younger peers would assign it to me. I did lose my temper at one point and reminded them that it was an acting class but other than that we got along fairly well.

Weeks into the course the instructor gave us our first actual performing assignment. We were to memorize and recite *The Lake Isle of Innisfree* by William Butler Yeats. Everyone in Ireland knows this poem, Everyone. If you were standing on the Number 10 bus and said, out loud, "I will arise and go..." everyone on that bus could finish this poem. It was my first introduction to Yeats and I loved it. I could see myself escaping from Dublin for the solitude of Innisfree just long enough for a respite from all that was taking place in Portrane. To practice at home, I would turn on the gas fireplace, heat up the bedsit and read the poem over and over in front of the mirror from Guiney's.

"I will arise and go now, and go to Innisfree,
And a small cabin build there, of clay and wattles made;
Nine bean rows will I have there, a hive for the honey bee,
And live alone in the bee-loud glade."

Whatever it was that got me to the emotional point of my classroom recitation, the instructor gave me the odd compliment that I had "brought a very different interpretation" to the poem. The acting class became very important to me. I could suspend the multitude of emotions that were ever present in Portrane and then revive them during class in a form that had a personal meaning just for me. Without question, I know that my inspiration always came from St. Ita's. I would take whatever role the instructor gave us and immediately layer it on top of the life of one my patients in Portrane. It was unavoidable; I was so caught up in what I knew of their pasts and of what their lives were like today.

Our big acting challenge was to be a scene from *A Life*, a play by the Irish author, Hugh Leonard. I was paired with Thomas, a very nice young man who had been in my improvisational group on several occasions. We were to learn our parts individually and then meet up on the night and perform the scene together for our peers. The instructor set a very dramatic scene of a young man and woman who lived deep in the country and were good, good friends. The young man fancied the woman, but those emotions never surfaced between them. There was a village dance, but he refused to go. The woman spent time at the dance with another man and ended up arriving home very late, shaming the family. Her irate father gave her several drastic options, one worse than the other, so as to clear her name and that of the family. Desperate, she asked her friend to meet her in secret. In this meeting, she tells him that she will be forced to marry the man from the dance if no one else can save her. He loves her, but he can't bring himself to reveal those feelings. But he is also jealous and feels that he must lecture her on her behavior. She is desperate. He is her friend; he loves her but he won't help her.

I practiced every night in the flat. Even though I was unfamiliar with the play, the scene that was described to me seemed to set my imagination streaming toward the past. I had been told that years and years ago, families had the power to admit their relations to the psychiatric hospitals for reasons other than their mental health. A baby out of wedlock, flirty behavior, shaming the family, or being in the way of an inheritance could be reason enough to lose your freedom forever. I couldn't take away the thought that some of the people I worked with may have suffered such a fate.

The night of the performance the instructor set two chairs in the middle of the room. Each pair of actors took their turn in front of the group. Thomas and I were the last pair to perform. Everyone seemed to take their cue from the instructor's placement of the chairs and they stayed seated throughout their readings. Having watched them, I asked for and was given permission to move around and away from my chair. Thomas remained seated. As I read my part, I moved closer and closer to him, begging him for my life and his help in saving me from a loveless marriage. At the end of the scene, Thomas' character stands, turns his back and walks away. When we finished, the instructor gave us our notes. Thomas and I met up again in the cloakroom when we went to fetch our jackets. Thomas had tears in his eyes, "I felt so bad for leaving you," he said, "How did you do that?"

"Kitty O'Doherty," I said, and we went for a pint.

Chapter 14 - Given the Day That's in It

Dublin had become an amazing source of sound for me. I could swear that whenever one of the numerous car alarms went off it was always to the beat of "Treat Her Right," by the Commitments. Irish music was everywhere. This was the time of The Corrs, The Cranberries and the plethora of boy bands. Clannad was huge. Frank and I drove for hours and hours on the narrow waterside roads of Donegal to hang out at Leo's Tavern in Gweedore with the hope of seeing Enya perform. She didn't, but the craic was mighty in her father's pub.

Maybe the music and the craic had fine-tuned my hearing because the sounds of my Irish experience seemed to register as the strongest of the five basic senses. True, when I first started working in St. Ita's, the smell was the overwhelming influence, but now my nostrils became desensitized to it after the first few minutes of entering a ward or a unit. Maybe because it was such a combination of dampness and mold and cleaning supplies that after a while it didn't cause a reaction. But the sounds would jolt me whenever I heard them. In the Children's Unit, Hugo's "Hsssss" would grab my attention no matter where I was in the ward. Francie, our youngest client, would throw himself on the ground and bang his head onto the floorboards. That sound could be heard throughout the passageway. At lunchtime, the resident who had placed the mitted fingers around my throat on our sunny day out would lean over the lunch table and headbang until the lunch was served. Strangely I never knew the gender of this resident. A huge helmet was always worn over and down the top of the head and he or she was never seen without a scarf over the lower half of his or her face. Early on I asked the name of this person but it was an Irish name that didn't reveal gender to me. Later I was too embarrassed to ask such a follow-up question. And there was Marco, a very small man who was verbal only in the sense that he could repeat what was said to him. Marco used to sit and smile and rock from side to side occasionally laughing with a sound that seemed too big to come out of his tiny body. He would emit this high-pitched giggle that arced up and out of him going higher and higher and then lower and lower before coming to a complete stop. Marco was great fun and enjoyed a day out more than anyone. Unfortunately, he was eventually barred from these excursions into town. As it happened, while crossing with his group in the middle of the street, Marco met an oncoming group of small children just leaving play school. Marco quite liked children. Maybe coming up against someone of his own size and stature felt welcoming to him. This time he stopped directly in front of one child and began to smile and rock from side to side. He wasn't about to be moved. In his enthusiasm, he let go of his amazing laugh and then, unfortunately, topped it off by looking the child directly in the eye and stating, "I'm gonna kill ya." Marco's expression could quickly go from light to dark and since he was at the exact eye level of the child, this provided a startling effect, to say the least. The teachers of the playschool complained and Marco's days out were curtailed. It seemed unfair because as it turned out, the nurses would often playfully wrestle with Marco and when they got him in a hold, they would hug him and say, "I'm gonna kill ya" just before giving him an affectionate squeeze and letting him go. For Marco and the nurses, it was all in fun. I began to wonder about the plan to move the residents into the surrounding communities. I was reminded how Vinnie's best friend was moved out in the middle of the night leaving him so traumatized that he habitually dragged his fingernails down his cheeks. Surely this need for the residents to be taught how to adapt to a new lifestyle would be included in their strategy.

The arrival of psychologists Niall and Imogen was a mixed blessing for the behavioral therapists and me. Our plans for the residents finally received recognition but we resented the fact that it was the arrival of the psychologists that gave us credibility. In Ireland, there was great cachet in being a psychologist and Niall and Imogen didn't hesitate to assume their roles as the anointed leaders of our workgroup. Deirdre adapted to this new hierarchy much better than I did. She held the same historical Irish admiration for psychologists but she realistically saw it as a way for us to get our programs moving. I resented the assumption that they would automatically be the leaders of a team that we had tried so hard to develop. Early on we took them on a tour around the grounds from the main building down to the children's unit. While we worked our way back to the Old Nurses' Home, I walked ahead with Deirdre. It was a slightly disingenuous effort to impress the new team members with my allegiance. While we slowly moved up the footpath I heard a loud, isolated sound that seemed to come from one of the large buildings on the grounds. It was loud enough to interrupt my complaining and ask, "What is that?" Since I had asked no one in particular, no one, in particular, answered me. It happened again. This time I looked up toward the top floor of one of the higher buildings where, from an open window, a shoe was flung out. As I stopped to watch, a second shoe, not a match, followed right behind it, accompanied by the same loud noise that I now recognized as a person screaming. As I watched, several more windows opened and several more shoes and other objects became airborne in counterpoint to the screaming of the residents. I caught up to Deirdre and asked again, "Why all the screaming?"

"What screaming?" she asked as she kept walking. I got her to stop and turned her to face the resident's hall. The rest of the group walked on. Perhaps their ears had grown numb due to years of working in mental institutions. Deirdre finally acknowledged the shoes and the screams coming out of the upstairs windows. She turned back to the group and we continued walking. Speaking to me from the side of her face she gave me a succinct two-word explanation, "Full moon," she said and she was right. That night a giant summertime moon glowed high in the sky over the top of the red brick clock tower at Portrane. And the shoes and the screams happened again; each and every time the day was the witness to the night of a full St. Ita's moon.

Niall and Imogen began to attend and manage our team meetups in the Old Nurses' Home. Their remit was to begin the work of identifying the residents who could move into the community or possibly into an environment that was not as restrictive to them as Portrane. The long-term objective was to close as much of the facility as possible in the coming years. This could bode well for some of the residents but not so well for those who had been working with me for many months. I begged and pleaded to the administration to let Hugo have the opportunity to try the day therapy in Coolock. With all his limitations, he would not be one of the residents to find a suitable reassignment. In fact, Hugo had been abandoned to Portrane for the very reason that no other facility would take him. Still, to me, he had shown an awareness that I wanted to nurture in another environment, just to see what that outside stimulation might do. And while the administration had agreed to the six-week trial period, it had yet to start. Imogen was less supportive of my plan but Niall agreed to help me get the plan in motion. He offered to meet with the chief of staff and begin to sort out the process that would get Hugo his one- day a week out of Portrane. But for now, the first to move would be Anthony.

Anthony was to leave his job in The Stores and be transferred to the south side of Dublin. He was delighted! His new placement would be less restrictive than Portrane. It was designed with areas for group living and many of the residents left the facility every day to work at sponsored jobs in the community. The magnitude of this move was not lost on Anthony. He totally understood what it meant to be leaving Portrane and even though it also meant leaving Kevin, Anthony was looking forward to the change. This south side facility was also considered as a possible move for Kitty. I asked to travel along with Kitty and her housemates when they went for an outing and a concert. I wanted to get an idea of what options were being developed for some of my clients.

As it happened, the groups that performed on stage were from various community-based facilities of the greater Dublin area. Kitty and her group were in the audience with residents from hospitals much smaller but similar to St. Ita's. I arrived in time for the closing act from Skerries, a beautiful seaside village just north of Portrane. If Kitty was to make a move, it was highly likely that she would be living in a group home with some of the people that were about to perform on stage. I was highly supportive of this possibility. Even though Kitty was diagnosed as deaf, she loved music and had performed in various Christmas shows at Portrane. I'd been told that she was a fabulous dancer and mime and I was hoping we could capitalize on that part of her talent.

I was very impressed with the Skerries group who had brought along their own Elvis impersonator in the likes of Finbarr, singer extraordinaire. Finbarr was a big burly man with coal black curly hair whose curls he brought forward and down over the top his forehead. He had managed to grow sideburns as well and he sort of shook his head, shaking his curls as he spoke, in a move that he considered very "Presley." From somewhere he had obtained a fake white leather jacket with fringe that also shook has he lumbered his way down the main aisle and up to the stage. As the music started he grabbed the microphone and began to sing along to "Jailhouse Rock." This was vintage Elvis, to be sure. He managed to move his thick frame in time to the music, occasionally thrusting out a hip or jabbing a knee forward in syncopation to the beat. The crowd went wild.

Finbarr closed the show to the delight of his screaming fans who crowded around him as he sauntered down the steps of the stage and into their admiring entourage. They all seemed to have autograph books open and at the ready while they clamored for him to sign his name. To this day I have no idea where the fans might have purchased those autograph books but Finbarr signed away, all the while maintaining his Elvis persona.

I found Finbarr to be very impressive but Kitty remained unenthused. I praised him to her but she just "shooed" me away to communicate her lack of interest. I wondered if she and Finbarr would be able to develop a friendship if she had the opportunity to move into the Skerries house. Finbarr seemed so comfortable in his surroundings and especially in his ability to communicate with his peers and the nursing staff. I sought out one of the nurses that I knew worked with him and asked what his prospects were for remaining in the Skerries house or possibly moving to another, more open, facility. "He seems so well adjusted," I said. She agreed that he may seem to have adapted well but she suggested that I might need a little more time to get to know him; just before this performance, they removed a five-inch blade from the inside of his boot. She assured me that he would be staying with them for a while.

The Old Nurses' Home was beginning to develop into a hotbed of energy, St. Ita's style. That is to say, while I was still in my office and on my own most of the time, I didn't feel the same isolation that I had during the days of the dark wet hallways with "Christeeeeen" echoing off the floorboards. The addition of the telephone helped me a lot for planning and I took to going down to the canteen and then coming back to my office for a working lunch. I was also getting so conscious of the mayonnaise and the chip butties and the propensity for starch that I tried to stay somewhere in the realm of the salad bar. I once stood in the buffet line with one of the nurses who, upon hearing my accent, began to ridicule the entire population of the United States for its bad eating habits. She had been to one of the southern states and regaled me with the description of the meal that she was given, big white biscuits on the side and gravy over everything. I tried to explain that the United States is a huge place with different habits and cultures surfacing in thousands of different and sometimes very tiny places. She disagreed vehemently but I didn't argue. I did notice that as she walked away from the buffet line, her plate was covered with lasagna and chips with a side of cauliflower and cheese sauce.

On one particularly dark morning, I arrived early to my office in the Old Nurses' Home. I wanted to finish up some work before going out to Skerries to have a look at the community-based service there. I had hoped not to come back to the office and wanted to get some things out of the way before the weekend. I was making loads of headway through the paperwork when I thought I heard a rustling noise coming from somewhere in the room. I stopped. I listened. Then it stopped. I kept working away on my notes when I thought I heard it again. I stopped. But this time the rustling continued. It seemed to be coming from the rubbish bin that was next to my desk just a few feet away from my right leg. I began to watch the rubbish bin. Nothing happened. The bins in Ireland are lined with "black bags" or garbage bags and they extend far over the top of the smaller, narrower dark metal wastebaskets. I heard it again. This time I stood up, took one step to the right, putting me directly next to the bin. I slowly leaned over and, bending slightly, I looked down into the darkness of the black bag. Staring back at me were the biggest, strangest, most vibrantly golden, glowing eyes I had ever seen. Whatever they were attached to stood still, and so did

I. Then I slowly took one step back to my desk and sat down. In my ignorance of not knowing what was in the bin, I began to think about how I might deal with it. My assumption was that it was a rat but I had never seen a rat before. I had no reference for size, but I had to admit, for my first rat, this one seemed huge. I didn't hear any more rustling so I supposed that we were both sorting out how to deal with each other. The weather was still pretty frosty so I knew my thick leather gloves were in my handbag. My plan was to put on the leather gloves, avoiding the possibility of a rat bite, grab the top of the black bag and then carry the neatly packaged rat out into the hallway. I put on the gloves, quietly and slowly, and then smoothly swiveled my office chair to face the bin. I began to lean over to quickly grab and close the top of the black bag when an image halted my progress...if I did manage to grab and close the black bag, and that the rat remained calm while dangling in the air, then what would I do with it? I would be standing in the hallway, holding a huge rat in a black plastic bag with nowhere to go.

I chose cowardice. I knew at this time of day I was alone at my end of the hallway but I was pretty certain that the ambulance drivers were sequestered in their office by the loo. I grabbed my briefcase and I quickly went down the hallway and put my ear to their door. I could hear the telly so I began to knock loudly while asking for help. One of the drivers came to the door and I spewed out that I thought there was a rat in the bin and then I made a run for it down the stairs. At least they would know who to call and I ashamedly left the rat and the ambulance driver to one another.

The following week I was called in to see a manager as soon as I got to work. For reasons I could not understand, having a rat in my office was a big deal. The news had gone all over the hospital. "The Yank had a rat in her office" was the talk of the place. I was given a seat in front of his desk while he perched tentatively on its corner. "Tell me what happened," he said. I explained as best I could, with my limited knowledge of rat capturing. He pressured me for a description; was it black or brown? Wet or dry? I did the best I could but to be fair, I didn't take a lot of time to note its appearance.

I explained that I had recently taken to eating lunch in my office and that the leftovers and paper plates would sometimes be stashed in the bin overnight. This was due to the fact that even though I was reluctantly given an office in the Old Nurses' Home, my existence had yet to be revealed to the cleaning staff. Maybe this had something to do with it?

He leaned back from his perch, folded his arms and shook his head. My lack of custodial support seemed to have an effect on him, or perhaps he thought my inconsistencies with black bag removal gave comfort to the enemy rodent. I don't know. But upon hearing my explanation, he rolled his eyes and said, "You are some gobdaw." In addition to never having seen a rat, I had also never been called a "gobdaw." I thought back to my sweet memory of Maurice calling me "tulip" and decided to pass on what I thought could be rat catching congratulations. Instead, I said nothing.

Chapter 15 - The Penny Dropped

The team was making great strides in our long-term goal of outplacing our patients. Anthony had moved and Hugo was to start attending the one-day a week program in Coolock. There was talk of Kitty making the move to that home-based program in Skerries and Delia was still assigned to the community house south of Dublin in Garrylough Mill. That the team was actually having an effect was testimony to the ethos of the Irish health services; psychologists were next to God. For those of us who had been on the ground doing the work, being next to the people that were next to God had its advantages. Still, for me, this was a condescending factor that really got up my nose. By now, for better or worse, I felt connected to the people that I was trying to help. I knew that the behavioral therapists felt the same. I couldn't really transition to treating them as "cases" but I had to admit that the administrative credibility given to us by the presence of the psychologists was the sole impetus that moved our programs forward. And by now, I had to accept that my California concept of teaming might never be adopted in my new country. In my naiveté, I had sought out all the staff members who were providing services to the same residents as myself. Nurses, teachers and behavioral therapists all agreed to meet once a month so that we could discuss our plans for our patients and combine our efforts toward a common goal. This was unheard of at the time. I was questioned on numerous occasions by original Pat, who had taken me around on my first day, as to why I felt it was necessary for all of us to talk. He even voiced concern that Aisling, the caregiver, sign language instructor and aromatherapist who was working with some of the most disturbed patients was "allowed" on the team. I found it hard to follow this logic. When I commented that the hospital had paid to train her in sign language and that she was the only person in the entire hospital who had that skill, he countered with the fact that she wasn't a nurse. Again, I was lost. He explained that some of the other nurses might object that she was on the team and meeting with other professionals. He repeated the fact that she wasn't a nurse. Had they complained? I asked. Not yet. I suggested that we worry about that when the time came. For all the times that we met, I never heard another staff member question her place on the team.

Our group met successfully for several months. We set agendas and common goals and we agreed to rotate the chairmanship of the meeting so that each of us had an opportunity to lead the team. Pat checked with me on a regular basis to see if the team was still intact. In my tenure at Portrane, this was the most contact I ever had with him. I finally realized that the thought of all of us meeting on our own made him extremely nervous. By our third meeting I "clocked" this suspicion and began to assure him that I had my doubts if the team would last much longer. This seemed to be what he wanted to hear and I was happy to go along with it just to set his fears aside so that the group could continue. After several months, members of the team were surprisingly pleased with our success and suggested that Pat be invited to attend as a member. They felt he should see how our experiment was helping us to communicate with our patients and with each other. I was the sole dissenting vote. I was pretty certain that open communication would not be considered a worthwhile objective. I lost the vote and Pat began to attend the meetings. Not long after that, the team voted to include Pat in the rota for team leader and again I objected. I reminded them that the team was based on all of us contributing at the same level. As a team leader, he might change the dynamic and our ability to speak freely. I lost again. Not long after that, he accepted their offer to be the permanent chair. They felt that his presence would give them more visibility. Not long after that, Pat pronounced the experiment a "complete success" and dissolved the team.

This need for hierarchy was solidly built into the system at Portrane. "Know your place" was still part of the national psyche and stepping out of it could bring consequences. Voicing an opinion was tapered and altered to a fine point, and depending on who was around, might only be delivered in a whisper. Even a simple straightforward question involving a time for lunch or a night out or a second drink would get an innocuous reply of "I don't mind" or "I'm not bothered." Was that a yes? A no? I longed for a definitive answer.

The presence of Imogen and Niall set our small therapist group into its own mini hierarchy. We all seemed to get along with Niall but, in the beginning, Imogene adopted quite a condescending attitude to the women in the group. As the only male, perhaps Niall felt his position was well defined but Imogen seemed to feel the need to establish herself as our superior. We were having none of this and we stood our ground whenever we felt the need. To be fair, there wasn't a cautious personality in the group and try as she might, Imogen could not establish herself as being above the members of the team.

Imogen's point of reckoning came several weeks into her assignment at Portrane. We were reviewing patient contacts and she asked about one patient in particular, the non-verbal young man in the locked ward that crawled around on all fours and hopped quickly to and from the pieces of office furniture. I told her that I had followed up on the speech therapy referral for that patient but that I had spent my time there hiding behind a desk chair with wheels. I told her that the nurses had warned me that the patient "…bites people that he doesn't know, especially women." She rolled her eyes and shook her head at my cowardice. It was true that the tall male nurse could have been winding me up, but I based my quick exit on the nurse's expertise. To be fair, speech therapy seemed like the least of the young man's needs.

Imogen assured me that there was no need to take the nurses comments to heart. She would demonstrate that there was a more professional way to go about dealing with this particular patient as well as the nurse's wry sense of humor. She volunteered to contact the nurses on the ward, meet the new patient and review her findings at our next meeting. The following week, when we arrived at the Old Nurses' Home, Imogen reported that it had all gone well. She had successfully interacted with the nurses on the ward as well as with the quick moving, lino-hopping patient. We were all temporarily impressed until Imogen, perched on her own office chair with wheels, delicately crossed her legs, right over left. There, directly in the middle of her leg, was a large bandage stretching directly across her calf. We said nothing but we all got along much better after that.

Niall became the biggest supporter of our efforts to convince the administration that the residents needed to be informed of the changes taking place in the hospital. At the time, the policy was to move people in or out whenever it was possible. Patients in the ward could wake up next to someone they had never seen before or to an empty bed where their best friend had been sleeping for years. Same sex relationships existed but were seldom discussed or acknowledged. The friend of one patient was moved out in the middle of the night to the disturbing reaction of the one left behind. When I suggested that the remaining resident might be depressed over the loss of her relationship, I was reminded that she, too, was a good girl and that pleasures of the flesh would not be a part of her thinking. And poor Vinnie continued to wander the hospital grounds hoping for the reappearance of his friend of many years. We managed to make a case for a transition strategy that would ease the patients into the plans for their change of location. Visitations were arranged and timelines were discussed. We knew that on various and differing levels, the patients were much more aware of the changes taking place than people may have realized. Change was something new to Portrane.

There would be no change of plans for Annie, a resident that I felt was one of the more communicative patients in St. Ita's. She had simply been there too long and was too institutionalized to adapt to a new environment. I had to learn to hedge my observations of people like Annie. While she communicated most deliberately with me, using mimicry or pantomime, her other behaviors, such as mood swings or bursts of anger, were unknown to me. I knew that she had a long time feud with a tall wiry, white-haired patient named John. They hated each other with a passion. He was as tall as she was diminutive but if they happened to meet up in the entryway or a hallway, they would turn their backs to each other, both of them emitting a snarling hiss. I could hear Annie, who was supposedly mute, suck in a chest-full of hospital air, giving her just enough power to squeeze out a hissy "bastard." To me, it was similar to Kitty destroying the library after Paris; I gave credit for sending a message in any form. But by now, my frame of reference for sending an "effective communication" was so drastically altered that when I came up against a resident who could make eye contact and initiate a connection on any level, I misguidedly felt that the possibilities were endless. This was a misconception that caused me to live with constant reevaluation and to defer to the nurses who knew the patients so well. Still, Annie remained as my main source of information for the whispered goings on in St. Ita's. This had been her home for a long, long time and she moved stealthily and silently in and around the dingy hallways with no one taking any notice.

Fortunately, the weather remained excellent throughout my first Dublin summer and there was no doubt that several days of sun could have a direct effect on everyone's mood. We spent lots of afternoons out on the back lawn behind the clock tower and Kitty and I took some day trips into Skerries. We were practicing for her possible move and I was developing a set of photographs that would help her to communicate in the shops and the pubs and in the community. She was very excited to make this move and Kitty, more than anyone, grasped the significance of the change in living arrangements. She would be out of the hospital and into a home. She was elated.

Hugo had also gone out on his first day trip to Coolock. It required a coordinated effort on the part of the hospital due to his need for transportation and assistance. Six weeks would be a good test of comparing the benefits to the cost. At the moment, the hospital was able to send Hugo to Coolock in one of the hospital ambulances but if the experiment should be a success, maybe his stipend could be used for a taxi ride once a week. According to the caregiver who accompanied him, simply looking out the window and seeing the new and different scenery was already pleasantly surprising him. I was elated with the possibility that the simple effort of a new experience would energize his other senses. I wasn't certain what to expect but even the smallest improvement could be a bridge to some other connection.

Frank and I continued to benefit from the beautiful weather whenever we managed to be in Dublin at the same time. He was back on the construction site, his holidays were over and Dublin was booming with development. There were skyscraper cranes covering the city center and the economy was poised to take off. My friend Eamonn kept encouraging me to buy a flat or an apartment in Dublin. I couldn't see it but he assured me that good times were coming the likes of which Dublin had never known. Besides, he pointed out, I had a job that was permanent and pensionable, that constant reaffirmation that such a job was the dream of any Irish civil servant. Political rumblings that the government was in trouble had begun to surface due to the mishandling of the extradition of Father Brendan Smyth. There was constant front-page news of a possible conspiracy between church and state to prevent the extradition to the north of Father Smyth, one of the first known pedophile priests. This was a simmering scandal that had the potential to completely take down the current Labor/Fianna Fail government coalition. It was fascinating to follow it in the papers and on the news. To me, the collapse of the government seemed like it would be a massive shakeup for the country but I was assured that the political system had it well in hand. Still, it seemed pretty unsettling and I couldn't see investing in a Dublin property. And to be honest, I wasn't completely certain that I wanted to be working in Portrane for the length of a mortgage. At the time, any mortgage had to be completely paid off by the time that the borrower reached the age of 65. My prorated payments would have a severe effect on my social life. I could barely afford my lino-over-dirt-floor subterranean flat. For the moment, I passed on making such a financial commitment and opted instead to enjoy the summer season that this year, actually, came with sun. So if I happened to be in Dublin at the same time as Frank or if I happened to be in the flat when the hall phone rang or if we both happened to be in O'Donoghue's on a Saturday afternoon, we made the most of the warm summer days.

We regularly walked up to the top of Dame Street to get fish and chips at Leo Burdock's. Burdock's was tiny and tight; there was always a queue out the door and up the street. This was the best place in Dublin to get fish and chips and it was solely for the purpose of takeaway. There weren't many places to plop down and eat around the shop so we would get our suppers and walk until we found a place away from the traffic and the noise. Frank would consistently tease me at my request for "light on the batter" as I'm fairly sure that no changes were ever made in the deep-frying process of Leo's fish.

On one particular Saturday afternoon, we had walked up to Burdock's and come away with just fish for me and fish and chips for Frank. We were starving and instead of looking for a place to eat we managed to squeeze onto the grass-covered verge that separated the lanes of traffic just at the bend of the road. It was sunny and bright and it was quiet enough as we spread out our newspaper-wrapped fish on the lawn. As always, I asked if my order had "light batter". My constant reference to calories both amused and annoyed him and he sarcastically assured me that not only was there light batter for me, but that he had asked that my batter be added to his fish.

It was an exceptionally lovely picnic on an unusually warm afternoon and I thought back about choosing to stay in Dublin and I was delighted with my decision. We finished up our meals and crumpled up the vinegar soaked newspapers rolling them into a soggy, solid ball. We were forced to mush our greasy hands against the already soggy newspaper to try and rid ourselves of the malt vinegar that still lingered on our fingers and thumbs. Burdock's is delicious but messy and my efforts were useless. I was about to stand up and walk back to the shop for something to help us tidy up when Frank, still sitting cross-legged on the grass, reached into his shirt pocket and pulled out a salmon colored napkin, handing it to me to wipe my face. I stared at the tissue in my hand as he gathered up our rubbish, stood up and walked away from me toward the bin. I couldn't believe it. Surely, I thought, no single man would select salmon colored napkins for his home décor, especially not a six-foot four-inch construction worker who lived on beer and batter. Frank dumped the trash in the bin and ambled back to where I was still sitting on the ground. He stooped down, held out his enormous hands and wrapped his fingers around my wrists. With his face close to mine, he lifted me up off the ground and then planted me back on the verge. I looked into his beautiful deep brown eyes and thought to myself, "Jesus, he's married." But did I say something? I did not.

Chapter 16 - It'll Be Gone Before You're Married

In true Irish fashion I opted to ignore what might be an unwelcome fact as to Frank's marital situation. After all, hadn't I ended up working in a mental institution because one little fact was omitted from my job interview? Wasn't I benignly roaming around with a married man who didn't see the need to reveal his status? Didn't I put my rent money down a hole in the ground the first of the month? Subterfuge seemed to be the strategy of choice. I was reminded of a butcher shop on Moore Street that, years ago, was frequented by my friend Una and many of her acquaintants. They would visit this butcher shop only during certain times of the week when a butcher, "who was known to them," was on duty. She told me how the butcher would weigh the meat, take their money and then give them the meat and in the fold of his hands, he would give back the money, too. "Times were hard," she said, "it helped us get by."

"But his employer," I complained, "is losing money. What about him?" This would invariably be followed with a shrug and/or a diatribe about "the man" or "the people" or "800 years of English oppression." One day while walking with her in the Ilac Center, I suggested that we go to the butcher on Moore Street and pick up some meat for a home-cooked meal on Haddington Road.

"Not possible," she said, "They went out of business years ago."

So I went along in my ignorance of the social mores of my adopted country. But with Frank, I was beginning to feel slightly guilty and fairly certain that I wasn't just putting my rent money but also sticking my head down the hole in the ground. I was sincerely hoping that Frank, as the indigenous member of the romance, would convince me that it was acceptable. By now I was familiar with No Divorce Ireland and the adjustments that people made to move on with their lives. Certainly Frank didn't hesitate to talk about his continuing relationship with the mother of the child; that she lived with her family and he was always welcome there. Why be so open about that and silent about another? I was fairly certain that the salmon colored napkin had not come from the kitchen of the father of the mother of the child, but I hoped, secretly, that it had.

But I wasn't the only one going through a social trauma. There was ongoing talk of a divorce referendum and that was causing lots of brooding self-analysis on the part of several of my friends. It seemed that as long as couples had no option to end their marriages, they lived their predestined lives in many adaptive ways. So pubs were populated with loads of men who just wanted to be out and about and didn't use their Friday night freedom for anything but drink. Wives went on holiday with their women friends and husbands never thought twice about it. Happy or unhappy together, they both welcomed the change. One Friday night I went to a hooley in Coolock to celebrate a couple's wedding anniversary. The music was mighty and I was surprised to see all the men standing on one side and all the women on the other. When I asked one of the women why the couples weren't mingling, she replied, "Sure, why would we? We see *them* every day," nodding toward the deep lines of men at the bar.

Sometimes the economics of a relationship would test the strength of the couple's companionship. When I worked at the clinic in Coolock, I met a lot of couples where the wives had jobs and the husbands didn't. It was simply fallout from the depressed economy of the time that women could find poorly paying but steady work and men could not. This was not unusual in the inner city and probably not any different than any other city with a high urban population. Mary would tell me about the history of this wife/husband - working/not-working conundrum. At the time, a child benefit check went out every month to the women who had given birth. Even if the father was present in the family, the check was always made out to the mother. Mary explained that this was due to the "auld days" when the men, who were often at home and unemployed, would get the check and "drink it away." Even Imogen, a highly paid psychologist who was married to another highly paid psychologist, received a monthly benefit check for her two children that was made out only to her. I objected to this financial support in one of our monthly meetings complaining that my 52% taxed monthly salary was subsidizing her income that was four times higher than mine. She shrugged. Shrugging was becoming an art form for me in Ireland. Omissions were constant and explanations weren't always forthcoming.

In Portrane, with our new team in place, we finally received the empowerment that we deserved. With two psychologists in situ, the administration began to take us seriously and our plans for the residents might finally see the light of day. This boost of energy was completely out of character for a group of people with permanent and pensionable jobs. The change in atmosphere also gave a woman on our team the courage to follow through on a trial marriage separation that had been brewing for some time; the fact that her husband also worked at St. Ita's definitely complicated the situation. In my limited awareness, it seemed to me that she had handled the situation extremely well, but to others, I said nothing.

This news reverberated around the nursing community in a way that made you think it was the first-ever marital separation known in the history of St. Ita's. If it wasn't, the male staff certainly acted that way. Not only did they give us the cold shoulder, but a good few of us were shunned, as well. Every once in a while I would overhear, "That Yank..." but I never gave in to the insinuation that my presence had raised anyone's consciousness. It simply wasn't true. I just stood by and watched as she became a strong advocate for the divorce referendum that loomed above us in the coming year. Divorce referendums had failed in the past, but this one was showing signs of passing into law even with the more outspoken support for rejection. The slow-growing positive backing was nebulous and suppressed but everyone felt its presence. It would be a topic of ongoing importance and agitation right up to a voting date that wasn't to take place until the following year.

This "no divorce" policy provided me with a prevalence of married but non-threatening men as neutral companions for weeknights and weekends around Dublin. I could skip work on a Tuesday afternoon, meet Brendan at the Screen Cinema for a matinee and then follow it with an early evening pub-crawl. Brian, the fabulous architect and fiddle player from New Year's Eve would keep me clued in on all the music around town. I would meet him in one place and then follow him to another. Eamonn would take me to business dinners at the nicest restaurants in Dublin where I met visiting EU businessmen and women. We'd end up in the Shelbourne Hotel and stay in the Horseshoe Bar until closing. It's how we met. One night Eamonn and I met up with his friend Denis just at closing time. The two of them announced that we would bundle up and walk the few blocks to The United Arts Club. I blindly trailed behind asking why we were going on when, obviously, the pubs were closed for the night. "Because," Eamonn informed me, "the club bar has an extension, a permit for an extra hour of drink."

Still dutifully following, I foolishly asked, "So we're walking six blocks in the drizzling rain just to have an extra hour of drink?" It was too late. I could not retrieve my incredibly naïve question. I could only watch it leave my mouth and escape into the chilly summer night air reminding my friends of my non-Irish status. I waited for the rebuke, but instead, both men stopped and turned to look at me. Then, in one smooth synchronized motion, they smiled, cocked their heads in the direction of The United Arts Club, nodded in agreement, turned back and walked on. They said nothing.

The United Arts Club has been in existence since 1907. It's housed in a cracked and splintered Edwardian building that reveals more history and personality every time a chip of paint peels off the wall. It was created on the heels of the great revival of art and literature that overwhelmed Ireland in the late 19th century. W.B. Yeats, Lady Gregory, Ellie Duncan, Count Casimir and Countess Constance Markievicz were all founding members of the club that, from the very beginning, always included both men and women. There is a buzzer at the door with a camera that identifies you to the barman upstairs. It's a member's only club but if you time your arrival to be seen at the door with a member, it's just as good.

The United Arts Club bar and its amazing cast of characters became a comfortable place for me. Even as a barely middle-aged woman, I was the youngest person in the club and I was fascinated with the stories that rolled off the tongues of the locals. On my first visit, I blindly followed Eamonn and Denis around the lounge and the bar, keeping my comments to a minimum.

I was very sensitive to my accent and had noticed, over the months, that hearing my California dialect was often the cause of a start-up discussion. I didn't mind that. Most people thought that I was on holiday and wanted to chat. But when they found out that I lived here, or had "stolen a job from an Irish speech therapist," then discussion often turned to argument, usually political and sometimes historical. I could never get over the intense conversations that could begin at a bus stop or just getting a cup of coffee. People seemed so informed and so well read and they were never shy with an opinion. It took me a while to realize that it was often done just for the craic but those boundaries were unclear so I kept my gob shut as much as I could.

That's why I was so surprised, one late night while sipping my whiskey at the United Arts Club bar, an American voice declared to me, "You're that Yank who is going to Budapest." I tracked the disembodied voice to a man sitting three stools over. Incredibly, he was right, I had planned a trip to Budapest.

"Do I know you?" I asked.

"Nope," he responded while sipping his whiskey through a slight east coast American accent. He definitely appeared to be enjoying my confusion.

"I've actually been to Budapest and back," I said. "Do you mind telling me how you know about my trip?"

He gave it a few seconds. Then told me that months earlier he had seen me reading a Budapest guidebook while sitting at the bar in the Gresham Hotel, totally on the other side of Dublin, and far away from where we were now. "I heard your accent when you ordered your drink."

I asked him if he was a spy but he turned out to be Pat the Yank, retired Marine Corp colonel doing graduate work on the GI Bill. He was a highly decorated Vietnam veteran who was fulfilling his dream of returning to the land of his birth. Several days a week he attended graduate school classes in Maynooth, and on the other days, he ran the office for a member of the Irish parliament, the Dail. This evolved into a great friendship with many, many nights drinking in the Dail Bar and several late nights in Jury's, securing my education into the Irish political system. He became a wonderful friend and another benign running buddy, but Jaysus, I thought, this country is just too, too small to think that you can get away with anything. I finally grasped that the philosophy is not to avoid doing things but to simply not acknowledge having done them. Everyone had their secrets; Ireland is a land of whispers. But if you don't acknowledge it, and everyone supports your denial, then it didn't exist; it's simply well planned, effective subterfuge.

My favorite person in the United Arts Club was Maeve, a retired public servant. She was the loveliest, most sardonic, well-groomed and acerbic woman I have ever met. She was sharp as a tack and would slyly and quietly let you know it. In Ireland, a public servant was forced into retirement at 65. Ready or not, Maeve had to leave her job, which she loved. She had been retired for many years by the time that I met her. Maeve never married and she lived on her own in a flat not far from the club. She had traveled some when she was younger but her preferred tourist location was the east coast of the United States. I sat next to her at the bar whenever I could find an empty seat.

Maeve was a slight woman with chin length, beautiful white hair that was perfectly coiffed and never out of place. Her nails were always done, I have no idea where she found a manicurist, and she was prone to wearing matching pastel sweater sets with the perfect set of choker length pearls. She drank red wine and the occasional whiskey and the barman knew to never let her wine glass go empty. Never. Other than myself, she was the only woman I knew who wore eye makeup and, like me, was totally on her own. She would sit at the bar, gingerly crossing her legs, and tell stories that often came with a sarcastic but witty conclusion. She slyly made comments under her breath that were hilarious and best kept between us. I idolized her.

Christine Lacey

Maeve kept busy during the day but the United Arts Club was definitely her home away from home. She would stay until very late and then walk home to her flat in the early morning hours. Members of the club pleaded with her to take a taxi or wait for a lift but Maeve would always decline. In the time that I knew her, she had been mugged twice and still she persisted in walking home on her own. I tried to keep up with her at the bar just to hear her comments but it was hard going. She was the most exquisite looking of women, soft-spoken and angelic to see but her wit and her drinking belied a woman of another ilk. One night while sitting next to her, Maeve's eyelids began lower in the middle of her sentence. I leaned toward her to hear the rest of her comment. She kept whispering as she uncrossed her legs and hooked her heels onto the lower wooden bar of the stool. Then in one slow and elegant move, her heels released, pointing her toes downward allowing her body to slide graciously along the perimeter of the barstool toward the floor. I panicked and moved quickly from my seat to grab her but her gaze remained with me, instinctively telling me that to panic would be the wrong thing to do. I stopped. With a bar full of people, she unnoticeably reached up for and then held on to my forearm. Halting her decline, she steadied herself and allowed me to slowly lift her up using my arm to place her diminutive bum back on her barstool. What style, I thought, and if anyone noticed, they certainly didn't acknowledge it.

Only once did I see Maeve outside of the club. It was on a Saturday night when Dublin was chock-a-block with people celebrating a rugby match. I was with a friend and we were absolutely hopeless at finding a pub where we could sit and talk above the thunderous telly noise and the pub conversations. We sneaked down a dark laneway and into the side back door of a pub off of Grafton Street that I didn't even know existed. Luckily the back of the bar was fairly quiet and seemed to have several snugs, private meeting areas, along the hallway that paralleled the busier part of the bar. Just as we opened the door, there was Maeve in the middle snug, with a man. I was lost as to what to do or say. I immediately thought that I shouldn't acknowledge her outside of the club and especially not with a gentleman. Having never seen her with, or heard her speak of, anyone, his very presence hinted at something secretive. But Maeve was ahead of me taking the lead, and introduced us to her gentlemen friend. We said hello and goodbye and moved on. The next time I saw Maeve in the club, she told me that they had been a couple for decades. Needless to say, he was married but their relationship had started and continued in spite of it. I kept her secret for decades. Years after she passed, I revealed her story to my friend Eamonn. He applauded my loyalty but he let me know that her love affair was common knowledge. It seems we all kept her secret, we said nothing.

Chapter 17 - As I See It, I Say It

The fabulous summer weather continued and I intended to follow the sun around Ireland as long as I could and wherever it led me. I made long-term plans for the Galway Races and then added the Ballinasloe Horse Fair, a suggestion from the teaching staff at the school on the grounds of St. Ita's. Sheelagh, one of the teachers, was adamant that I seek out Madame Lee when I eventually got to Ballinasloe and have her, and only her, tell my fortune. Having your fortune told was a major part of the horse fair experience but I couldn't see the connection. I wondered about Sheelagh's emphatic insistence to have my fortune read, especially when The Church, as far as I knew, was just as adamant about not seeking out fortune tellers, palm readers or tarot card dealers. Evidently, the fantasy of revealing your future lived quite happily next door to a church which claimed that only religion could show you the way. Sheelagh was the chief source for all things spiritual and I was more than enthusiastic about meeting Madame Lee but the horse fair was still weeks and weeks away. To feed my now piqued curiosity, Sheelagh sent me down to the Irish Psychic Institute on Wicklow Street off Grafton Street. I met with John, a lovely, older Irish man with a long, curly, grey beard who was soft spoken and all knowing. John had lived in numerous countries before coming home and spoke with a warm kindness and what felt like an all-consuming insight. John told me many things but his strongest message to me was that I would not be going home to America anytime soon. He felt strongly that I had been grounded by growing up in America with its astrological element of "earth" and that it was time for me to experience Ireland and its element of "air," the sign for emotions. It was time to be responsive instead of rational and he assured me that my earthly upbringing would hold me together. I had my doubts. I felt that I was already swimming upstream with Frank and St. Ita's and that *not* thinking might be my downfall.

Still, things seemed to feel as if they were progressing at Portrane, what with Anthony and Hugo out on their placements and plans in the works for both Kitty and Delia. A group of us took a drive to Garrylough Mill to see the place that might be a home for Delia. It was a beautiful location. The building was set up against a lovely grass-covered hill with wildflowers popping out all over the hillside. It had been part of a working mill and there was a slim little stream that ran along the property with a large wooden water wheel at one end, fairly close to the building. It was Irish Picture Postcard Perfect. The team agreed that acquiring the property would be an excellent venture and the long process of working through the acquisition was soon underway.

Hugo was now into his third visit to the center in Coolock. I was delighted with the participation of the members of the group and Marie, the group leader, let me know that Hugo seemed to be enjoying it. Hugo's language was limited so he tended to respond with a head move or a laugh as a reaction to his surroundings. I knew that Hugo was a flirt but I kept this to myself. I'm fairly certain that the staff felt, given his disabilities, that Hugo had lost interest in the opposite sex. My support of residents "interacting" was not always shared by my peers. In a lecture class with the psychiatric nurses, I commented on how flirtatious a much, much older resident acted whenever he saw an attractive woman. He would laugh, maintain eye contact and use complete sentences, all good stuff in the speech therapy handbook. It's true that his closing line was an offer to reveal his appendectomy scar, "from St. Vincent's," but he never showed it, at least not to me. I called him "connected." The nurses called him "randy."

As it happened, Hugo seemed to develop an attraction to one of the young, female caregivers working in the center. Marie had her suspicions but there was nothing to back them up until the third of his six promised visits. The clients had been moved into a circle for a communication game. The caregiver was away for the morning, having left to do the messages. When she returned, the activity was still going on. So as not to bother the group, she entered through a side door that opened up into a workroom, adjacent to but behind, where the group was meeting. She closed the door and raised her voice to announce her return. "That's me finished," she said.

Hugo turned his head in the direction of her voice and said, "Oh, you're back." I was beside myself. This was Hugo being aware, spontaneous and initiating a timely and appropriate social response. It may seem like an overreaction to a four-word comment but both Marie and I knew the significance of his reaction. The next morning, I was ecstatic to report this development to the team where I was duly informed that Hugo would not be getting his promised remaining three sessions. He wasn't even allowed to go back to say, "goodbye."

Nothing that Marie or I could do was going to change this decision. The administration had promised Hugo a six-week trial period to placate us from pursuing a long-term move and we had agreed to that proposal. Halfway through the placement, we had seen progress. But a caregiver voicing the opinion that, "They can't teach him anything there that we can't teach him here" had left an impression. That may have been true if the programs in Coolock were also available in Portrane. But Marie had designed something special for people like Hugo. In Portrane, he was well cared for and he was minded but the most exposure he ever received was when he rode around the Children's Unit with his stomach flat on his skateboard, eye level to everyone else's ankles. My defense was that growth can come from a change of scene or sound or stimulation. Just getting Hugo into his wheelchair, moving him outside into the warm sunny air and then into a taxi where, once a week, he could look out the window as he went down the motorway was giving him stimuli that he had been denied for years. But no, his visits were finished. My astrological experiment with "air," the element of emotions, was taking a toll.

When I got home that night to Haddington Road I was overwhelmed with one central emotion; disappointment. If an agreement from the administration that was supported by the team and backed-up by my boss could be wrenched out of existence without any discussion, then I had my doubts about our plans for the other residents. I knew that I couldn't face the Friday night crowd so I opted for a night in and a Chinese takeaway. The "Chinese" on Baggot Street made an excellent chicken curry that was my favorite new Irish comfort food. Cushioned on a bed of rice, the side dish was always a large order of chips with curry sauce. Due to what people felt was an unusually high number of cats disappearing from the neighborhood, the local Chinese restaurants had been instructed to use an entire chicken breast when making up this dish. We wanted no doubts about the origination of the smaller bits of food that floated in the golden-red, spicy curry sauce. Unfortunately, having an identifiable chicken part did make it harder to eat when you were wobbling your way home from a night out.

Standing in the middle of the bedsit, the only place I could stand, I started to change my clothes before heading up to Baggot Street for my meal. The night air was still a little sharp and I had turned on the gas heater just to take away the chill. I hung up my coat in the tiny wardrobe and moved closer to the heat. As I pulled my jumper over my head a piece of wool caught in my earring. I moved closer to the heater so that I could see the reflection of the earring in the oval mirror from Guiney's that hung above the fireplace. It gradually loosened and I pulled the sweater up and over my head. It was just then that I caught sight of my reflection where I saw rows and rows of bright red welts, crisscrossing my back in a slightly symmetrical and horizontal fashion. I let out a scream and a comment, "That figures," and then I burst into tears. I had never experienced such welts before and I knew they didn't come by way of a sweater brought from home. The assumption that they had to come from stress and sadness kept me in tears for a good long while. When I recovered, I walked up to Baggot Street for my dinner. While waiting for the fully developed breast of chicken curry, I went to the off license to buy the least expensive bottle of Jameson's and a ten pack of Silk Cut Blues. I collected the curry, walked back to the flat and planted myself tightly into the corner of the tiny single bed. I turned on the telly for reruns of the Late, Late Show and then I ate all of the chicken, most of the chips, drank half of the whiskey and smoked nine of the cigarettes.

The disappointment over Hugo's placement got me to thinking about changing jobs. The offices of FAS (the Irish word for "grow") were government-sponsored centers for job seekers and they were peppered all along the streets of Dublin. If John, the psychic, was correct and I wasn't going home, then maybe a career move would be in my best interest. I had a background in corporate communications and television production so I started to shop the job listings whenever I walked past a FAS center. Available jobs were described on a handwritten, pale orange, 4x6 note card that was then stuck on the office window with Sellotape. Openings weren't plentiful but there were a few that definitely matched my background. My enthusiasm lessened each time I read the bottom line of every job description, "Applicants over 45 need not apply." Placement counselors would not even read a CV if the applicant was in this age bracket. Youth was given all the leverage, and regardless of age discrimination, it was obvious that anyone over 45 was judged to be well past their "sell-by-date." Career moves weren't an option for people of a certain age. Like it or not, a secure job was kept, finding another was just too dodgy. Job counselors found it hard to believe that I would consider leaving my permanent and pensionable job in Portrane. True, my motivation was vague. I explained to one counselor that I wanted to wear a suit, meet co-workers for coffee and know that they wouldn't spit into my cup during the conversation.

Not surprisingly, I had no luck at FAS. But a friend organized a meeting with the head of Ardmore Studios, which was experiencing a revival in the mid-1990s. This was partially due to the support of Michael D. Higgins, the Minister of Arts, Culture and the Gaeltacht who was instrumental in bringing film production into Ireland. I took a day off of work to have the meeting in the morning and then head off to the Galway Races in the afternoon. Frank was also going to the races but I didn't plan to meet up with him. I was trying to distance myself from what I thought was becoming a tricky situation. I sprung my "interview suit" from the back of the wardrobe followed by a feeble attempt to apply my first ever contact lenses. I hoped to look younger than the dreaded age of 45. Perching over the tiny sink in the bedsit loo, my face four inches from the mirror, I got them in well enough, but unfortunately, I couldn't get them out. For hours I poked and pulled and flooded my eyes with solution. When I finally got them out, sometime in the early hours of the morning, my eyes were the same shade of red as the St. Ita's induced welts crisscrossing my back. I got to the interview, but I wasn't called back. I'm sure I looked like the Yank who moved to Ireland and couldn't stay off the drink. My career path was settled.

Dejected I headed out to Galway for the races and what was touted as one of the biggest and liveliest meets of the year. It was a gorgeous day and I drove around and around Galway looking for a place to stay. I hadn't booked a room but things were quieter then and my philosophy, as a single traveler, continued to rest on the belief that there is always one single room left. And there was one, just at the edge of the city. I dumped my bag and made my way out to the races. It seemed like a combination of gambling, drinking and the county fair all rolled into one. After several races, I made my way back into town where I located a restaurant with a long queue. An elderly gentleman waiting just inside looked to be in need of assistance so I helped him over to a bench where he could rest while he waited for his table. As he sat down the cuffs of his trousers lifted slightly showing off the most colorful pair of socks I had ever seen. I complimented him on his stylish choice and then his name was called for his dinner. Before he wandered off he thanked me for my help and then he bent over, close to my ear and whispered the name of a horse and the number of a race. Straightening up to leave, he extended a boney index finger and with a quick wink he thumped me twice on the shoulder. I smiled back even though I was slightly unsure of what had just happened. I waited a while longer then gave up on the restaurant and headed over to the Great Southern Hotel. Sheelagh had assured me that the Great Southern was the place to be. Galway was absolutely jammed with people from all over the country but I managed to make my way into the hotel bar and find a stool at the very end of the bar next to the wall. I had every intention of holding onto that seat for the duration of the evening. There was great music and lively chat and when I turned around there was Frank.

Now Frank had very mixed feelings at finding me in the Great Southern Bar. He was already miffed at me for refusing his invitation and heading out on my own. In fairness, I did tell him about the job interview but he considered that to be a silly waste of time given my permanent job status. He couldn't understand my interest in the film business and considered the whole idea to be frivolous and far-fetched. Our differing backgrounds were beginning to edge themselves ever near the surface and they were bringing our differences with them. Still, we were in Galway for the races and it was impossible to not have a good time with all the craic and the craziness that came with it.

We left the Great Southern and headed out for a night of food and music that lasted late into the morning. The weather was mild and dry and everyone was in good form. We arranged to meet the next day and I headed back to my own single space. I was staying on until bank holiday Monday to visit the Aran Islands but Frank was leaving the next day to get back to work.

Very late the next morning we met up in Eyre Square and went immediately to buy an Irish Times and find a place for breakfast and the crossword. Doing the crossword puzzle in the Irish Times were some of the best moments we had together. We could be in a betting office or a café or a pub or on a train and we would squish up into the corner and work the puzzle. Sometimes the newspaper came in and out all during the day and at various times of squishing. He always finished the puzzle, always. I did it, once.

We found a betting office next to the restaurant and shifted between watching the horses and finishing our meal. Then we found a betting office next to the pub and we bet between drinking our pints. I was astonished to see that the winner of the afternoon race was the horse that the elderly man had whispered in my ear. He sailed easily into first place and stayed there, winning a pot full of money for people smart enough to bet on him. I told Frank the story of the lovely man with the crazy socks who had whispered in my ear. Frank was amazed that I hadn't told him so that we could have placed a bet on the horse.

"You got a tip!" he kept saying, "You got a tip!" My learning curve for betting shot up by 100%. Evidently these valuable tips often floated around the racetrack and elderly men with crazy socks eating in expensive restaurants were often the place to find them. I regretted that I had said nothing.

Frank was still upset that I was staying on and he was going back to Dublin. I was trying to limit the time that we spent together but I was too cowardly to deal with it directly. This evasiveness was causing friction between us. Rather than address my concerns about his marital status, I left it up to waffling excuses like "needing time on my own" or some other cowardly explanation. He didn't buy it. All he wanted to do was be together. It was brilliant fun and terribly exciting so why would we stop doing something that felt so good? I left him in Eyre Square sitting in the little Red Golf when I went off to buy my ticket for the Aran Islands. When I came back, he was sitting on the driver's side of the car with his arm wrapped around the top of the steering wheel. The door was open and he had one long leg curled up perpendicular to the seat and the other was stretched out, reaching way into the next parking space. The radio was on, the volume was up and I could hear Linda Ronstadt's voice emerging from the little red Golf. "Desperado" was peeling and pleading all along the warm air that floated over the tops of the cars in Eyre Square. I knew that "needing time on my own" wasn't going to go much further.

He got out of the car and we walked across the square, down a tiny side street where he had found a space to park his aging Vauxhall. It hadn't been running very well and I was concerned that he could make it all the way back to Dublin for work the next day. I knew that he could clock to within five miles how far he could go when the gas gauge read "empty" and he often drove without much petrol in the tank. But now the Vauxhall had developed a fierce leak in the radiator. He assured me that it wouldn't be a problem. Then he popped the bonnet and asked me to mind the car while he slipped across the street to a little corner shop and came back carrying a small paper bag. He handed me the bag then he opened the radiator cap and started the engine. Out of the bag he took a half carton of eggs and he gave them to me. As the engine heated up, one by one, he cracked the eggs and poured them down the steaming radiator. When the sixth egg had been well and Chevy poached he replaced the radiator cap, closed the bonnet, kissed me goodbye and headed back to Dublin...Desperado, indeed.

Chapter 18 - An Irish Solution

In Portrane, I had to accept that my plans for Hugo were done and dusted. It felt like a major setback in my attempts to "do something" irrespective of the low level of expectations that were put on my position. I began to grasp the true concept of Aisling's caution, "They need you to be here, but they don't want you to do anything." My frustration was gaining momentum and I sought out Mary's help during our debriefing in Coolock. I told her how disappointed I was that Hugo was not going back to the clinic. I admitted that I had almost lost my temper and barely avoided making an emphatic gesture when I left the meeting at the hospital. Mary was also frustrated and empathic. She raised her right hand with her arthritic fingers all curled down and inward toward her palm and moving her wrist, she shook it furiously, up and down, as one unit. "I know," she said, "if I could lift my middle finger, I'd flip them off, too." I knew that I still had Mary's full support, so with the help of the team we moved forward with plans for Kitty and Delia.

The placement for Kitty was a shared room in a large, two-story home located in a housing estate in Skerries. There was a caregiver on duty, day and night, and the residents had differing activities throughout their week. Finbarr, the knife carrying, highly successful Elvis impersonator, had a job during the week, as did several others. Kitty would not be employed but she would have walking access to the village, which would suit her just fine. I made several trips to Skerries to map out Kitty's route to the village. At each juncture of her walk from home to town, I positioned her at an obvious landmark, had her point toward the next direction she should take and then I took her photograph. This picture guide would lead her over to the village and back to the house giving her some well-earned independence. Due to her deafness, we spent a lot of time practicing to look in all directions before making any move at all. The walk to the village included several busy intersections and two sets of train tracks. Kitty had to be on a constant visual alert, as she would never hear the train coming or the car turning. In addition to the map, we created a communication book that would help her to order in restaurants or ask for assistance or make a purchase.

We made our first successful trip into town and our reward was a cup of tea in the local pub. We selected a table and then it was Kitty's job to get the attention of the barman and order the tea. By now, Kitty's confidence had grown, giving her the courage to increase her vocalizations. By simply using her voice she was improving the clarity of her speech and this made her more willing to try to speak to people in differing situations. I was especially proud of her when she demonstrated such grace at being asked, several times, to repeat her sentences. She never lost her patience or her control. She continued to smile, maintain her eye contact and sometimes she would lightly touch the arm of her listener just to make one more connection. She was one of the most highly motivated people I have ever met. The more I got to know her, the better I understood her frustration at leaving Paris for St. Ita's and then destroying the library in her wake. Her need to communicate was powerful and she was willing to try anything to build that bridge.

Kitty went up to the bar, and when the barman came over, she flipped through the communication book to the picture of a teapot and a cup of tea. She used the sign for, "Hello" and then pointed, as practiced, to the picture in the book. But as she pointed she also voiced, "Cuppa tee, peese." He looked at her quizzically and without asking for a repetition, she comfortably provided one.

The barman understood and asked, "Where are you sitting?" as he scanned the room. She must have understood this gesture and she pointed to where I was waiting. "Right away," he said, but before he moved from the bar she took hold of his forearm.

"Sooka?" she volunteered and he nodded his understanding. When we had finished our tea, with sugar, we took a walk around the village for some window-shopping before mapping our way back to the house. She was delighted with her progress. I had never seen her so pleased.

When we returned to the house and Kitty had gone up to her room, the nurse on duty asked if I could take some time to interview some of the other residents to assess their need for communication assistance. She said that she could set me up in the sitting room but at the moment the visiting chiropodist occupied it. We had yet another cup of tea and when the chiropodist had finished and gone, the nurse pointed me toward the sitting room door and off she went to get the residents. I knocked at the door even though I was fairly certain that the room was empty. I had learned that due to heating costs, all the doors to rooms in Ireland were kept closed, and knocking and waiting for an answer was a priority in Irish etiquette. I knocked and waited and when there was no answer, I went into the sitting room and heaved my briefcase and notebook up on a nearby table. I positioned a chair next to the table and across from the couch where I felt the residents would be the most comfortable. Evidently the chiropodist also felt this was the optimum position because as I sat down I saw, at my feet, the largest pile of skin and toenails ever-accumulated in one sitting room. I tried to be pragmatic about their existence, but the combination of colors and lengths gave a slight turn to my stomach. I reversed the position of the table and chair before meeting the residents and giving the nurse the feedback that she was seeking. Regular toenail maintenance was right in line with the facial hair trimming that I had seen in St. Ita's. I hadn't thought much about the men being in need of a shave but the women often had a good set of facial hair as well. I was told that its rapid growth was due to hormones and medication. I would see the women with a fair bit of hair on their chins and their lips and then it would be gone. As it happened, there was a scattered schedule throughout the hospital where men in one ward were shaved on one day and the women on the other. Given my half Portuguese heritage, I thanked God for my Los Angeles electrologist and I made a mental note to never again visit Kitty on the heels of the visiting chiropodist.

By now I had become good friends with Pat the Yank, the retired American colonel. His major in Irish studies was a great support to him in his part-time job at the Dail. The TD, the representative, that he worked for came from Cork and Pat helped to manage the Dublin office. Pat was a staunch supporter of a United Ireland and was outspoken with his attitudes and his opinions. The negotiations for the Northern Ireland Peace Process were just beginning and Pat was extremely helpful in guiding me through the political process now underway. But we actually bonded over his misassumption of my support for an American presidential candidate when, as it turned out, both he and I had voted for the renegade. Pat was my academic mentor and taught me a great deal about the history of Ireland and its politics. He invited me to go with him out to the Wicklow Mountains to a pub called Johnny Fox's. Pat believed this pub to be a stronghold of local republicanism and wanted to exercise his academic awareness in a place that supported his ideas. Mary had reservations about me visiting that pub. "That's where the American girl went missing," she warned.

I was undaunted and agreed to go with him. By now I felt I had accumulated a significant amount of time in the Dublin pubs and was well able to handle the strategies and expectations. For example, there is a lot of body contact when trying to negotiate your way through a pub crowd to get to the bar or to find a table. No matter what body parts are touched or jostled, this physical contact means nothing when compared to the goal of ordering a pint. I had a friend visiting from California and we happened to go for a drink at O'Shea's The Merchant just after an All Ireland GAA Football Match. There was standing room only and we got separated while trying to order drinks. When I finally found her she was beet red and flustered and giving out about the rude and obnoxious Irish men. To be fair, this had never been my experience, so I asked her what had happened. She complained that the men were all over her, pawing her and touching her with very unwelcome gestures. When I asked where she had gone to get the drinks, she pointed to a section of the bar, just in front of the taps for draught beer. She had positioned herself directly between hundreds of post-match, GAA supporters and their access to Guinness. Good or bad I couldn't say, but I assured her that her womanly charms were never in danger.

Politics were ever present in the various Dublin pubs as well. I was in Searson's on Baggot Street one night for closing at 11:30 pm. I was just finishing up a conversation with a friend when the lights went up and music began to play. I was whooshed off my bar stool when my friend waved her hand at me and then indicated by repeatedly lifting her chin that I was to get up and stand somewhat at attention. People began to sing to the recorded music and I eventually recognized it as the Irish National Anthem. This seemed a bit of a heavy-handed way to finish a fun night out in a pub but I loved hearing everyone singing the National Anthem, in Irish, at closing time. So I wasn't surprised when Pat and I drove up the mountain to Johnny Fox's that after dinner and drinks the national anthem began to play. I was well able for the reverence presented and the silence expected. But at the end of the National Anthem, one strong voice began to sing "A Nation Once Again" and everyone in the pub forcefully joined in at the chorus. For the first time, a cease-fire coming from the Northern Ireland Peace Process was beginning to feel like a reality. People dared to have faith that there might be an end to the conflict. The feeling of hope was palpable. I could never learn the Irish words to the National Anthem but I proudly hummed along with the rest of the Johnny Fox patriots.

When I returned to St. Ita's on the Monday morning, Annie was there to meet me in the entryway. I was beginning to have an immediate sense of dread whenever I saw her standing and waiting for the little red Golf. Seldom the purveyor of good news, she couldn't wait for me to get to the front door before dancing through her current pantomime. This performance had an immediate dark tone as she extended her index finger, made several wide circles around her head, turned the finger into a fist and then jerked her fist upward. I went inside with her to reception and made a motion for her to do it again in front of the clerk at the switch. He watched her movements and then he confirmed, "Yes, a nurse hanged himself on the tree down in the schoolyard." Annie beamed at having her message relayed. I went quickly up the stairs of the Old Nurses' Home where a team meeting was about to start. Everyone was talking about the loss of this nurse who was well known and especially well-liked by the patients throughout the hospital. It was a tragedy beyond belief and the team set about discussing how to handle this loss with the residents. We had been trying to convince the administration that the feelings of the residents should be taken into consideration when changes were made to their lives in Portrane. We were concerned that as people moved out and new people came in, the residents and their friends who were affected by these moves should be given some sort of warning or rehearsal. We had been working on ways to possibly use visuals to communicate these changes and hopefully lessen the stress experienced by the patients. But the loss of this nurse had a widespread effect; all over the hospital people were talking about his death. The tree where he hanged himself was the tall, lone tree that grew between the hospital outbuildings and the schoolyard. We couldn't be certain but it was highly likely that some of the residents may have seen the body as they walked along the well-used path. The ramifications of this were heartbreaking.

After the meeting, I happened to see a manager going hurriedly into his office. I followed him and asked if I could have a word. I told him about the team meeting and suggested that we might set up some sort of counseling for the patients who appeared the most traumatized over the loss of this nurse, that they might be more disturbed by this act than we knew. He listened and nodded and nodded and listened and then he stood up to face me with an attitude that I hadn't seen before. "It's been seen to," he said, in a huffy, exhausted but very conclusive manner.

Hesitatingly, I commented, "That's good news. What's been done?"

He turned his back to me and dryly confirmed, "We cut down the tree."

I had so much to say, but all I could do was hold back the tears and say nothing.

Chapter 19 - This is It. This is Just It.

———————

Aisling's observation had become painfully clear but to not "do any-thing" just wasn't in my remit. I opted to avoid giving in and to instead become selective about my future battles. I had lost my fight for Hugo but Anthony was doing well, Kitty was delighted to be in Skerries and Delia had visited the house in Garylough Mill and loved it. I still had Mary in my corner giving me massive amounts of support and assis-tance and that together with the overwhelming truth that the pubs were fun, the music was mad, the craic was mighty and the sun was still shining meant that I wasn't ready to go home just yet.

Having said that, it had come to light over a pint in O'Donoghue's that Frank *was* married and he seemed pretty happy about it. The fam-ily didn't live separately nor did they build a wall made of plywood down the center of the house. The question was asked in a fairly direct fashion during a betting session on a Saturday afternoon. He was total-ly flummoxed about my somewhat delayed consternation given all the time we had spent together, but I felt that I had to bring some sort of emotion to the table. I needed at least a semblance of righteousness if I was going to use ignorance as an excuse for downplaying my instincts.

I shouldn't have worried. Frank came off as something of a good-na-tured soul and a man who was well able to compartmentalize. In ad-dition to me he had been, and to some extent still was, involved with the mother of the child. He was content being married, the relationship having been somewhat predestined. It took a bit of a push because of a ten-year age difference but he was happy. It was all about balance.

My protestations about ending "our situation" fell flat. He countered with the fact that we had been having a wonderful time; no one had been slighted, so obviously, there was no problem. I suppose that I was hoping that he would seem sad, or sorry, or a little bit guilty because I was certainly feeling guilty. But I had no intention of carrying all the guilt especially when I had been following his homegrown Irish romantic lead. Up until now, I had met all sorts of couples who were managing their unhappy marriages in whatever ways they could. I knew that lots of couples had learned to live without the option of divorce and carried on with their separate married lives and their new relationships. I had several friends who had left their wives or husbands and set up housekeeping with their new partners. They made it easy for their children to visit the other parent and the priest always baptized any new babies that came along. This made me question the comparative weight of sinning in Ireland. I couldn't understand how divorce was so evil and yet having children out of wedlock got a pass. "Sure 'tis all for the child," I was told. I guess we didn't want the little "babaí" missing out on eternal salvation, but I never got the feeling that their parents would be eased out of heaven either. There were lots of fine lines in the Irish Catholic-social psyche and I thought that Frank was working one of these loopholes for us. But no...he just "was" ... in the most existentialist of interpretations. I couldn't judge him closely enough to guess if he had done this before but I admit to thinking that meeting me might be something strange and different for him; there still appeared to be a sort of cachet at being involved with a foreigner, even an older American woman. As my friend Pamela says, "You only get to be exotic once you cross an ocean." She never mentioned I might have a "sell-by-date."

Frank and I did not make any decisions after this first round of facing the music (in-between betting on horses and drinking pints) but I knew

I would be bringing it up again. The concerns were totally mine and my whinging about breaking it off caused him to react with an anger that I hadn't seen before. I had seen his temper flash but never toward me. My hollow and defensive protestations over right and wrong were totally lost on him. He held to his "no harm, no foul" philosophy but slowly over the next days and weeks, I increased the distance between us. Finishing with him was going to require some sort of action; talking was getting me nowhere.

In St. Ita's we started preparing for Christmas even though it was months and months away. In the therapies and down in the schoolyard the teachers and the nurses got out the poems, the music and the construction paper to start working on scenes for the upcoming Christmas concert. Residents began to practice poems and learn songs that they would perform for the public at the holidays. At first, I was appalled that the patients would be performing on stage for the local community. It had a bit of a "sideshow" feel to me and I was against it. But I began to see how the residents absolutely loved this break from the daily routine and welcomed the opportunity to do something different. They painted sets and worked on costumes with Christmas carols playing in the background. My guess is that most of them, at some time, had experienced positive feelings toward the Christmas season and this, plus the opportunity to do something different, made their day to day existence much more bearable. I think the staff felt the same. They worked very hard to bring the residents together for practices during the week and organized rehearsal sessions in the large multipurpose room with a stage. Just leaving the wards to move through the hospital and practice together on the stage had an overwhelmingly positive effect on everyone. Never mind that Christmas was months away. It was a welcome change throughout Portrane. All in all, there was a feeling of "lightness" that hadn't been there before. After seeing their enthusiasm, I was a willing participant and supporter. Among my clients, Kitty had a significant part in the show. Apparently she was an excellent dancer and responded beautifully to the music even though her hearing was almost nonexistent.

I also volunteered to drive former residents from their work locations up to Portrane for the rehearsals. This is how I met Emer. Once I collected her from her job, it could take us a while to get across town to the hospital. We were often together in the little red Golf for a good bit of time. I became quite fascinated with Emer and her personal story that, over time, she told very concisely and eloquently. Emer must have been in her early fifties when I met her, much the same age as Kitty. I enjoyed talking with her and she was very forthcoming when she spoke about her personal experience. I told her that one day I hoped to write a book about my time in Dublin. "Jaysus, Chris," she said, "tis my story you should be writin'."

At a very young age, Emer was placed in an orphanage even though, unknown to her, she had a sister somewhere. Eventually that secret was revealed but Emer was never able to find her. Because she found it difficult to learn to read, Emer was placed in a home for what she called "backward" children. Judging from the way she was speaking with me, I could assume that her language developed appropriately; her communication skills were relatively very good. By the time she was eleven she had learned to read but it she still defined herself as backward. As soon as she reached her teenage years, she was sent to work for the Church. She was apprenticed to a much older woman who put her to work doing the cleaning and ironing for the local priests. Once she had shown Emer the work for the day, the woman remained silent for the rest of their time together. By the time she was seventeen, Emer was doing most of the work and the constant silence was driving her mental. She managed to run away but she was found and brought back to the church. When she ran away for the second time, that was considered proof of a "mental handicap" and she was admitted to St. Ita's where she remained for thirty years. When I met her, the health board had found her a job and a place to live and she was managing her life fairly well. She was quite proud of her checkbook and her ability to mind her finances.

As it happened, Emer had been a "regular" in the St. Ita's Christmas show each of the years that she had lived in the hospital. Now that she had an outside job, she was brought back to participate as sort of a "ringer." She knew the annual routine and the staff could depend on her to perform without a hitch.

My volunteer assignment to work with the residents on their Christmas show performances was an added break for me, as well. I enjoyed going down to Lissenhall to collect some participants or helping them with their parts in the wards and down in the schoolyard. I teamed up with nurses and teachers to pump enthusiasm into their performances and everyone was excited to be preparing for the show. I wondered if we could maintain this enthusiasm for the months to come but we didn't seem to have any difficulty keeping the momentum going. Even residents like Hugo who would have no actual part in the show got caught up in the excitement of people coming in and out of the ward and the practicing of songs and dances that he could hear going on somewhere. I saw more of St. Ita's during the Christmas concert rehearsals than I did in any other time.

I believe my moving around the various work locations and the many wards of Portrane was responsible for my sheer panic when one morning I woke up in the little single bed of No. 292, terrified and blind as a bat. The alarm had gone off and Morning Ireland had come on but I couldn't see the button on the radio to stop it from bleeping. I couldn't even see the radio. Somehow I fumbled around and managed to turn off the noise and then I just sat still trying to assess my situation. I wasn't in pain so that seemed like a plus. Then I gingerly touched my eyes and felt something brittle covering my lids and all along the base of my eyelashes. For once the coziness of the flat, what the locals call "homely," helped me in my efforts to feel my way to the toilet. The space was so small that I knew to move slowly along the edge of the bed, dragging my fingers to the end of the duvet knowing that it would stop just short of the doorframe. Once past that, I could find the door to the toilet on the left. The only thing that I could think to do was to put a warm face cloth on my eyes and see if that would dissolve whatever was clinging to my lids. Then I remembered that I didn't have hot water on demand, so I had to work my way around the flat to the kitchen and find the switch that would start the hot water supply. With my fingers trailing along the walls, I flipped the switch and slowly backtracked to the toilet where, if memory served, a facecloth was still hanging on the towel rail. I reached for it and pushed it into the sink where first I soaked the cloth, then I soaked my face and gradually, my eyelashes became slowly and systematically unglued. My fear temporarily subsided as my eyelids sluggishly retracted but it quickly returned when looking back at me from the tiny mirror over the sink were the pinkest eyes I had ever seen, and they were mine!

I found some coins and went into the hallway to ring the hospital and let them know I wouldn't be in. Surprisingly, I still didn't know what was wrong with me. I just kept soaking the cloth and keeping the warm compress on my eyes. It seemed to help and when I felt better, I got dressed and headed up Baggot Street to the chemist. Obviously, the chemist had no difficulty in diagnosing my secondary bunny characteristics and prescribed some drops for conjunctivitis. As it happens, conjunctivitis is pretty common around places like Portrane and some of my co-workers were surprised that I had sidestepped it for so long. The drops were very successful, for a while, but the illness didn't clear up as soon as promised. I went back to the chemist who asked me if was taking any other medication. I assured her that I merely soaked a facecloth and kept the warm compress on my eyes. It certainly made me feel better. She began to shake her head. The facecloth, even though it was being rinsed out in hot water each time, was causing a reinfection in my eyes every time I used it. I began to think that between the hepatitis, the conjunctivitis and the welts, creating "The Portrane Guide to Personal Healthcare" wouldn't go amiss.

My pinkish eyes got me a few days off of work although Frank questioned my illness. He rang the flat several times and unusually I was home each time. I begged off getting together due to my illness, but since things were getting strained between us, he thought that I was creating my own excuse to avoid meeting up. This was the first I had seen of this jealous behavior. He found it easier to believe that I would succumb to the advances of another man than to a hefty shot of bacteria. Given our situation, he was tripping headfirst over a keg of Irish irony especially since I had not given him any reason to doubt me. His reaction was reminiscent of the other men in the pub who assumed that a woman of my age, on her own, would be helpless to fight off the patois of the ever-charming Irish male no matter what his or her age. This both surprised and annoyed me but I filed it away for future reference. Somehow I knew this jealous streak would come back to help me rather than haunt me. Besides, I have to admit that I welcomed this temporary social/anti-social benefit of pinkeye. It gave me some time to sort things out and helped to set the plan in motion for us to finish. He still refused to talk about the change in our relationship, continuing to believe that there wasn't one. I envied his ability to just live his life but I truly believed that there were issues at play here, issues that he would never, never talk about with me.

As my eyes began to pale I went out for an afternoon of shopping and I stopped to have a look on Grafton Street. The weather was still fine and having some time on my own was a welcome blessing. I had plans to travel to Galway for the upcoming Ballinasloe Horse Fair, so even though I was looking forward to a great weekend, the conflict with Frank wasn't far from my mind. To the non-pink-eyed observer, he and I were nowhere close to being a good match. But he was so smart and so clever and I still found him interesting and funny. He had written me poems and lovely letters when I was fairly certain that he had let go of his poetry skills years ago, along with his hopes to be a teacher. I could not get him off of my mind as I wandered through the women's department in Switzer's. There was absolutely nothing in common with our backgrounds, our education and our life experiences. Did that matter? Maybe those were the previously unseen differences that seemed to be surfacing now. How he thought we could go on was a mystery to me.

In the shop, the piped-in music was taking over my thoughts and it seemed to be having an effect on the other women shoppers as well. As I reached down to check the price of a jumper hanging off a circular sales rack, I perceived an audible hum. Their mid-calf skirts swished left, then right as they purred through the chorus of the now so appropriate "My Baby's Got a Secret." Even their sensible shoes shuffled languidly in time to the music. I couldn't help but join the softly murmuring shoppers in supplying back-up for Madonna. Ireland is a land of secrets, musical and otherwise.

Chapter 20 - Nil All

I put my love life on the long finger and got ready for the Ballinasloe Horse Fair in County Galway. I had first read about it in the novel *Scarlett*, the manufactured sequel to *Gone with the Wind*. I thought that the tale of horse-trading, pony rides and sulky races was totally fictitious; fodder for Scarlett's return to Ireland. But The Ballinasloe Horse Fair is one of Europe's oldest and largest horse fairs dating back to the 18th century. When I discovered that it was not only fact but also an historical event I put it on my list.

Down in the Portrane schoolyard, Sheelagh reminded me about her recommendation that I meet up with Madame Lee and have my fortune told. Ballinasloe was the place to do it. Madame Lee had told Sheelagh's fortune with uncomfortable accuracy and she insisted that my questions would all be answered behind what I thought would be a pile of manure and a circus tent. I was still unclear about the link between reading your palm and selling your pony, but other than agreeing to suss out Madame Lee, I said nothing.

I was able to encourage a friend to go with me to Galway and after a long drive we ended up in Ballinasloe late in the afternoon, the day before the fair was to begin. We had wandered a bit off the main road when we sidetracked through the town of Mullingar looking for lunch. Our food options were limited, so true to form, we stopped in a pub for soup and brown bread. I hadn't traveled through County

Westmeath before and found the area to be a hub of cattle ranches. Once at St. Ita's, I had overheard a nurse describe another woman's features as having "legs like a Mullingar heifer." I was never too sure if that was a compliment or an insult but after driving through the town, I figured it out.

In Ballinasloe, we booked into a hotel that overlooked the expansive open area around and behind the church that was to hold the horses and all the exhibitors. It was totally void of activity of any kind. This was a massive piece of property to be completely and totally empty just a day before the second biggest horse fair in Europe. The increase in the population of the town was another matter. It was buzzing. Every place was packed out with the most colorful of customers. The fair holds a long-standing tradition with the Travelling community and the girls especially go all out for the fair. There were big hoop earrings and dramatic makeup, lots of exposed midriffs, long, long hair extensions and high-heeled boots that topped off way above the knees. The fair is a serious place of business for the Travelling community and hundreds of horses are bought, sold and traded during the run of the fair. But to the neutral observer, it really feels like a good-natured, massively extended family reunion. There was great craic all around the town and we weaved in and out of the pubs before heading off to bed after the long drive from Dublin.

When we woke up in the morning and looked out the very same window of the night before, the area was now chock-a-block with people, horses, caravans and carnival rides. The transformation was amazing. The traders must have come during the early morning hours and staked out the best spots for their horse-trading and living areas. We got dressed, and after breakfast, went directly down to the fair which, close-up, looked like a combination of horse show, rodeo and carnival midway. It was fabulous. We wandered around for hours watching the horses being moved in and about with overpowering voices and deals being negotiated and made. One of the locals heard our accents and good-naturedly asked us if we had been "kicked yet?" Seeking to avoid this painful rite of passage, we wandered away from the livestock and went in search of our destinies through fortune telling.

We set out to find Madame Lee, but after traversing the length and width of the main trading area, we couldn't find anything that looked remotely like a place for palm readings and crystal ball gazing. We finally gave up and asked a guard if he knew of her. Since we were certain that she was the one and only famous Madame Lee, we couldn't understand how he wouldn't know, straight away, where to guide us. When we finally explained that we were looking to have our fortunes told, he directed us down one aisle and over another three. We walked down one row, passing horses and traders and buyers and riders and then crossed over through three rows of bridles and blankets that evolved into ring tosses and one bright blue and red tilt-a-whirl. As we turned the corner we stopped dead in our tracks. There, directly in front of us, were more than a dozen caravans, lined up in two rows, with each of them posting a bright glittery sign reading "Fortunes Told," or "Palm Reading'" or "Psychic Truth Teller." Amazingly, loads of people were queued up for each and every one of them. In our naiveté, we thought that we would be secreted away in private to participate in this ceremony that was so adamantly frowned upon by the church. Obviously, the pope didn't intimidate the patrons of the Ballinasloe Horse Fair. Still, we had yet to find *our* Madame Lee in this psychic menagerie, and not being psychic, we had our work cut out for us; the title of "Madame Lee" seemed to have been bestowed upon the majority of our caravan dreamers. She/they were everywhere!

At first, we joined a few queues and started our own "Vox Pop" interviews looking for the one, true Madame Lee. As it happened, most of the people who had lined up for their readings were either already loyal to the psychic inside or they had heard something wonderful about her and they were sticking with the recommendation. Our objectives were mutual so we kept searching for our personally recommended Madame Lee. Luckily Sheelagh had given me an elaborate description of her caravan, which at the time, seemed like a useless detail. But now, as we wandered through the rows and rows of mollusk shaped modes of towed, two-wheel transportation, I was glad that I had listened so intently to Sheelagh when she oozed about her fortune telling experience and had described the surroundings in which it took place.

We found Madame Lee toward the end of the second row of caravans. Once we saw it, there was no need to look any further. The caravan was painted a brilliant, bright silver, the color of a fresh mackerel's belly. The sides and the windows were trimmed in both pink and black. It had a pink-fringed shade that just barely crept down the middle of the large center window; its pink pull-tassel dangling in the breeze from the open doorway. The caravan practically throbbed in the Ballinasloe sun. The queue was very, very long but by now we were committed. We took our place at the end and then we began to ask the other people waiting if they had been to Madame Lee before? The comments were stellar, easily one hundred percent customer satisfaction. What a woman! We heard amazing stories of predicted pregnancies, diagnostic help with illnesses, of course, there was exceptional advice in the love life department and there was even a second generation Madame Lee fan with us in the queue. We all took turns getting bottles of water as we waited in the sun for our shot at the crystal ball.

When our turn came we chose to go in together. The color scheme of silver, black and pink carried on to the inside décor. Dolls of many sizes in elaborate and frilly costumes rested on black and grey pillows trimmed with pink fringe. There were loads of family pictures and many of them were historical in nature, old family pictures that showed people dressed in native costume. I sensed that there was an interesting story behind this love of fortune telling and the Travelling community. Madame Lee did reveal in very brief detail how her family had come from Romania through England and then over to Ireland. I made a mental note to ask about it later; I hoped that she might tell me more. My friend took the seat at the roundtable offered by Madame Lee. We knew that she was hoping for a first grandchild so we had decided that this would be our "test secret." Just how much, we wondered, would Madame Lee really be able to reveal? First, there was a palm reading and then, surprisingly to us, Madame Lee actually did bring out a crystal ball and asked my friend to gaze into it, which she did. Among other things, Madame Lee assured her that a grandchild was coming, that it would be a girl and that she would be healthy. My friend was over the moon. Psychic success. Then I took the chair across from Madame Lee, folding my hands and holding them still as I rested them on the triangle of black velour that most likely served as both shawl and tablecloth. I can't say that too much news was forthcoming. She seemed to echo John, the previous psychic, and she supported his precognition that I was in Ireland for a reason and that I would be staying for a while. It's true that my mind was full up with my romantic situation in Dublin; maybe that kept me from missing the focal point deep down in the misty crystal ball. I did my best to apply my most sincere gaze but other than messages about work and money and professional success, the answers I was looking for were not revealed.

We thanked Madame Lee, and to be fair, we both felt that she was worth the wait. With the session finished, she took a few minutes to chat and then, as she walked me to the door, she smoothly lifted the top card from a pink candy dish that rested on a silver and glass table by the door. Ever so slyly, she slipped the card into my hand folding my fingers over it. Then she let me know that when the fair was finished, I could find her sparkling, silver caravan, with the parking brake on, in Lucan, a town just outside of Dublin. The address and the phone number were on the card. She assured me that she would be there when

I wanted to meet up again. It was true that I had some unanswered questions, but even though she was encouraging me, I had my doubts that another session would help. Then, just before stepping out of the throbbing caravan and into the mid-afternoon sun, she gently grasped my elbow and with her head close to mine she whispered, "That man you're seeing...let him be. He's not yours." I tucked the card deep into my pocket but I said nothing.

It seemed ordained that I should follow through with leaving Frank given Madame Lee's celestial advice. I knew it was the right thing to do but I just hadn't had any luck doing it. I greatly admired my colleague in Portrane for making the hard decision to leave her relationship and enduring the social pressures that accompanied that choice. Certainly, hers was a more difficult one than mine but I didn't have the leverage of a strong decisive move when my relationship was based on intermittent social outings. Somehow, I would have to make Frank understand that we, as a couple, were past our mutual sell-by-date.

Back in Dublin on a Saturday afternoon, Frank had left a message on Friday to meet at a new pub up the road to watch the rugby. I hadn't talked with him since being away in Galway but my housemate Tess had Sellotaped his message to the phone. As I was standing in the hallway with the message in my hand, the phone rang again and I answered it. It was Frank. We had a very brief conversation and he gave me the directions to the pub where he was waiting. I repeated them and then after agreeing to meet, I hung up. I went out the front door of the subterranean bedsit, up the three steps to the front of the building and stood in the middle of the residence car park. I was motionless in front of No. 292 still holding the message in my hand. I knew that if I turned left to meet Frank, things would go on for a while but that our ending was inevitable. If I turned right and went somewhere else, there would be hell to pay. Not only would I be standing him up, I would be missing a big rugby match and that was unforgivable. The sound of his voice on the phone indicated that he had been out and about for some time and that a significant amount of drink had been taken. If I waited much longer, I would be in trouble for showing up late. I gave it just a few more minutes and a little more thought, and then with respect to Madame Lee, I turned right.

I walked down Haddington Road and turned left onto Northumberland Road and then directly into a pub called Kitty O'Shea's. There was a great crowd in the pub and I fell in with a group of five businessmen from Edinburgh who had come over to Ireland to play football on an organized outing. They were all new to Dublin and when the match ended I bundled them up and took them on a pub-crawl all around the town. The irony of the night wasn't lost on any of us, five Scottish men on the tear in Dublin being taken around the local pubs by an American woman. As the night went on, two of the men left for their hotel and I sent two others onto Joy's nightclub. That left the last single Scotsman, Duncan, so we went on to have one more drink before ending the night. Surprisingly, Duncan and I got along really well and for a time, my upcoming conflict with Frank temporarily left my mind. Duncan and I exchanged telephone numbers but I couldn't see how we would ever meet up again. He was quite the gentleman. He even saw me home to No. 292. Still, this chance outing and innocent flirtation gave me the confidence to prepare myself for the inevitable. Meeting the Scottish men proved that single men of a certain age were out there; you just had to cross the sea to find them.

The next day I was ready for the phone call that I knew was coming. I had a full cafetiere of coffee at the ready and an explanation at the less ready but getting readier. I kept the door to the hallway open so that I would be the one to hear the phone if it should ring. Duncan and I had talked and talked until past closing time so I had a bit of a lie in and I was pretty sure that Frank wouldn't be out with the crack of dawn either. Just around one o'clock, the phone rang. When I answered, Frank was very direct and simply asked me where I had gone. I told him I had gone to Kitty O'Shea's, and without any help at all, he jumped to the obvious next assumption. "Did you meet up with someone?" he asked. And since I could conjure up a fairly realistic picture of the night before, I pictured Duncan, and I said that I had. I knew, given our previous discussions, that the only thing that would make Frank leave me without discussion would be jealousy. So I related the picture of the last night's Scottish pub-crawl and let him think whatever he liked. His comment took me by surprise. There was a brief pause and then I heard him say, "You cunt."

My response was quick. I had a flash of anger and a change of tone and I immediately responded with, "No one talks to me like that. I'm done." I hung up the phone.

Now the "C" word, as my friends and I would call it, was reserved for the worst of women and became an even worse insult if a woman was using it to label another female. I was crushed that he would use that language with me. I knew that I had set the argument in motion but I was demoralized that he would resort to such a slur with what felt like minimal provocation. By now I had learned to say cardigan and jumper, toilet and pee but I couldn't bring myself to use the "C" word.

I was deeply and dramatically wounded...but not for long. My Irish women friends came to my cultural rescue. They assured me that I needn't have been so offended. This was just another word to let someone know that they were "acting the maggot"; or being a gombeen, a wanker, a langer or an amadán. I had unknowingly ended my relationship with a simple, cross-cultural overreaction. My righteous indignation was short-lived. I was an eejit.

A few weeks later Niall and Imogen called us together for an emergency team meeting. We met to discuss Anthony's unscheduled return from his community placement. This was a huge setback given that Anthony had been doing well and by all reports was happy living there. We were told that Anthony was being readmitted to St. Ita's due to his violent behavior but no specific behavior was mentioned. As far as I knew, Anthony's primary social interaction was flirtatious but never violent. When we assembled in the Old Nurses' Home, Niall informed us that Anthony was being sent back because he had attacked someone with his wooden leg. The ambulance had been dispatched to collect him and bring him back to St. Ita's. It was a disaster. The team set about making a plan for his arrival but I was left with my doubts. "How," I asked, "could Anthony attack someone with his wooden leg?" My question was ignored but I persisted. If he removed his leg in order to hit someone, surely the potential victim could outrun the hopping assailant. Or if he removed it, and sat on the floor, possibly swinging it around and over his head, couldn't everyone just walk away until he tired? Anthony would have to have been traumatized on some level to cause such a reaction. My questions were perceived as meddling and I was instructed to accept the decision and support the plan in whatever way was necessary.

But the following month, when the team met again, I had gathered just enough gossip to push for clarification. Niall revealed that Anthony had been violent, but it had nothing to do with his wooden leg. After many months, Anthony was told that his mother was coming to visit. He got dressed up, gold chains and all, and sat outside the reception office waiting for her to arrive, and he sat there, and he waited, for hours. As it happened, his mother had cancelled the visit, but this had not been clearly communicated to Anthony. When he finally realized that she wasn't coming, he stood up, and with both legs planted firmly on the ground, he picked up his chair and chucked it through the office window.

The failure wasn't Anthony's. He had been institutionalized almost his entire life. His skills at dealing with frustration and disappointment were limited, and while his behavior may not have been acceptable, it was certainly understandable. Anthony loved living in the community and I've always felt that we let him down by not finding another placement for him. Ten years later, when I was working in Galway, the national television station recruited a camera crew to go into Portrane and create a four-part series called *The Asylum*. I'd never used that label when I was there, and hearing the state-sanctioned use of it put me off just a little. The program chronicled the final closure of the many wards and the outplacement of the remaining inhabitants of St. Ita's. From all observations, the camera crew was well received by the residents who must have enjoyed "making a movie." I watched with great interest and then I saw Anthony, bouncing in front of the camera; after ten years he was still there.

Chapter 21 - See You Next Tuesday

Now so, my attempts to end my relationship by fostering a fictitious relationship were undermined and somehow supported by my ignorance of the local lexicon. My flash of Portuguese fury toward Frank scared him, especially since he felt his comment was appropriate and harmless coming from someone who had been so rudely stood up. I was in his world. He was right.

I decided to take the blessing from whence it came. I hadn't meant for things to end so tempestuously but at least it felt that they had ended and that was the desired result. Frank and I had always met on an inconsistent basis so it wasn't that difficult to avoid running into each other in the next few weeks. Things were proceeding as planned in St. Ita's, so for me, there were lots of events to occupy the time. I booked a trip to London to meet with friends and that helped me to stop thinking about being away from home for the holidays. I was told that Dublin would be extremely quiet during the Christmas and New Year's breaks. Everyone goes home to the country; the town would become deadly calm and annoyingly peaceful.

As far as business goes, it came to a complete stop. I was told that anything I might need to do would have to wait until after the new year even though we were still weeks and weeks away from Christmas. I found out that "after the new year" meant February. I thought I had acclimated to the work ethic of Dublin but working through the winter holidays was another style altogether. I had strips taken off me when I rang a woman in the council to sort something out for a resident. I was told that the woman who could help me was on her holidays. So I asked who was taking over her duties while she was gone. "She's on her holidays," was repeated to me. I said I understood but I was just wondering who her back up would be while she was away. "She's on her holidays," was repeated for the third time. I eventually got it, holidays were sacred as were the almost six weeks over Christmas that we patiently waited for things to get back to "normal."

Strangely, the pace at St. Ita's picked up with the excitement surrounding the Christmas show. Posters announcing the program were now put up all around Donabate, the village that surrounds the hospital and its environs. I foolishly asked if the program would be used as a fundraiser but this thought had never been entertained. There would be two shows over two nights and a full crowd was expected for both.

Surprisingly, after our chance meeting in Dublin, Duncan contacted me from Edinburgh. He called my office in Portrane and when I answered, he asked if "this was a good time to speak?" I remember thinking that I had not been offered such a professional courtesy since being in Portrane. We spoke several more times and we made a plan to meet up after the first of the year. My fictitious liaison to escape from Frank was taking a twist toward reality. Maybe God does love a tryer, after all.

In St. Ita's, we lost another of our residents. Francie, the youngest patient in the hospital passed away. I was told that he died of a brain tumor. Given that he used to repeatedly slam his head down on the concrete floor, I wasn't surprised that his injury was cerebral in nature. Some of the staff hypothesized that he continuously hit his head due to the pressure or pain that he couldn't describe to us. We will never know. Several other, older residents passed during the cold Irish winter. By now, I was getting used to seeing the long, dark hearse curve slowly down the tree-lined avenue as I was driving up. Annie was working overtime at keeping me informed.

Weeks after our row, I received a letter from Frank. It was written on pale blue stationery with light blue ink. At some time during the past week, he had slipped it through the main door of No. 292 and one of my housemates had lodged it between the alcove and the coin phone. It may have been there for days sandwiched between the throwaway ads and the menus for the Chinese takeaways. It had a title and a message:

"Bridge End"

"Hello there, Chris," Frank went on to say,

"Well, I'm just sitting here listening to 'Desperado' and wondering what went wrong with us. It was a relationship, a something I ain't witnessed for a long time and yet pressure was there to keep it from being the simple, happy affair type thing (or is there)? Maybe. I wouldn't dream of letting you be hurt (sad, tears, etc.) and yet, as you say, I said some interesting things...not meant and I'm really sorry for it.

You'll always be there in my mind.

Missing you, Frank xx"

Jaysus, could I feel any worse? My music loving, poetry writing, Guinness guzzling giant man from Donegal could really turn a phrase. I missed him too, but I knew that I might still be living in the movie script, as Mary had described, and that Frank and I would never have a happy ending. I let the farewell stand. As farewells go, it was one of the loveliest.

In St. Ita's, the staff turned its attention to the Christmas performance. I attempted to entertain some of the residents as they were waiting to go on stage for their practice but I'm fairly certain that only a bit of my California humor made the translation. By now, most of the staff and the residents were used to my American accent and my boisterous laugh. Any attempts to display my pseudo-Irish wit were more or less tolerated by the nurses and especially by the patients who graciously maintained their good manners at my efforts. I overheard one of them say, "She'd be great if the TV were broke, like."

On the first night of the Christmas performance, I borrowed a video camera from Mary and interviewed some of the staff and the patients as they were waiting to go on stage. This was met with varying levels of success and failure. In the dressing room, I saw Orla being primped but I could tell that she still wasn't using her dentures. It was just as well. I think she was an extra in the crowd scene. Minimal talking required. I can't say that anyone enjoyed having their hair brushed or their make-up patted on and then smoothed all over their faces. Sensory issues prevented lots of them from relaxing through the process. Most people squished their features inward toward their noses and endured the tap of the powder puffs as the teachers spackled their faces and enhanced their features with black eyebrow pencil. Billy was the exception. He was absolutely buoyant and seemed really eager to perform. When I asked him if he was nervous, he gave me a resounding "no" and maintained a posture that was composed and nonchalant. As it happened, like Emer, he was a seasoned performer with years of Portrane show business behind him. He was really looking forward to the next two nights.

I tried to interview Angus and Fergal, two older gentlemen who were inseparable around the hospital. They would generally try to avoid me but tonight they were with their caregiver, Edel, who was trying to encourage them to speak to me on camera. They were having none of it. It was understandable. Whenever they saw me coming around a corner in St. Ita's they would both head off in the opposite direction. I didn't take this personally. I often saw one of them hitching up his trousers as the two of them wandered off. There was always the faint smell of urine about them and my guess is that they had an ongoing urge to sneak a forbidden pee. I foiled their efforts more than once. My proximity with a camera was having a negative effect on them. If Edel couldn't convince them, then no one could. Edel was a good-sized woman with a great smile, a big laugh and a mound of long, dark, curly, reddish-brown hair and with what seemed like a permanent seaside tan. She could pass for a Fiji Islander. During my time at Portrane, she was relentless at asking me to be one of the supervisors when the staff took a group of residents on a pilgrimage to the holy city of Lourdes. I declined, saying that I preferred to have my holidays without a religious overtone. She called me shortsighted. "You'd be surprised," she said, "at the craic you can have when the right people get together in Lourdes." The Irish don't go looking for the craic; they bring the craic with them.

Before going into the auditorium I managed to find Emer already in her costume and sitting in the makeup chair. I turned the camera toward her and attempted a word of encouragement by saying, "Hi Emer, knock 'em dead."

This appeared to be a poor choice of words as a worried expression came quickly over her face. She glanced furtively around the room asking, "Who said that? Who said that?" When she realized that I was behind the camera she gave me a quizzical look. She seemed to have real concern for me. "Chris, is that you? Are you all right, Chris?" she asked.

I changed my words of encouragement to "Have fun out there!" which seemed to suit her much better. She gave the camera a wave and a big smile, "Cheers!" she said and then headed for the stage.

I went into the auditorium and found a place to stand in the middle of the side aisle close to Edel. She was sitting next to Angus and Fergal and just down the row from Hugo and Marco. I staked out my spot and focused the camera on the stage. Even after all the practice sessions I still didn't know what to expect. A small table with one chair was placed on the floor in front of the stage. Two residents, Patsy and

Maureen, eventually took charge of the table, Maureen in the chair and Patsy moving up close in his wheelchair. They waited there while the audience filled in the empty seats. I didn't know Maureen but I knew Patsy from my visits to the Day Center where Cormac minded him most days. He was chunky and round, bald on the top of his head with a smidgen of black hair over his ears that horizontally half circled the back of his head. He might nod to you when you spoke to him but he was usually just giving it a "go," his expressive language was limited to a few short social responses. He loved to sing and whenever there was music, he would keep the rhythm going by extending his left arm out and away from his body and the wheelchair. Then he would lift it way up and spin it into floppy, uneven circles. Patsy was a great man for getting himself around the hospital and everyone knew him. He loved an audience and that seemed to be his role tonight.

With the crowd seated, the curtain opened and one of the nurses came out onto the stage in the role of show presenter. Patsy waved at the audience and started the applause. The nurse-host welcomed the crowd and introduced the first act. On the stage was a set that depicted Mary Street in a Dublin of long ago. It was populated with many residents either standing or milling around in front of it. They were dressed in the costumes of the day. Many nurses and teachers were similarly dressed and they folded in and out of the scene, gently guiding or encouraging or comforting the residents so as to give them success with their practiced part in the show. From somewhere a tape machine began to play a Christmas carol and this was the cue for anyone and everyone, including the audience, to sing along. As he heard the music, Patsy started to conduct us by waving and circling his animated musical left arm. The music seemed to calm the performers on stage and, with the guidance of the nurses, they performed their parts by moving about and across the stage. The street scene had shops, a flower vendor, a wandering guard and several "fires," giant flaps of shiny red paper waving from big, round, metal tubs as if to keep the carolers warm on this winter night. This allowed for many residents to have their moment; I saw Marco with his characteristic sideways bob weave down the street guided by a caregiver; Maurice faked warming himself at the fire, laughing all the time and Billy parked his wheelchair right down in front, singing away at the top of his lungs. When the carol finished, Patsy wound down the audience by slowly lowering his left arm and hooking his hand onto his less mobile right side where he waited for the next act.

Emer appeared to be the lead singer through several songs while the nurses and residents provided her with back up. Kitty and Alice came out with their heads poking through what looked like white sheets that covered their bodies. Each of them was wearing some sort of a metallic wig, one with shiny blue strips and one with shiny red strips. The wigs were cut directly across the forehead and left long at the sides giving them a sort of shiny Egyptian look. After their song finished, Alice re-appeared wearing the same costume and standing at the top of a short ramp accompanied by a tall male nurse in an old-fashioned coat and tie. They both began to sing/ lip-sync to a 1959 Cliff Richard hit, "Living Doll." This was a huge crowd pleaser. Patsy was able to whip the crowd into a tepid frenzy at every chorus. Even though it was 35 years old, this song brought down the house. It reminded me of Frank being so fond of Dean Martin and a style that in no way represented the music of the day. Music memory is a very powerful force and I had to wonder where some of these people might have been when they heard this song hit the "top of the charts" 35 years ago. Maybe for some of them, it brought back pictures that were "pre-Portrane."

A lone Irish singer followed this duet. A young resident named Damien walked out from the left side curtain, went to the far end of the stage and sat down on the top step of the temporary stairs that were placed parallel to Patsy's wheelchair. He was a young man, for the St. Ita's population, most likely in his late twenties or early thirties. He wore a long-sleeved, yellowed, open neck shirt with the sleeves rolled up to his elbows. His hair was long, black and wavy and he had a full mustache that curved down into the corners of his mouth. The auditorium went dark with the exception of one spotlight that came on just as Damien took his place on the top step. He held a microphone in his left hand as if to act the part of a singer and he lifted it to his face waiting for someone to hit the "on" button of the tape recorder. The music started and Damien began to sing along to "Ringsend Rose." But Damien's voice came out strong and true and he melodically overrode the voice on the cassette. He brought such emotion to his song that he captured everyone in the auditorium, all of whom joined him in singing along with each and every chorus. It was a sad and powerful delivery. The audience was captivated.

After a huge round of applause for Damien, the lights came up in the auditorium and a sketch starring some of the nurses and a good part of the teaching staff took over most of the stage. I turned the camera away from the steps and toward the center stage, fixing it in one position as the sketch began. The jokes seemed to involve a good many of the staff with the punch lines coming mostly from innuendo. The nurses and teachers had created a mock radio station that was having difficulty broadcasting due to technical problems. The sports reporter was overlapping the fashion reporter who was overlapping the political reporter and so on. It was fast and clever and by now I knew enough people that I got most of the humor. Then the sports reporter announced that "The director of patient services was spotted at the top of the Cusack Football Stands…" This appeared to overlap with the fashion reporter who interrupted by saying, "…where Chris Lacey could be seen sporting a pair of frilly, green knickers." Looking through the camera lens, I thought, that's me; they're making a joke about me. And for the first time, I felt connected, in a good way, to Portrane.

Chapter 22 - It Does what it Says on the Tin

The rare Irish summer had ebbed away causing life around No. 292 to be plunged back into darkness. I had overcome my fear of the gas-burning fireplace and revved it up many late afternoons and most nights. I promoted my hooded, two-tone insular jacket to daytime duty and I bought boots and hats to ward off the cold and damp; the wind was just too strong for an umbrella. My bedsit view of the car park and my eye-level view of the tires on the little red Golf became one big blotch of wet, grey, streaky tarmac.

My first holidays away from home were approaching and while I had no urge to return to Los Angeles I didn't relish the idea of being on my own. I was constantly reminded by my co-workers that Dublin would be deadly quiet so I was happily looking forward to a trip to London. An American friend was visiting there and he offered me the chance to housesit with him through to the New Year. Before I left I managed to meet up with Kitty, and using a calendar and some travel icons, I demonstrated to her the dates that I would be going away and when I would be coming back. We were working on increasing her signing vocabulary and she was making loads of progress. It was surprising that signing hadn't been attempted in the past. I was excited at her ability to match the pictures with the movements but even more impressed with her ability to retain and use the signs taught in our previous sessions. The more time I spent with her the more I wondered what her future might have been had she been diagnosed in a different place and time.

Her willingness to learn new things continued to captivate me and her desire to communicate could not be suppressed. By the time we finished the session, I was certain that she understood that I would be back to see her in three weeks' time. She seemed content with that information and when I left, I received one of her famous big kisses tossed from mouth to hand to Irish air.

I almost made a clean Dublin getaway but a hiccup occurred when I looked up from packing my suitcase to see Frank's frame looming large from the top of the bedsit window. I pretended not to see him but from his height, he could see me over the top of the shabby white curtains. He tapped on the window, "Hello? Hello?" in this funny high pitched tone that so betrayed his size. He had come by the bedsit to give me a birthday present. The hope of reconciliation must have been at the very top of the hidden agenda; "I could feel it in me water". I let him in but when the subject came up I stood my ground. Frank quickly lost his temper and threw the gift on the floor. When it hit the ground the wrapping paper came loose and an audiocassette of Sheryl Crow rolled across the creepy brown paisley carpeting. He took one long, giant step and captured it, tossing it to me as he turned toward the door. I glanced at the song list on the back. He explained that he had chosen it because of the song, "All I Wanna Do." I didn't get it. "It's about people who work in Los Angeles, wash their cars at lunch and work at the phone company." He was right, that had been my pre-Dublin existence. I was impressed that he'd paid that much attention to the wandering stories of my California lifestyle. It was right up there with "Desperado" and I was touched. But for Frank and me it was a fairly sad reunion. My emphatic refusal to pick up where we left off made him very emotional and he started to wonder about his chances to ever be "really happy." He implied that part of the problem was that he was ten years younger than the mother of the child as well as his wife. That hit me where it hurt. Even though he had brought me a birthday present I was the only one who knew the gap between our ages. I had a quick, twisted reaction to his outburst, becoming defensive of his life partner and probably older women in general. I blurted out, "I'm ten years older than you are, too!" This seemed to have a frighteningly sobering effect on him.

From way up on that Donegal spinal column, he looked down at me and almost blubbered, "Why does this always keep happening to me?" as if we women of a certain age were his personal cross to bear. Emotions aside, I shooed him out the front door but I kept the cassette.

Arriving in London at Christmas was nothing short of magical. Every inch of Oxford Street was decorated with lights and tinsel and gigantic Christmas tree ornaments. London at Christmas was on My List and I wasn't disappointed. There were single and multiple carolers, pinging tin drums, the many incarnations of Father Christmas and chestnuts roasting everywhere. My housesitting friend and I had made plans to prepare a home cooked Christmas Eve dinner and to go out to a big hotel for New Year's Eve. No sooner had I unpacked when he threw a spanner in the works; an American couple living in France was coming for Christmas dinner and would be staying for the entire week. Two days after their arrival the three of them decided to feck off back to Paris on the Eurostar leaving me on my own for the rest of the holiday. Supposedly they had struck up a business deal, but I was abandoned nonetheless. My only choice was to regroup; I was quickly becoming very efficient as a traveling-single-mature-female-forager.

The next day I headed back to Dublin for the New Year and unpacked my holiday wardrobe into No. 292. It wasn't quite what I had planned, kicking off the New Year all alone back in my bedsit. I hoped to be sipping champagne in the Savoy but instead, I forced myself to walk up to Baggot Street. Starting in O'Donoghue's I made a personal New Year's promise to have one drink in every pub between Baggot

Street and No. 292 before the night was through. At midnight I would wend my way home and cross off the evening as first ever solo Dublin New Year. Luckily the night had attracted some musicians and what started as a spontaneous duo expanded to a quintet. In comparison to other nights, it was quiet, but there definitely was a good-natured holiday buzz. I was saved from my solitary whiskey sojourn.

After a few hours, the musicians headed off to The Pembroke where there was room in the back with chairs for music. I didn't know any of musicians or the customers so I slinked into the back of the pub and found myself a seat at the far end of the bar, last stool, against the wall. The music was mighty and the number of musical followers grew exponentially as the sound permeated the chilly outside air. I don't know why these musicians were out on their own or how the music moved from place to place, but for me, all alone, it was the saving grace of New Year's Eve. I stayed until way past midnight and got to know Brian, the fiddler, who in addition to playing the violin also bred racehorses and was one of Dublin's most successful architects. Con, who played the squeezebox, the accordion and the guitar, also sang beautifully when he was sufficiently encouraged or jarred or both. The crowd was small but lively and we stuck together until the barman moved us out. From then on, on any given lonely weekend, I could find Brian and Con and follow them to numerous music pubs all over Dublin. It wasn't sipping champagne at the Savoy but that New Year's Eve got me through many an isolated Dublin weekend. I valued and nurtured that connection for the all of the time that I remained living on Haddington Road.

When the holidays were over, Duncan and I decided it was time to follow up our phone calls with some actual physical contact. I was delighted to make the journey to Scotland. I had been to Edinburgh once before and loved it. It was only an hour's flight from Dublin to Edinburgh and I quite liked living the fantasy of working in Ireland with a sweetheart in Scotland. Without Frank, my cavalier attitude about love and romance had returned but now I was starting to hedge my bet. Maybe my chance for finding a companion and happiness was here, in the Land of Air. Maybe John the Psychic was right and this was the place for me to be.

The first weekend I flew to meet Duncan we toured around Edinburgh, which was dazzling. I booked a B&B in *New Town*, circa 1767, and we met up in different parts of the city over the long weekend. The weather held and we partied well into the night. Somewhere by Charlotte Square, he went looking for a small pub on a side street to have a drink before closing. When I pointed to one that seemed to meet the description, Duncan, who had never been married, was dismissive. "We can't go in there," he said, "That's where the divorced people go."

I returned to Scotland a few weeks later and this time I stayed in the guest room of Duncan's flat. We walked the Royal Mile and toured Holyrood Palace. We found multiple pubs with happy hour menus that provided various ways to eat haggis. Haggis became the prerequisite for all our future happy hour stops. We got along really well while sizing each other up as possible long-term candidates for love. I was ready to commit but I could sense that Duncan was uncomfortable. I made a note to check this hesitancy with my Celtic sisters. That Sunday night, Duncan walked me to the check-in at the Edinburgh Airport and we made plans for a meet up in a few weeks' time. I was now EU trained to travel with carry-on baggage only. This left time for Duty Free shopping, a non-negotiable part of the trip even on an hour-long flight from country to country. No one was going to let discounted cigarettes and whiskey slip through their boarding pass. On this trip, I was in the middle of an extremely long queue with barely enough time to get to the cashier before taking off. I was just about ready to put back my whiskey and Toblerone chocolate when a representative from the airline walked through the Duty Free asking those of us on the Dublin flight to make our way to the gate, the plane was scheduled to leave. I was about to obey the rules when the man in front of me lost his temper. In a strong Dublin accent, he demanded to know where the airline "got off" not giving us enough time to shop. I found it hard to get my head around this concept; how could the airline know when we had arrived at the Duty Free and how much time each of us would need? But the passenger in front of me was dead certain that his rights had been violated. As I watched this drama unfold I decided I would follow my Irish countrymen. They didn't move. I didn't move. And the plane waited for us.

After hearing of the struggle with my trans-sea intimacies, my female Irish friends were adamant that this was a warning sign and that I should run away as fast as I could. I thought their judgment seemed a bit harsh and I chalked it up to our cultural differences when it came to men and sex. One evening six of us were walking arm in arm, three abreast along the river under clear, coal black skies and a big full moon. It was in the early hours of the morning, three Irish women in front and in the back, two Australians and me. Those of us in the back were raving as to how the Irish men were the best lovers we'd ever had. The Irish women totally disagreed and tried to disqualify our sexual boasting with one disparaging question, "Had drink been taken?"

We Greek-chorus-backed, "Who cares?"

As far as Duncan was concerned, I wasn't ready to give up just yet. He was a lovely man who actually listened to me when I spoke about my work and he seemed to be sincerely interested in my job at Portrane. When he was younger, Duncan had volunteered at a center for people with learning disabilities so he had some cop on for my work at St. Ita's. After several trips to Edinburgh, Duncan came to visit me in Dublin and traveled with me for a quick trip to Portrane. Some of the residents were out in front and when they saw the little red Golf coming up the avenue they walked over to the car park to wait for me. It was a beautiful afternoon so we had the windows down with the volume on the radio turned up high. Kevin, who loved music, quickly came over to the car. As I parked, I warned Duncan to roll up his window before Kevin got any closer. But as Kevin approached Duncan's side of the car, Duncan, ever the gentleman, extended his hand out the window to properly introduce himself. Before I could stop him, Kevin bypassed Duncan's hand and instead took hold of his elbow. I watched as Duncan's arm, shoulder and upper back were pulled up and out of the way while Kevin simultaneously tried to crawl head first through the window to grab "the music." It only took a minute before Kevin realized that the tape machine was out of his reach and he let go, bouncing Duncan off the backside of the passenger seat. No harm was done but it was a great introduction to Portrane. Months ago I might have panicked, but now I found the whole thing amusing. It was then that I realized how desensitized I had become during my brief career in this Irish asylum.

A few weeks later Niall and Imogen called us together for an emergency team meeting. We met to discuss Anthony's unscheduled return from his community placement. This was a huge setback given that Anthony had been doing well and by all reports was happy living there. We were told that Anthony was being readmitted to St. Ita's due to his violent behavior but no specific behavior was mentioned. As far as I knew, Anthony's primary social interaction was flirtatious but never violent. When we assembled in the Old Nurses' Home, Niall informed us that Anthony was being sent back because he had attacked someone with his wooden leg. The ambulance had been dispatched to collect him and bring him back to St. Ita's. It was a disaster. The team set about making a plan for his arrival but I was left with my doubts. "How," I asked, "could Anthony attack someone with his wooden leg?" My question was ignored but I persisted. If he removed his leg in order to hit someone, surely the potential victim could outrun the hopping assailant. Or if he removed it, and sat on the floor, possibly swinging it around and over his head, couldn't everyone just walk away until he tired? Anthony would have to have been traumatized on some level to cause such a reaction. My questions were perceived as meddling and I was instructed to accept the decision and support the plan in whatever way was necessary.

But the following month, when the team met again, I had gathered just enough gossip to push for clarification. Niall revealed that Anthony had been violent, but it had nothing to do with his wooden leg. After many months, Anthony was told that his mother was coming to visit. He got dressed up, gold chains and all, and sat outside the reception office waiting for her to arrive, and he sat there, and he waited, for hours. As it happened, his mother had cancelled the visit, but this had not been clearly communicated to Anthony. When he finally realized that she wasn't coming, he stood up, and with both legs planted firmly on the ground, he picked up his chair and chucked it through the office window.

The failure wasn't Anthony's. He had been institutionalized almost his entire life. His skills at dealing with frustration and disappointment were limited, and while his behavior may not have been acceptable, it was certainly understandable. Anthony loved living in the community and I've always felt that we let him down by not finding another placement for him. Ten years later, when I was working in Galway, the national television station recruited a camera crew to go into Portrane and create a four-part series called *The Asylum*. I'd never used that label when I was there, and hearing the state-sanctioned use of it put me off just a little. The program chronicled the final closure of the many wards and the outplacement of the remaining inhabitants of St. Ita's. From all observations, the camera crew was well received by the residents who must have enjoyed "making a movie." I watched with great interest and then I saw Anthony, bouncing in front of the camera; after ten years he was still there.

Chapter 23 - A Dog's Dinner

Things were looking bleak for the team in the Old Nurses' Home. Hugo was back in the Children's Unit and Anthony had returned to his old job down in the basement organizing supplies for The Stores. I suppose, if they could, the two of them might say that they enjoyed the adventures that got them away, even if only temporarily, from Portrane. It wouldn't have been the third act that I envisioned for them but somehow this inbred feeling of Irish acceptance always seemed to permeate and overtake dreams. Maybe it was necessary for survival.

Still, Kitty was flying and thoroughly enjoying her living situation. When I met up with her after Christmas, she took me on a tour of her wardrobe and showed me absolutely everything that she bought at the Christmas sales. She was delighted with her new possessions: hats, scarves and handbags. I was impressed that she remembered and continued to use the signs that we learned before the holiday break. Her ability to retain information was indicative of a person with some good, resilient cognitive skills. She constantly amazed me. Kitty and I partnered up for the annual Portrane field trip to Winter Funderland on the south side of Dublin not far from No. 292. My role had become fairly eclectic and I was happy enough to volunteer now that I was no longer worried about being strangled by Majella or petted by Raymond or bitten by John the lino-hopping resident. We had all become comfortable with each other. Kitty and I rode the Tilt-a-Whirl and the Spinning Cups and we harassed Maurice about losing his toupee when everyone, but me, went on the Top Spin. I wasn't long there when Kitty dismissed me with a condescending wave of her hand. She had spotted a man that she fancied from another community placement. I wasn't bothered. It was just another sign of normalcy.

After the holiday break, the team met up to begin the completion of the next move, opening the new community placement in Garrylough Mill. Delia was now officially linked to this reassignment and she was scheduled to move in the next few months. With hospital permission, Delia and I celebrated her upcoming move as well as her thirtieth birthday with a pub-crawl around Dublin. It took a bit of doing to get permission for an evening out and I'm pretty certain that I enjoyed it more than Delia. I had an inkling that she went along just to please me. We went to several pubs and finished up at the Horseshoe Bar in Shelbourne, a sight that Delia, who was a true Dub, had never seen before. Several of my friends happened to be there that night. Delia met them all and held her own with the local craic. Most of the residents of Portrane were well able "give you stick." I can't say that Delia was all that impressed with her night out in Dublin. The bigger thrill seemed to be that we were out, at night, in the little red Golf, and away from Portrane. She was on her best behavior and because she was on medication, she wasn't even tempted to take a drink. I was impressed with her maturity. The nursing staff didn't particularly appreciate our excursion; it's possible that I was acting above my station but I was never very sure of where my station began and ended. Our outing may have been frowned upon by some of the staff but that didn't keep Delia and me from talking about it for days to anyone we could corner in a unit or a schoolroom or at a table in the canteen.

The move to Garrylough Mill was of primary importance to those of us on the team but the rest of the hospital was totally immersed in the upcoming tryouts for the summer games of the Special Olympics. This year the qualifying athletes for the Irish team would be going all the way to Connecticut. The practices and the trials for the Special Olympics was a boon to the residents of Portrane. Not unlike the Christmas

Concert, it was a chance to break the monotony of the daily St. Ita's existence. Delia was in good form and feeling pretty confident about her athletic abilities. Combined with her excitement about creating a new identity outside of Portrane, she was feeling positive and independent, even a little cheeky. It was great fun to be around her.

Things had settled into a comfortable pattern with my job now established in Portrane and my love life emerging in Scotland. It felt like I would never return to California although I was now well aware that even my highly sought after *senior* pay wasn't going to provide me a very comfortable long-term Irish lifestyle. I know that people felt I should be appreciative of the salary that I was given but with 52% going for taxes it didn't allow for much in the way of take-home pay. I could see why people remained in the same organization for decades waiting for an opportunity to open up for them. Claire, another therapist, and I used to get together and spin entrepreneurial ideas that might merge with the Celtic Tiger. There was a huge shortage of speech therapists and the services were valued highly given the need and the length of the waiting lists. We'd buy that pack of Benson Hedges, find two seats in the back of a Baggot Street pub and trash out our future money-making opportunities. Our fantasy was to open a day care center somewhere in the south side of Dublin. With the growing economy, loads of jobs were opening up. The women were going back to work in droves leaving the grannies to mind the children. A center run by two speech therapists couldn't help but make money. But in the end, I was having too much fun and Claire took a post in Saudi Arabia. In one year she saved enough money to put a down payment on a house in Dublin.

With Portrane fairly well sorted, Mary asked me to spend time in Coolock testing some of the children in the special needs classes while setting up a program for the children in the Travelling community. There were two full classes of children diagnosed with special needs but I couldn't find any current testing on any of them to establish a teaching strategy. At the time, they were being taught in the same way as the other children, only slower. Specific learning disabilities were seldom identified so most issues with learning were swept under the umbrella of "mental handicap." This is how I ended up working in Portrane; I said "specific learning disabilities" and the interviewers heard "mental handicap."

One little girl, Rose, in the special needs class, was constantly getting into trouble with "Sister" due to her bad behavior. In the testing room, it became obvious that she wasn't able to sit in the chair long enough to finish a task. Eventually, she slid off the chair and made herself comfortable on the floor and I continued with the testing. My goal was to complete the test, *how* it was completed was another topic. Her inability to stay seated could have been an indication of balance problems or sensory issues that kept her from feeling safe and organized in her own space. Her resulting scores were relatively high and I was delighted to report them. I added the observation that "Rose can't focus if she has to sit in a chair for long periods of time, and that in fact, she successfully completed some of my testing sitting quietly on the floor." I was delighted with this additional information that could change the learning environment for Rose but I needn't have been.

"Well, we can't have that," Sister said, and without looking at it, tossed the report in the lower left-hand drawer of the grey metal desk.

When I had finished all the testing I asked to meet with the parents of Alan, a 12-year-old boy who, for me, had also tested within normal limits. My results indicated a reading disability but his other skills were age appropriate. His parents were lovely and listened intently as I explained why I didn't feel that he was mentally handicapped, but that he might be dyslexic. They nodded in agreement. "Yes, our older son is mentally handicapped, too." No, I tried to explain, Alan has a reading difficulty, but his other skills are fine. "Yes, it's the same with our other mentally handicapped son." I couldn't get them to understand the difference between Alan being taught in a class for special needs students when his difficulty was based in reading. They kept comparing the brothers so I finally asked them what had happened to their eldest son? "He owns his own garage," they proudly told me, "he can take an engine apart and put it right back together. He's got three people working for him."

"Well," I said, "you can see my point. Obviously, if he's successful with his own business, he is most likely not mentally handicapped."

"Oh, but he is," the father said, "he can't read a word in the manual."

This correlation of reading to mental handicap was the ethos of the time and a constant source of frustration to me. Children were going to school at the age of four and were expected to learn to read on a preset schedule, ready or not. I couldn't help but think of Emer in Portrane, thirty years earlier, and how her inability to learn to read at the appointed time resulted in her being bequeathed to the church at the age of fourteen.

I left all of my reports with the substitute teacher who would be there until the end of the year. Three months later I went back to ask her how the teaching suggestions were working. She explained that the reports were all alphabetized and in the filing cabinet. "But you read them?" I asked.

"No," she said, "I'm only the substitute. Those reports are best left for the teacher who'll be back next year."

It never occurred to me that the more open-minded staff members would be found in Portrane. At least our team was willing to undertake some new ideas even though bringing them to fruition was still a struggle. Delia's placement was my last strong hope but even that hit a snag early on. I came back to Portrane on a Monday morning to find everyone in a panic over an incident that took place at one of the trials for the Special Olympics. It seemed that Delia was participating in a large group that was being supervised by a caregiver named Oliver. They knew each other well from years and years of co-existing in Portrane. The day was warm, the competition was exciting and Delia was in good form, having an afternoon out and knowing that her move to Wexford was on the horizon. At the end of the long day, and for whatever reason, Oliver lost his patience and hit her with an open hand across her cheek. By the time they returned to St. Ita's, the story had made its way around the hospital and back again. Even Annie could act out the details.

My first response was to find Deirdre and the other behavioral therapists to see if what I was hearing was accurate. They felt certain that some form of punishment would have to be handed down if only for the fact that there were many members of staff at the event. In a way, it sounded like Delia was almost fortunate to have been struck before an audience but I'm certain she would have preferred that the entire incident be ignored. I had gotten to know Oliver over the past year and expressed my surprise to the three therapists that he had lost his temper in such a way. He seemed very easy going and he was hugely popular with the residents. "That's just not like him," I said. The three of them looked from one to the other, but to me, they said nothing.

When I found Delia she was beside herself with emotion. There was no calming her. She was racked with guilt and felt responsible for irritating Oliver to the point of anger. She blamed herself for teasing him. No matter what I said Delia was certain that the nursing staff would rally behind Oliver and punish her by taking her name off the list for the move to Garrylough Mill. She could see all of her dreams disappearing in the haze of an afternoon outing. I had never seen her so agitated. I pontificated that no one was allowed to hit her but she minimized my input with her horrible description of the reality of the situation, "You don't understand, Chris, you can go home, but I have to live here!"

Oliver was put on unpaid leave causing him to lose his local accommodation. A co-worker gave him the use of a small, compact one-man caravan that he pitched on an area just off the hospital grounds and he lived there while his case was being considered. This had a combined effect on Delia; she felt a slight sense of vindication but his presence on the grounds was an unnerving reminder that she had caused a major disruption to the hospital hierarchy. It created intense paranoia on her part. She continued to believe that the staff would cancel her upcoming move and abandon her to Portrane for the rest of her life. The team managed to send her off on another trip to Garrylough Mill just to put her mind at ease, and for a while, she was back to being her old self. In true Irish fashion, I invoked a prayer that I had heard in Coolock telegraphing a wish that Delia would stay that way, "Touch wood, please God," I whispered while knocking on one of the ancient door frames of Portrane.

My Scottish romance was going nicely with me off to Edinburgh several times a month. I was happy to do most of the traveling. Staying in a fourth story Georgian flat, within walking distance to Princes Street, was miles ahead of my subterranean Dublin bedsit. Duncan was an excellent tour guide and we covered a good bit of Scotland that spring. He remained hesitant about our romance and the only thing more awkward than the relationship was not talking about it. This attitude was certainly different than the freewheeling sexual freedom that seemed to come from the Irish men, drink being taken or not, and it didn't seem to be a universal Scottish trait, either. I had been in Dublin for several Scottish rugby matches and witnessed the total debauchery that the Scots brought with them on match day. Once, leaving the stadium at Lansdowne Road in blustery weather I watched a Scotsman tackle a friend from behind and skid with her, head first, along the icy footpath. As they both burst out laughing the wind caught his kilt and lifted it over the top of his head, answering that age-old Scottish question. On another match day, Kathleen, Una and I were walking along Baggot Street just behind two Scotsmen also in town for a match. As the traffic went past, one of the Scotsmen turned quickly, bent over and grabbed the hem of his kilt. Then he pulled it up past his nose, exposing himself to the wide-eyed occupants of the Number 10 Baggot Street bus. Kathleen and I were speechless, but Una's only comment was, "I can't believe he was circumcised." Go 'way," she chided us, "don't tell me you didn't notice."

I knew now that Duncan's childhood had been pretty strict but when I met him in Dublin, he was traveling with a fun-loving group of friends and that seemed to indicate those issues were in the past. So I set about trying to enhance our budding relationship. Una cautioned me again "Training, if it's required past a certain age, is never a sign of something good." Since I wasn't permitted to talk about it, I attempted to enlighten him in other ways. One night I took him out to dinner in a lovely little Swiss restaurant. I waited until we had consumed most of a bottle of wine, then I took off my shoe and slowly lifted my "stockinged" foot to his lap. I let it lightly rest there, waiting for him to realize what was happening. He made wide-eyed, eye contact with me and I started to slowly and rhythmically move my toes up and down. His eyes dropped and he reached for the wine bottle to fill our glasses. My foot stayed in motion as he poured. Then I raised my wine glass and sipped in time to my dancing ankle. Duncan did the same. It was fortunate that we had finished most of the wine, because as my foot moved faster, Duncan's grip became tighter, and he squeezed the wine glass so firmly that its pieces shattered across the table. I said nothing, but when we left the Swiss Restaurant, I hoped that we had finally left neutral territory.

Chapter 24 - Tis Yourself!

Luckily spring seemed as if it was actually going to arrive this year, but having said that, it would be some time in coming. At first I thought that the constant dampness was making me delusional, but Mary confirmed that yes, it really was only raining on the weekends. This was disappointing but manageable as long as the country was on its way to drying itself out. The cold left invisible patches of black ice on the ground, which terrified me no end. One late afternoon while heading out to the cinema, the little red Golf slid backwards off the asphalt of No. 292 and accurately parallel parked itself on the other side of Haddington Road. I left it there. The danger of black ice was bad in town but it was an even bigger problem in Portrane, with its closeness to the sea. One of the locals told me that more than once the bus to St. Ita's had hit a patch of black ice and then slid slowly down the incline, parking itself inside the lounge of Keeling's Pub. It was scary enough but it still sounded safer than the little red Golf and I got back on the bus until the weather improved.

I didn't mind. I could sort all the bus routes and the ambulance runs. By now I was desensitized to the ambulance smell and I knew most of the patients so I didn't mind getting a lift if I needed one. Getting the bus back into town was easy enough although it meant waiting with Archie, current in-patient and former fiancé, who still wanted us to get married and run away to Rush. We were often at the bus stop with Delores, a long -time outpatient whose paranoia would make all of us circle the roundabout rather than queue anywhere near her. Delores would spot someone on the other side of the road and point at them while she raved as to how it was their fault that the bus wasn't coming. "Tis her with the black pullover!" she'd scream, pointing at a person on the other side of the footpath. "Wanda's black pullover is keepin' us from gettin' to town." Once she started ranting she wouldn't stop until the bus arrived and all of us, including Wanda, got on with no problem.

On the bus trips in and out of town, I would often see passengers blessing themselves with a swift and efficient sign of the cross. Out of boredom, I created a bus ride distraction by trying to peer out the window and locate a church before the up-down-across-across gesture was completed with a kiss to the first knuckle on the right hand. I got pretty good at it on the Portrane to Dublin run but several older and faster believers were continuously beating me to "amen" when to me, there was no church in sight. This Catholic phenomenon was explained to me by Brendan, a Dublin resident and former believer.

"There doesn't have to be a church," he explained, "There just has to 'used to be' a church." This would require a deep knowledge of building demolitions and church remodeling so as to never miss a chance for heavenly credit.

As the weather began to warm, my landlord Eoin Bowen, introduced a new money making scheme to the irritation of those of us living in the flats on Haddington Road. He ejected our cars from the blacktop area in front of No. 292 and then resurfaced it, painting assigned numbers in each space. Vertical steel bars were added that required a key to release them, opening up the space so the car could enter. Once that was completed, he rented out the spaces to the people who worked in the advertising agency housed in the remodeled Edwardian building across the road. This was a huge disadvantage for those of us renters who had cars. There were far more flats than offices on Haddington Road and the street could get chock-a-block with motors and no place to park them. Luckily for me, I became friends with Stuart, agency man and new owner of the parking space that peered directly into my subterranean flat. Every morning his headlights lit up my bedroom cum sitting room cum kitchen. It created a sort of friendly urban awareness of our very distinct lifestyles. Stuart parked his new, sleek BMW just in front of my shredded, off-white Irish curtains and I would meet him coming in just as I was going out. One morning Stuart stopped me in the car park and slipped me a copy of the key to his steel-bar-barred-parking place. From then on he'd leave me his "away" working schedule and spared me many a rain-soaked morning and night. I know that Stuart had my best interest at heart, but I also believe that some joy came from putting one over on Eoin Bowen. It was similar to being locked in the pub during Holy Hour or getting free parking on the double yellow line or having a TV without a license. There was always great joy in getting away with something.

I took advantage of the car park resurfacing to leave my initials forever in the wet cement of Eoin Bowen's annoying new project. By now I had certainly taken up residence in No. 292, but by its very temporal existence I was reminded daily that I had no real home and no one looking after me. There were weekly reports in *The Irish Times* about people being found dead in laneways or doorways or on the banks of the Grand Canal. No one had reported them missing and when their bodies turned up their names would be posted in the newspaper. Many would "be known" to the guards, but there would be no address, just the expression "NFA" or "No Fixed Abode." True, I had made contacts and acquaintances but no one knew or cared about my comings and goings. I knew that if my body turned up soaked and sullied, *The Irish Times* would report it as "Christine Lacey, of No Fixed Abode was found dead today, on the banks of the River Liffey." So I took a sharp stick and into Eoin Bowen's newly poured cement I carved my epitaph, "LaceyNFA", documenting the reality of my Irish existence directly onto and into Haddington Road.

The eve of my second St. Patrick's Day rolled around and Pat the Yank and I appropriately rolled along Baggot Street in celebration. Of course, there would be a parade down O'Connell Street but it consisted of multiple flatbed trucks and Irish dancers trying to stay upright as they danced to music blasted from a cassette tape recorder. In Ireland, it was just another holiday, a day off work and a chance to go on the tear but not much was done in the way of an organized celebration. If you were lucky, like this year, this saint's day came on a Friday and a three-day weekend loomed ahead of us. It was the hat trick of holidays. That meant the chance to leave town or visit the family in the country. Pat and I managed to meet up at O'Donoghue's and sequester two seats in the front of the bar near the area reserved for the musicians. We were in for the duration.

When it was my shout, I went up to the bar, and I think I started a conversation with this man I had been eyeing throughout the last few months. That is to say that I think I was the one who started the conversation, but later he revealed the many times he had seen me in town and he could repeat overheard parts of my conversations using a fairly accurate American intonation. He had dark eyes and black curly hair and an accent that would make your heart melt. He was originally from West Cork with time spent in Cork City and Dublin and this had modified his speech into a deep-pitched melodic Irish inflection. A Cork accent can be difficult to follow, it can be a singsong sort of medley, but his voice was musical, wafting in and about the smoke from a constantly lit cigarette. He always wore a white shirt, open at the neck, with the sleeves rolled up to his elbows exposing strong, dark-haired muscular forearms. His smoking style had the panache of the 1930s. He had this Bogie habit of taking his cigarette out of his mouth by placing three fingers across the top, his thumb just below and his pinkie slightly extended. He would slowly remove the cigarette in this way, and then he would speak, his luxurious accent and dark eyes moving in absolute rhythm. Sometimes bits of tobacco would stick to his lower lip and he would gingerly peel them away with his other hand, never taking his eyes away. Then, just as casually, he would replace the cigarette letting it rest on his lower lip while waiting for a response. He already knew my name but I was introduced to him that night as Liam. He had fashioned a way of abbreviating my last name in a slow, modulated style, easing it out so that it sounded as if it had two syllables. "Now, La--ce," he would say, or "Another drink, La--ce?" It made me feel like I existed in that finely made web of intertwined silk threads.

I blamed my flirtatiousness on my ongoing Scotland saga. It was nice but still not titillating. "Nice" was not my objective when I made this change of cultures and I was seriously rethinking the fact that I was using logic as a measure of my current romantic success. Duncan and I had just recently returned from a trip to Madeira, a beautiful Portuguese island off the northwest coast of Africa. We'd done some local traveling around Scotland but this was our first trip away, and on some subconscious level, it was probably a make or break weekend. For his part, he authoritatively declared that we "could get married" and for my part, I coerced him into the huge bathroom where I had filled the blue and white tiled tub with bubble bath. Taking his hand, we looked down into the tub and I invited him into the warm, dancing bubbles. "We can get in there," I whispered.

"Won't the water dissipate," he asked? I didn't look up from the semi-enticing foam but I wondered about our future as we stood sweating in the steamy Portuguese loo.

I was captivated with Liam but I had learned my lesson about Irish men and their various forms of marital status. He didn't wear a ring, but that was hardly a warning sign in a country that simply assumes that you are married as soon as you reach a certain age. I was now of a mindset that Irish couples got married by way of an Irish musical chairs sort of process. Couples dated for a while and when they reached a certain age, it was as if the music stopped and you married whomever you were dating at the time. It also helped if your friends were getting married. The "marriage-knock-on-effect" was powerful. Getting married was expected, and given that contraception had only been legal for 15 years, marriage at a certain age solved a lot of life's little problems.

This expectation of marriage might have been one of the reasons that the campaign for the divorce referendum was heating up. I was learning a lot about "marriage breakdown," the two-word euphemism for divorce that wouldn't cost you the farm or condemn you to hell. It was the only option allowed under a constitution that contained an absolute ban on divorce since its adoption in 1937. Couples could officially opt for this form of separation, which allowed them to lead individual lives while legally allocating funds for spouse and child support. If it wasn't done officially, "marriage breakdown" was still an allowed description of the situation, but women might not be availed of legal financial support. At the tax office one woman complained, that having been abandoned, she was now being taxed as a single woman even though she was legally married and supporting three children. A citizen in the office overheard her complaint and to him, it was a denunciation of the Irish constitution. In the middle of the government office, he loudly accused her of sedition. It became clear that the debate on the referendum would have as much to do with the status of women as it would about ending a marriage. With no divorce available, remarriage was not an option and couples adapted in whatever way they could. One female supporter of the "Vote No" campaign made the headlines with her rationale for maintaining the status quo; "People who are separated shouldn't be allowed to remarry. The fact that they failed the first time proves that they are dysfunctional."

I wondered about Liam's marital status but not enough to delve into it at the moment. I would take my time starting something new with another Irish man of questionable availability. I made my way back to Pat the Yank and took my seat in front of the musicians playing madly just under the window facing Baggot Street. Pat had become a good friend and confidant in the last year. There was something comfortable about wandering around Dublin with another American; it required less explanation and allowed for more acceptance. Pat knew about my romance with Frank and he liked him very much. He told me that he had seen Frank in O'Donoghue's on the previous night and that he appeared to be in exceptionally good form. Frank had stopped in for a few pints and announced that he was on his way to catch the ferry to England. He was going to the races in Cheltenham! I couldn't believe it. Almost a year had gone by since he had warily confided in me that getting to the races would be his dream come true. I knew the importance of this seemingly simple trip to England, and while I was delighted to hear Pat's news, with respect to Frank, I said nothing.

Chapter 25 - A Spanner in the Works

As it happened, Frank was so excited to be fulfilling his dream of going to Cheltenham that he spent a good portion of his betting money buying drinks for everyone in O'Donoghue's. He was having such a good time that he celebrated through several ferry crossings and almost missed the races altogether. His timing was just more evidence that God loves a tryer. He got there and he won.

In St. Ita's, day-to-day life seemed to warm with the spring weather. It was amazing how a little sunshine could affect everyone's outlook. Kevin was especially brightened up and even chattier than before. He seemed to be everywhere that spring, following me around, looking for cigarettes and grabbing my wire-rimmed glasses. Kevin could knowingly test your patience; once he saw the slightest expression of annoyance cross your face he'd break into a big smile and begin his third person chant, "He's a pest. He makes you weary. Are ya hungry?" and then he would turn away, escaping down the corridor with his big grin intact. Those phrases were his mantra for months. But he still responded with "Ah loves ya" whenever he would stand still long enough to have me fix his twisted braces.

St. Ita's is built on a large site with loads of open spaces enclosing the multiple red brick buildings. Down the lane and away from the main entrance there is a large empty field and it was announced that for a week this spring it would be occupied by the Big Top of the traveling circus. This particular homegrown Irish circus had been touring around the country for decades and the anticipation of its arrival was irrepressible. The circus managers proclaimed a free afternoon performance for the residents of St. Ita's and we all set about organizing who would go and how we would get them safely down the avenue.

This was more difficult than it appeared. While it seemed logical that everyone would want to go, sitting in a dark tent under bright circus lights with an enthusiastic audience could have a powerful effect on some of the residents. They might ask to go, but walking down the lane and traipsing through the grass to enter a large dark tent might make them turn around and head back to their beds. The staff knew who would want to go, who could be trusted to go and who wouldn't lose the plot when the ringmaster loudly welcomed them to the show.

Kitty and Kevin, Maurice and Annie, Delia and Anthony, and my other clients could all make it down there with a minimum of assistance. I was asked to help by collecting Buck and pushing him in his wheelchair down the laneway and into the tent. Buck had just celebrated his 64th birthday in conjunction with another anniversary, that he was admitted to Portrane thirty-four years ago, on a temporary placement.

I was told that Buck had cerebral palsy with spasticity. He had no teeth and no dentures but even without them, his speech was fairly intelligible if and when he chose to speak. He had great time for Aisling, his caregiver, and he would give her a big toothless smile whenever he saw her coming down the corridor. One afternoon she gave his wheelchair a spin and chased around it staying right alongside of him. "Buck will think I've been drinking," she said.

He threw back his head laughing and said, "You never drink!" which was true. Slightly muffled and rounded, we could understand him very well.

Buck had difficulty with his hearing and I offered to spend some time with him to try and sort it out. In the activity room, I spoke closely to the side of his head to let him know that I was going to move his wheelchair backward to a table. Just as I got him in place, he revved up his feet and scooted away from me totally in the opposite direction enjoying a great gummy laugh at my expense. When he came back to the table I asked the nurse what activity he should do and I was told to give him the choice of drawing a picture or doing a jigsaw. I asked him, but he couldn't hear me and I was afraid to speak too loudly into his ear. He helped me by pointing to his right ear and saying, "This ear is deaf." He chose, instead, to put pegs into a board, a task that was supposed to reduce the spasticity of his fingers. He began to put the pegs in the holes by gingerly moving the pieces from his crumpled left hand into his twisted right one and then slowly moving them into position. A blue peg fell to the floor. Before I could get it, he moved his chair and bent forward towards the floor. I paralleled his move but he didn't need me. He slowly reached down and picked up the blue peg. As he worked the peg into the slot, Annette, one of the nurses, came in to visit him. She asked how he liked living in Unit J. He shook his head "no." She recited the names of the many people who worked with him in the unit. It wasn't that, he likes everyone, so Annette said it for him, "You just don't want to be here," she said and he agreed, nodding his head.

As he worked the pegboard Annette spoke of how Buck gets depressed and when it happens, he won't speak or listen to anyone. He will stay in his room and pull the covers up over his head. I can only imagine his sadness, watching him struggle to grasp the blue peg from the ground, not wanting any help. He must battle for everything; he's alone and in a wheelchair that he doesn't really need but there's simply not enough staff to let him try moving about in a walker.

I took his right hand in mine and asked him if it hurt as I straightened out his fingers. He shook his head. His fingers were not spastic but soft and flexible. I rubbed them gently, massaging them. From my purse, I got a small bottle of hand cream and rubbed it into Buck's hand. I asked Buck about his hearing and if he would wear his aid if I could get it fixed. He nodded his head, "Yes," he would "try." When I brought back the repaired aid, he crimped up his fingers and rummaged in his pocket. Then he slowly pulled out a £5 note and folded it into my hand. "For yourself," he said. My refusal to take the money was causing more stress than calm so I asked him if I could get him something, what would he like? "A j-j-jacket," he told me. I went to several little shops in Dublin and found him a lightweight coat perfect for the spring weather but when I brought it to him, he had lapsed into a deep depression and wouldn't accept it. I left it in his room although I never saw him wear it.

But on the day that the circus came to town, Buck was in fine form. When I went to meet him in the unit he was bundled up in a big heavy coat, with a scarf around his neck and a red knit hat pulled down tight and over his head. This was how he dressed to go outside. It was more than what was necessary for our short walk in the sunshine but sometimes the ritual has to be respected. We rolled out to the front of the building where we met up with Patsy and Hugo and everyone else who was walking or wheeling down the avenue. We must have looked like quite a procession. Once inside the tent, our mobile contingent was organized to the left of the center ring. Kitty and some of the more mature residents were in seats to the right and everyone else was up in the bleachers. Aisling had even managed to corral Kevin to a spot where he wouldn't roam. It was a fabulous afternoon and when it was over we all poured out of the tent and waited in the warm sun for our turn to be safely escorted back up the avenue. I was just a few feet away when I looked over my shoulder and saw everyone smiling and laughing while patiently waiting and enjoying the heat. It was the perfect picture of the perfect afternoon and by sheer impulse, I had the idea to take their picture. When they saw the camera, everyone struck their favorite pose under that gigantic "Circus" sign. I hesitated; through the lens we appeared to be straight off the set of a Fellini movie. I put down the camera but it was too late. Everyone, especially Anthony, had already struck their favorite pose and there they were, waiting for me to take the picture. And so I did.

In Scotland, I managed to close out my own personal circus with a letter to Duncan. We had talked at length on the phone but I was pretty sure he wasn't hearing me. I went with the theory that visual rather than auditory would work for him so I wrote everything out in a letter. He was very sweet and after reading it, he confirmed his understanding of my heartfelt exit. We decided to meet for one more weekend in Edinburgh, and strangely enough, each of us had brought break-up gifts for the other. Duncan gave me a little antique ring and I gave him a pink dress shirt. Duncan, who was colorblind, managed this dilemma by only wearing shirts of blue. He had rows of shirts in hues of blue. I just hoped to leave him in a blaze of color. He wore it, but only once. I've always felt that I was the one pink shirt in Duncan's compressed, but very blue, relationship wardrobe.

That weekend was memorable for many reasons, the pink shirt being the least of them. Since I was going to be away for a long weekend, I had left Duncan's telephone number with a friend of mine in St. Ita's. She rang me on that Sunday night to warn me that things at Portrane had taken a turn for the worse. It had been a beautiful spring day in both Portrane and Edinburgh and we were all looking forward to what was going to be an unusually warm spring and summer. But on that day, she rang with news to prepare me for the tragedy that would be waiting on my return. Oliver, whose investigation for allegedly striking Delia was ongoing, was still living in the caravan down at the boundary of the hospital grounds. On this day, he had invited several friends to the caravan for Sunday dinner. As they walked down the grassy pathway, they could see Oliver waving to them as he stood framed in the doorway of the tiny mobile home. When they got closer, Oliver appeared motionless and then, with no warning, the little caravan erupted into flames with a force so strong it kept them and everyone else from reaching him. It was horrific.

When I got back to Portrane I had never seen such widespread sadness. It was the day of Oliver's funeral and everyone was beside themselves with grief. Delia was in tears, Kitty was in tears and every resident I saw was visibly shaken with the news. For Delia, her feelings of remorse took on insurmountable proportions. She had been living with the guilt of being the sole participant in an incident that had taken Oliver away from the other patients and then banished him down to the caravan below, but now he was dead. And the mysterious nature of his death could do nothing to erase her feelings of blame. She was devastated.

We all did our best to help her deal with the numerous and confusing emotions that must have been whirling around her head but none of us could comfort her. I tried speaking with her on the way to the funeral, even hinting that maybe she shouldn't go. And for the first time I think I saw deep and personal cynicism in her eyes. How could I possibly know what she was thinking or how she was feeling? Through no fault of her own an old friend had died and yet she felt responsible for his death. She believed that other people blamed her as well. Her personal sorrow was laced with the fear that losing Oliver would cost her the only chance she'd ever have to leave Portrane and start a new life away from the oppressive clock tower and the chipped red brick buildings. As I spoke, she seemed to watch rather than listen to me. When the tears began to spill over her cheeks she turned from me, put her head down and silently and decisively waved me away. She said nothing and I could think of nothing more to say.

Chapter 26 - Chancing Your Arm

The tragedy in Portrane would settle itself over time. Oliver was gone but the strong indoctrination of the Catholic Church helped the residents to deal with his death. All of them had grown up in the belief system of the Church whether it was during their time at home or their time in an institution. Its structure was layered over their day-to-day existence and the order of life and the consequence of death were never questioned. The fact that the funeral mass was held in the chapel on the grounds of Portrane did a lot to strengthen their feelings that the order of things was maintained; Oliver was with God. But for Delia, the Catholic process provided only conflict and the team agreed to prioritize her move away from Portrane and into the community.

In Dublin, Liam and I met up periodically on the odd Thursday or Sunday night. He was at loose ends when I met him and was temporarily house sitting in a little ground floor flat on the north side. He was recently separated; his family had moved back to the country. There was more work for him in Dublin and it wasn't uncommon even for happily married fathers to work in the city and return on the weekends to the family home. Liam hoped that using work as his reason to be away would lessen the stigma of his marriage breakdown. And even though it was becoming more and more common, serious effort was still made to camouflage it from the family and the neighbors. It wasn't all that hard to do. Dealing with geographical separations is deeply embedded in the Irish psyche. Historically people have had to leave the small island and go wherever work could be found. At least in this day and age, they could come back for a visit or a wedding or a christening. This is different from the separations that came in famine time when families would have funerals for their loved ones before they boarded ships to wherever because they knew they would never see them again.

I tried not to tie up Liam's loose Irish ends in an American square knot but I remained cautious about his separation. He was unemotional and pragmatic when the subject came up. He went home when he could and he assured me that this was how the process worked in non-divorce Ireland. I bounced these behaviors off of Mary whenever I saw her and she agreed that this was how people managed to move forward with their lives, keeping the sacraments of the church while holding their heads high at the butchers.

Liam was my best audience. I loved to hear his deep Cork-laced Irish laugh when I talked about the rat in my office or the tortured Golf or the guards calling to the flat. I was open and honest with him and I felt, for the first time, that my humor and my American-ness was not only appreciated and understood but also fascinating and appealing. He gave me stick for holding out on the romantic part of our relationship and teased me unmercifully when I would evade any behavior that might suggest to observers that we were a couple. To some people I was still "that blonde American woman," and my comings and goings were worthy of a comment whenever the pub conversation lagged. I even avoided holding hands with him while walking about St. Stephen's Green. I was intent on waiting for enough time to go by to confirm that his separation had taken hold. It was just as well. Not long after I met him, Liam made a spontaneous trip home to the country. He informed his employer that he would be working from home, then he bought a ticket for the next train out of Dublin. To me, this cavalier attitude toward his chief source of income seemed pretty risky but my Irish work experience was limited to the health care industry; maybe things were different in an Irish business.

He seemed to be gone for quite a while. At least I think he was gone. I didn't see him around Baggot Street and he didn't come by the flat. No messages were left at the communal coin phone and nothing came in the post. I was back to being on my own but it wasn't much of a muchness; I was used to it by now. I did miss our occasional weekday happy hours. In Ireland, private time was sacred and everyone was out the office door at 5; leaving lots of evening time for music and drink. It was expensive though, so happy hour was short, and people would go home, have a meal, get cleaned up and go back out again at 10. With work not starting until 9 the next morning, that left a very civilized work schedule. If I met up with Pat the Yank we would go off on a tear looking for Brian the fiddle-playing architect. This made for some wildly memorable, musical weekends in numerous Dublin pubs, but without my knowing it, the Irish double standard was still playing havoc with my reputation. I thought that I had blended in with the Baggot Street crowd after shielding myself against Carlos, who wore his advertising on his undershirts, but I was wrong and my inability to recognize this left me on the back foot defending my singleness. Even the male friends who innocently roamed around with me left me alone to deal with this. One night, out on my own in O'Donoghue's, the barman implied that Pat the Yank and I were having an affair. I should have ignored it but instead, I sloppily denied it, pointing out that Pat's wife had just been here for a visit, and hadn't the barman himself seen us all out together? He shrugged. My ability to carry on with someone else's husband while the wife was around only made me more of a jammy bitch. I went to Pat with these false accusations in hope of having my honor defended, asking him if he had heard the gossip. He had heard it, many times. "Did you deny it?" I asked.

He smiled, "Do you think I'm crazy?" he asked. Pat, who was easily twenty years older and happily married, was delighted to remain innocent while having his reputation enhanced.

Considering that I was living in the capital of the country, I was hardpressed to understand how my comings and goings could be of any interest to anyone but my singleness remained an oddity for all the time that I lived in Dublin. I suppose I should have expected it from the pub crowd but I was disappointed that my male friends secretly believed this, too. One night after an evening of music, Brian gave me a lift back to Haddington Road. When he pulled up to the flat I thanked him, then he reached over, cupping his hand around mine and squeezing my fingers. He confided to me, quietly and sincerely, that he was a happily married man and that it would serve me better if I would "find a single man to give me what I *needed*." I commented that his attitude might be a bit over the top when all I *needed* was a lift to No. 292. Brian was a white-haired grandfather, even older than Pat but he was a man, and therefore, a prize. The Irish women faulted the Irish mammy for this centuries-old social phenomenon. Twenty years after the introduction of the International Year of the Woman and we were still being reduced to husband-hunting-maniacs. I suppose that was to be expected given the assumption of marriage, the limitations of birth control, no divorce and the fact that not long ago, women were expected to give up their public sector jobs as soon as they married. The Irish woman who remained single had a lot to take on. Maybe this was why, historically, more women than men emigrated and when they left, they travelled alone.

Eventually, Liam showed up at No. 292. His spontaneous exit had cost him his job but it was time well spent. With his personal issues sorted, he was back in Dublin looking for work. We went for a pint at the Beggars Bush and he announced that he had taken a room across the road, and now he too was a resident of Haddington Road. He felt his prospects were good and he had several interviews lined up. As we laughed our way through happy hour, I gave his situation a lot of thought and then I offered to support him for the next few weeks while he settled on a job. This was totally against my nature and even though I had moved to a foreign country without knowing a soul, risk-taking was not really in my remit, especially when it came to my minimal salary. But Liam had impressed me as an honest straightforward person who was now in a difficult situation and needed some help. He was smart and funny and I found myself strongly attracted to him. He was so heartfelt and realistic in his feelings about the marriage break-up that I did my best not to layer any American value judgments on his decision. This concept was still socially challenging and I knew from going through it with other Irish friends that it took a lot of courage to take that first step. When I was with him, I felt a deep give and take in our conversation that I hadn't felt in years. Liam could mirror my feelings with his own by verbalizing such deep emotion that he built an immediate closeness between us. We seemed to be talking with each other all the time. I very consciously decided that I would take what I thought was my last chance for love and make the leap to trust him. If it went pear-shaped, then so be it. I wouldn't blame Liam or second-guess my decision; I would chalk it up to my Irish experience and I would say nothing.

But Liam didn't find a job in a few weeks, or in a few months. It was quite a test for a new relationship. My financial support for him included everything except rent and child support. I kept my promise and said nothing but Liam kept a little notebook and each day he entered the cost of the cigarettes, the pints, the bus fares and the food. Most days after work, he would walk across the road and I would do the cooking. We stayed in more than we went out and numerous pints turned into the occasional bottle of wine. Only two of the burners worked on the little cooker in the flat, Eoin Bowen wasn't much for maintenance, so our most popular evening meal was a stir-fry with rice that could be cooked on half a stove. I included vegetables of many colors into the stir-fry, creating a veggie learning experience for Liam who was used to corn and peas. He totally lost the plot the night I brought home an artichoke. He did love the addition of balsamic vinegar to his diet, a totally unknown condiment, and he annoyingly lost loads of weight due to his newly balanced and pint-less diet. I didn't lose any weight but I gained the title of Queen of the Slap Up Meal.

Liam eventually landed a job working from home and he set about renting a computer to start earning some income. I admired his perseverance. It held him over for several months until he took on a permanent job in Ballsbridge, not too far from the flat. Once the paychecks became steady he took out the little book and showed me all the entries from the past weeks and then he sorted out a schedule to pay me back for even the smallest pack of cigarettes or the one glass of Guinness. He also called when he said he would and showed up when he said he would and I was delighted with my decision to put my faith in him. He teased me about my ongoing attempts to keep order in the little bedsit and this included my Calendar of Irish Writers, blu tacked to the wall, where I entered my daily experiences as if it was a diary. He would read it aloud while I was cooking and then prod me to expand on the one or two word comments. It didn't take much encouragement for me to amplify and embellish; I was still living in that movie script of Mary's and I wanted to remember all of it. Liam would listen and laugh and ask me questions, it was heaven for a story-telling speech therapist. One night he complimented me on my emotive delivery and gave all the credit to our shared ethnic background. I emphatically denied it. "I was raised Portuguese," I told him.

"That may be," he said, "but when you tell a story, you're Irish."

Chapter 27 - A Leg Up and a Leg Over

Liam quickly settled into the new job in Ballsbridge. The money coming in relieved some of the family tension and it helped to bolster his self-esteem. We were able to become more of a 50/50 couple although the stir-fry dinners and balsamic vinegar remained a part of our everyday living. As it happened, Liam turned out to be quite a good cook and he would often bring fresh fish home from the shop at the bend of the road on Baggot Street. It appeared that he was well-liked at work and he enjoyed setting off in the morning with a bit of purpose and success.

Even the weather had taken a positive turn and stayed bright for the entire day with not even the shortest of breaks for drizzle or rain. I finally realized why Mary would lapse into some kind of euphoric trance when she spoke about the weather of 1983. We were quickly approaching another such phenomenon; 12 years in the making and it looked like summer was on its way. The days are long this time of year in Ireland and it was amazing to have the sun last well into the evening. One night Liam was working late and I offered to collect him in Ballsbridge. When I left the flat at 9:30 in the evening, I had to linger at a stop sign while I put on my dark glasses, the sun was so incredibly bright. The entire population of Dublin went crazy with the heat and I went with it. The communal relief of the break in the weather was palpable having come out of months and months of hailstorms, freezing rain and black ice. On a weekend that Liam was away, I took the little red Golf, a blanket and a book and went to the seaside for the entire day. The following Monday morning the Irish Times ran a headline describing the huge number of people who ended up in emergency rooms across the country due to iridescent, self-inflicted sunburns. Even I suffered and had to miss a day of work after being totally and summarily scorched. Mary was good-natured about it but she wondered how I, coming from Los Angeles, could be so thick as to overdo it in the sun. I admitted that she was right. My only defense was my overwhelming joy at being in the heat, wearing a minimal amount of clothing and ending my bedsit hibernation after living life for so long as a hedgehog.

When the sun is out in Dublin then all is right with the world and I had every intention of capitalizing on this universal feeling of good-will; I would make Ireland a tourist destination not only for myself but also for Liam. Before separating, he had become a creature of marital habit, so in addition to expanding his list of condiments, we decided to broaden our traveling horizons as well. He was a willing participant in the venture but he attributed its start up to my American attitude. He was quick to make note of what he thought were the differences between our two cultures. One night we were in a crowded music pub. All the tables were full so we couldn't get close to the musicians. I noticed two free chairs at the back of the crowd and then, toward the side of the pub, there was a little table. I simply moved the table over to the two available chairs and we sat down and enjoyed the evening. I didn't give this a second thought, but to Liam, this was an act of social rebellion. "Only an American would think to move the table," he said. This logical, common sense gesture seemed unworthy of comment but I chose to take it as a compliment. As our relationship progressed, Liam continued to observe numerous differences between our two outlooks. He managed to put a positive spin on it but sometimes it felt more criti-cal than complimentary and seemed more about gender than ethnicity. I hadn't forgotten the ever-present double standard but I couldn't see Liam as holding on to this belief. He was too smart. I chalked up his attitude to a lack of exposure and set about increasing his comfort zone with this new American woman.

In Portrane, the weather continued to work its magic. When we could, we were all outside, sitting on the grass or taking walks around the grounds. The anxiety levels dropped with the warm weather as people became more tolerant and easy going. Residents went swimming or horseback riding; those who could ventured into Swords on the bus and stayed away as long as they could. Those who couldn't found a place in the sun and remained there, contentedly immobilized in the heat. Even Kevin adopted a mellower attitude. When I stopped him so that I could adjust his braces, he turned to me before leaving and said, "I'm a quiet guy today, aren't I?" Kitty was enjoying her placement in Skerries; she was definitely one of the success stories of the new placement process. We still had issues with patients being dropped off at St. Ita's at all hours of the day or night, some of them with no understanding that they were leaving their home or their hospital and coming directly to us. This could cause an elongated period of adjustment not only for them but for everyone else living with them in the ward. All around the country, residents who couldn't adjust or had nowhere else to go would have to settle in Portrane; their next and last destination. It would take a while to sort out the changes needed to alter this process but things were getting better and our efforts to move people into the community were progressing. Garrylough Mill was almost up and running with Delia planning to move in the next few weeks.

Until now I had been exploring Dublin on my own unless someone visited from the States. When they did, I booked in as many things as I could between their holiday time and my work schedule. A friend working in London popped over to me for a long weekend in Dublin. The first day we drove to Meath to visit Trim Castle on the River Boyne. His motivation was to see the castle from Braveheart, mine because my Norman ancestors were its builders and early inhabitants. Not that my ancestry gave me any credibility as far as the Irish were concerned. One night in a pub on Northumberland Road, an Irish American friend from Minnesota and I got into a heated discussion with an elderly, cap wearing, chain-smoking Dubliner. My friend's surname was Connolly, and as the argument became more intense, the Dubliner turned his back to me and spoke only to her. He dismissed me by pointing a crooked finger across his chest and in my direction. "She's not Irish like we are," he sneered. My Norman heritage and 800 years in the country were no contest for a Connolly even if she was from Minnesota.

Perhaps the keeper of the Trim Castle felt the same. Once we had finished exploring, we headed back to the big iron gates that guarded the entrance. While they had been wide open when we entered, they were now closed and padlocked. We had no way out. We walked around to the small building where we had met the gatekeeper but he was nowhere to be found so we headed back to the front gates. Grabbing hold of the bars, we tried to coerce the passersby for help. Someone must have relayed our plight to the guards because eventually an officer appeared with an extra set of keys and set us free. We apologized for the inconvenience but he acted as if he had heard it all before. He graciously assured us that it was no problem but as he walked away we heard him whisper, "I wish he'd stop locking up the Yanks."

Liam seemed to be feeling positive about work and family; he always had a £20 phone card so that he could ring home from the corner call box. It was early days for us so I didn't ask many questions but I did wonder as to how the separation was going. The publicity surrounding the upcoming divorce referendum was heating up and I found myself living through the real-life turmoil of how this constitutional change would affect an Irish family. On the occasional Friday I would drop him off at Heuston Station and collect him on Sunday, but when he stayed in town, we made the most of the time.

My friends from St. Ita's had given me loads of local recommendations and I followed through on every one of them. I took Liam to all my favorites. I dragged him across the Glasnevin Cemetery with the sole intention of ending up in the haunted Grave Diggers Pub. Liam had never been to the cemetery where the famous patriots Michael Collins, Charles Parnell and Daniel O'Connell are buried. The pub, also known as Kavanagh's, opened in 1833. It's full of wooden seats with snug-like partitioned areas. I was told that in the old days, late in the evening, the gravediggers would quietly come in through the door in the dark, back part of the pub and warm themselves by the fire. The spirits, so they say, came in with them. But my favorite place was St. Michan's, a Protestant church in the Smithfield area of Dublin. This was part of the deep inner city that during the week was given over to horse-trading and flower selling. It was still part of an earthy Dublin of another time. St. Michan's was hard to find and not always open. But once inside it was extremely beautiful, with extraordinary woodwork and a beautiful organ from the 1700s where Handel had supposedly played The Messiah. A picture of this organ was on the current £20 note. One night, out on my own, a punter saw me hand one of these notes to the barman. He put his hand out to stop me from paying just to tell me the story about the church, the organ and its inhabitants below. Under the church is an ancient dungeon where four mummies were unearthed in 1956. Their origin is uncertain, but it's said that one of them, The Crusader, will bring you good luck if you reach through the bars that protect his crypt and touch his mummified hand. I touched him, sure, who would turn down a chance for Irish good luck?

Living in Dublin as a couple became a new adventure altogether. We went up to Derry, out to West Cork and over to Castletownbere. Liam's family originated in the west but he had not been back in years. He showed me the little two-room school house where he spent his first few years with his left hand tied behind his back. Like me, Liam was left-handed and the first "citóg" in the family. "Citóg" (KI towg) was my first word of Irish. I picked it up early on because people, watching me write, quickly labeled my "abnormality." At the time, being left handed still stood out from the crowd. Fortunately for Liam, several of the younger brothers and sisters also developed a dominant left side and his parents gave in to their handedness. It was just too complicated to keep that many one-handed children out of trouble.

At Castletownbere we found the endpoint of our trip, the cable car to Dursey Island, the only cable car in Europe to cross the open sea. There is only the one car and it moves between the stations on a haul rope. An islander told us that it was built to transport livestock from the island to the mainland, specifically, he said, to carry a man and a cow, if you could fit in a few sheep, all the better. It was the only time I saw a religious side to Liam, blessing himself as the cable car lifted off. We never left the rickety car to set foot on the island. We went over and back and then straight into the pub.

Truth be told, things were going very well. We became a normal couple around Baggot Street, blending in with Pat the Yank and Brian the architect. We spoke of visiting Belfast in the autumn and London at Christmas. I got serious about collecting the tokens from the Superquinn where I did my grocery shopping. Enough coupons could earn tickets to far off places like Barcelona. We even talked about a trip to the states.

Reluctance gave way to trust as we held hands during those walks around Dublin, our relationship having been accidentally sanctified one post-dinner night in No. 292. Liam had arrived with haddock in hand to celebrate his now permanent employment. That Baggot Street fish led to bottles of wine, a kiss and a cuddle and a bedsit sleepover on a chilly summer night. The next day, on the Calendar of Irish Writers, I marked the occasion with one word, "Oops." When Liam read it, he mentioned my "lack of romance" but I let it stand. The Irish are all about the chat, but for now, I added nothing.

Chapter 28 - Acting the Maggot

With bittersweet feelings, we moved Delia away from Portrane and down to her new life in County Wexford. She was over the moon at her new digs and sure, why wouldn't she be? At 16, Francie, may he rest in peace, had been the youngest person in St. Ita's; however, Delia, at 30, was still young and ready to be out on her own, well, out on her own with a twenty-four hour a day caregiver and a psychologist on call. Still, she would have her own space, a village nearby and a chance to meet flat mates who would fill up all the bedrooms in the house. Her excitement was infectious, and even though we knew it was an experiment, we all hoped for the best.

The summer rhythm of Portrane settled into a more sedate autumn cadence where politics on many levels took over the casual chat. The talk was full of concern for the women who were infected with Hepatitis C due to a contaminated blood by-product. And to complicate things even further, Ireland was still getting its head around the issue of HIV. A campaign to promote the use of condoms was launched to help with AIDS prevention but it was tricky; the effort had to support good health while not supporting casual sex. The gay population still appeared to be closeted, so being diagnosed with HIV / AIDS was perceived mainly as a heterosexual problem. More panic set in when down in Waterford a youthful priest announced from the pulpit that a young, blonde, HIV-positive woman with an English accent was marauding through the town of Dungarven avenging her infection. He announced that she had already transmitted the illness to five local men and that at least eighty more were at risk. She was christened the "Angel of Death," her sexual revenge having been revealed by an anonymous parishioner's revelation in the confessional. People were publicly fearful and verbally outraged but the local health board staunchly contradicted what they classified as gossip. While the priest's declaration sent many men to the health board to be tested none were found to be infected. Nor had the young woman ever been identified or located. Still, the members of the parish considered the priest to have their best interests at heart, and while no proof was forthcoming, they stood by their "local hero."

Interestingly, the double standard that was so obvious in the city also bubbled to the surface in the country. The "Angel of Death" was the talk of the town for weeks and weeks. The chat shows were full of condemnation for this wicked sexual predator who had allegedly coerced more than eighty feckless men into her bed. One female radio caller condemned her by stating that "Some of those men are married and now they'll give it to their wives and those children will grow up with no parents. She should get everything that's coming to her." No mention was ever made of the cheating husbands and no Angel of Death was ever found.

This intense publicity was pushed aside by the debate surrounding the upcoming divorce referendum. The government had allotted £500,000 to publicize the debate and the upcoming vote. As the sitting government was pro-divorce, the opposing parties complained that this was public money being spent to influence the vote. The government retaliated with a plan to use the funds to educate but not to influence the decision of the voters. As the months closed in on the vote, the debate became more and more intense. In Coolock, one of the administrative assistants asked me pointedly, "I suppose you have a vote?"

"I do," I told him. I explained that I had registered immediately upon taking up my post.

"And," he pressed further, "I suppose you're going to vote 'yes?'" I told him that I didn't believe that you should suffer through the rest of your life due to one poor decision. "And now you want to turn us into America," he challenged me. I gave that some thought. Other Catholic countries had divorce: Spain, Portugal and Italy. I felt he was going a bit over the top comparing his island of four million people to the entire population of the United States. I thought about Ireland and how much I had come to love it; if I could, was there something I would change?

"No," I said, "I don't want to turn Ireland into America. I just want the toilets to flush."

The campaign for and against divorce was a fascinating foray into Irish politics. While I perceived it as an issue of personal freedom, many perceived it as an issue of family heritage. A significant number of my younger Irish friends were staunchly against the divorce referendum. I couldn't understand their reluctance to at least have the option of leaving a broken marriage. But one of them explained that if the parents broke up, and the father remarried and had more children, then who would get the family farm? The possibility that the founding family might not inherit their own land was a thought not to be entertained. In Portrane, a lunchtime discussion became heated with Pat pounding on the table and declaring that the constitution guaranteed a lifelong marriage. "If that's so", I countered, "then where's mine?" Political humor was evidently out of place at lunch so I left the table hoping to avoid the obvious recommendation of solving my singleness with a trip to the Lisdoonvarna Matchmaking Festival.

The advertising posters for both pro and con began popping up all over Dublin. I was surprised at the number of themes that took the husbands to task and implied, that on the whole, the men were mostly to blame. Women were portrayed as victims and their lives would be tragic if the men left and tragic if the men stayed. In a country where the policy of women having to give up their jobs once they married still lingered in the collective memory, divorce was considered by some to be totally to the advantage of the men. Family abuse was also a constant theme and increasingly brought up by the pro side of the debate. Both sides countered but with a similar theme, the con side produced a poster of a family with both parents and two children supported by the declaration, "If this was *your* daughter would *you* destroy their marriage?" The pro side produced a picture with a mother and two children stating, "If this was *your* daughter *you'd* give her a second chance." It was a powerful debate.

In the midst of all this politicking, Liam and I decided to plan a trip to a warmer climate. I redeemed my grocery tokens for two airline tickets and a city break to Barcelona. Unfortunately, I developed a severe respiratory infection just before we were to leave that had all the signs of spoiling the trip. Both of my ears were totally blocked and I couldn't hear a thing. Reluctantly, I left the flat one afternoon and walked down the street to the local general practitioner, who had offices above the pub, and was known locally as the Doc in the Box. He confirmed my diagnosis but insisted that there was nothing he could do. My professional concern about being on an airplane with two blocked ears made me pester him for his reciprocal professional concern. He reneged and I left with a prescription to go and "suck on some boiled sweets." Not the most medicinal of recommendations, I went to the chemist to fill this prescription and surprisingly left with a bag of hard candy. I tried not to worry. He had finished our appointment by walking me out the door and assuring me the worst thing that could happen is that both my eardrums would burst.

Ears be damned, our to trip to Spain was a huge success. Until then, I hadn't realized how little Liam had traveled. Early one morning on the second day of our trip, he took off on his own to explore the city's outdoor markets. He came back with his first pair of Bermuda shorts and equally rebellious leather sandals. God knows they would never see the light of day in Dublin but he was happy as Larry to expose his legs from knees to toes in Barcelona. These "firsts" were a constant reminder to me of how different our past experiences had been; even the introduction of balsamic vinegar had expanded his horizons. When we returned to Dublin we attended a big kick off for a nighttime city celebration just over the bridge on O'Connell Street. We bundled up and ventured out to the River Liffey to join the crowd. With the Celtic Tiger gathering political and economic force, the promised display of fireworks would be a showy demonstration of the city's new wealth. The weather held and the fireworks went off, glistening over the dark, oozing water that framed Dublin's city center. Liam was dazzled. On the walk home, he confessed that it was the first time he had ever seen fireworks. I wondered what he would make of the Golden Gate Bridge?

We began to make plans for a move to California with the hope of a career change for Liam that would massively increase his prospects and his income. He was anxious to try his luck in America; his gambling instincts had taken over and fused with the attraction of California and the Silicon Valley. I was somewhat reluctant. He had shown several signs of jealousy in the past and while I found it unnerving I chalked it up to our cultural male/female differences. He always seemed to see the light once we had talked it out, but for me, it was an uncomfortable emotion that often seemed illogical and useless. I went to Mary with my concerns about Liam as well as with my thought of leaving Portrane and returning to the States. Mary was, as always, supportive and understanding. I was well past our agreement of staying for six months and sorting out the post for an Irish therapist so my job was ready for a transition. I hoped that one of the younger therapists from Coolock would step up and take advantage of the promotion but they all turned me down. "You've just told us too many stories," was the defense of their total and complete rejection. So I unofficially discussed my resignation with Mary and told her of the plan to start over in California. She agreed that as a new couple, we should try a life in the States. "Besides," she said, "you've lived in his culture for a while now; it's time he learned about yours." So Liam and I made a plan; I would leave a few weeks ahead and find us a place to stay; he would follow. A friend offered us a sublet in the Haight/Ashbury district of San Francisco. That intrigued me; there would be a lot of "firsts" in the Haight.

Still, there was one last lingering winter to get through before returning to California. In Portrane, the hallways and wards were buzzing with the preparations for another Christmas concert; once again the diversion of the holiday created an energy and an excitement that simply couldn't exist at any other time of year. My Irish adventure was about to end and it saddened me to think of leaving the patients and the staff who had, without intending to, kicked off my incredible learning curve.

The rain lashed down on the day of the vote for the divorce referendum. It was dark and foreboding, freezing and wet. I hadn't received the notice of my polling place so I spent the first part of the morning combing the neighborhood to find my place of registration. When it got late, I headed off to Portrane but I was overwhelmed by traffic in the city center. The vote was taking place on a Friday so hundreds of people were already lined up at the bus loading areas to head home to vote in the country. Given that many people perceived the divorce referendum to be about land, they were heading home to vote in a show of support for the family home. People didn't really change their registration once they moved to the city. They remained loyal to their area of family heritage. Voting choices could often be associated more with a party affiliation than with a personal choice. People tended to vote in support their party, which was the party of their parents, and often the party of their grandparents. The voting was expected to be very, very close. Once when discussing voting options with a much younger friend of mine, I tried to counter her belief in one party's recommendation with the view of another. She wouldn't hear of it. "I couldn't disappoint my grandmother." was her response, "She always supported Fianna Fail." Unnecessarily I pointed out that her grandmother was dead but I still lost the argument.

Just like the masses of voters standing in the rain waiting for the buses, I also headed out early from Portrane. The polling places were operating under extended hours so that people could get across the country in time to vote in their home counties. I parked the little red Golf on Haddington Road, bundled up in rain gear and went across the road to see if Liam was home from work. When he answered the door I asked if he wanted to roam the neighborhood as I looked for my polling place. He suggested the Boys' School just up the road and I admitted that it was the one place I had overlooked. He picked up his umbrella and we walked just up the road to the school by the church. I was delighted to see my name crossed off the registrar as I cast my first official ballot. I waited for Liam to vote but his name wasn't there. When we walked out into the chilling rain on the way to the pub I asked if he had voted somewhere else in the city but no, to vote he would've had to go home to the country. "It's just as well," he said, "I would have voted 'no.'" I glanced at him from the corner of my eye and wondered what that meant to the future and our move to the States; I wondered, but I said nothing.

Chapter 29 - Come to Mine

The referendum passed but only by the most narrow of margins. Divorce was now an option but people didn't flood the courts as prophesied by the opposing party. Hardly. In order to be divorced there was a built-in waiting period; the couple had to prove that they had been living separately for four of the last five years. To a young woman, this waiting period could be disastrous if it coincided with her time to start a family. So married people continued to live separately and start new lives with new partners and begin new families.

Liam's quiet but emphatic lack of support for the referendum left me confused and questioning. Mary had explained the varying perceptions that could surround an Irish divorce not only in the eyes of the Church but also in the repercussions for the family and even in the neighborhood. I had no interest in pressing Liam for this decision but I sensed a conflict in his unwillingness to back the amendment and his participation in our new relationship. Mary was helpful but I needed more; I needed Madame Lee.

I still had the business card that Madame Lee had surreptitiously slipped into my hand when I left her caravan at the Ballinasloe Horse Fair in Galway. I always felt that since she had psychically peeled away the truth of my relationship with Frank, there was a soft spot in her romantic Gypsy heart for me and my naive involvement with Irish men. Just as she had said, with the fair season over, her caravan had set its parking brake in Lucan and she was taking appointments for personal sessions. I booked one for a Saturday afternoon and made my way to Lucan, not without a bit of meandering for lack of direction. I parked the little red Golf in front of the shiny silver caravan with its hot pink trim. The weather was fine and the sunshine bounced off the silver coating so that the caravan virtually throbbed in the light. Inside the caravan, the decorations were the same, the pink fuzzy tassel still dangled from the pull on the window curtain and the lampshades glistened with silver trim. I remembered the many, almost historical, family pictures that rested on every flat surface in the sitting room. I commented on one that happened to be a picture of her grandparents before they had settled in Ireland. Evidently Madame Lee's caravanning lifestyle was indigenous to her family history and not uncharacteristic of their centuries-old life pattern. I found her to be even more fascinating in this less harried encounter but I had to forego my curiosity about her or lose my time to sort out my own personal destiny. First, Madame Lee wanted to know if I had followed through on her recommendation to end my relationship with Frank. I assured her that as difficult as it had been, yes, I had followed her advice. But now I found myself in a new relationship and wondered if she could see any need to forewarn me as before. We spoke of many things with questions asked and answered, and in the end, Madame Lee gave me, and us, her Psychic Seal of Approval.

Bolstered with this newfound psychic energy, I went to Mary and officially resigned my position. The job search had to be posted, routed and waited for but Mary knew that given St. Ita's historical reputation within the Irish therapist community there would hardly be a clambering of applications. She finally settled on an Irish therapist named, what else, Mary, and gave her a lead-time of several weeks before taking over. Therapist Mary came to spend one morning a week with me before we did the official hand-off. I found myself to be strangely proprietary about St. Ita's, my clients and my friends in the hospital. So much that happened had affected me personally, and whether it was fair or not, I had the strange sensation that I wanted her to take it personally, too. Instead, she viewed it as a job, which would most likely save her from skin rashes, conjunctivitis and getting choked while being transported in the minivan. When I escorted Mary around the hospital to introduce her to the staff, someone would always ask her if she had heard the story of the rat in what was my, and soon to be her, office. Each and every time they asked, she reacted viscerally to the tale. Unfortunately for her, she confessed to anyone who would listen, that of all things, rats were her biggest fear. By now I had learned to "take the piss" with the best of them so each time someone brought up the rodent, I embellished the legendary story of the rat that came in from the cold to take up its winter lodging in my wastebasket. As I spoke, her shoulders retracted into her frame, her body cringing at the very thought of such vermin. I knew, by now, that you never revealed your weakness in an Irish conversation; it left you vulnerable to all comers. Unfortunately for Therapist Mary, I wasn't the only one who noticed this; so at each welcoming introduction, the story was told, her fear was revealed and the rat became bigger and bigger.

I took Mary around to as many wards as I could just to give her a feeling of how things were done in St. Ita's. Improvements were numerous since I first arrived on the isthmus and I wanted to spare her some of that learning process. I tried to be overtly professional but I had invested so much emotion in Portrane that at times I wasn't certain that I was really and truly ready to let it go. Mary seemed to be absorbing the overall picture of the place, but at times, I think she felt that I was being a bit too dramatic. On her last visit, I took her up to a ward with some new patients and cautioned her to follow my lead with the timing of getting safely into the ward. I'd become accustomed to the rhythm of quickly unlocking the door, getting inside, and turning, just as quickly, to lock the door behind me. I explained the process to Mary and she nodded passively at my instructions. I took out my dangling ring of keys and slowly opened the door allowing Mary to go in first. Rattling the big tooth key into the ancient lock always caused some noise and alerted the residents that someone was coming in. I moved as swiftly as I could, letting Mary in and coming in quickly behind her. But she left me little room to close the door and with just that smidgen of daylight, a resident came flying through the air, passing over Mary's head. He curled his fingers around the top of the open door, angled his body toward the wall and pushed his feet against it using all his strength to pry it open. This was truly a valiant effort, but not only did it defy gravity, it simultaneously broke several laws of physics. The patient made a loud bang against the door and then slid slowly down to the floor, crumpling at Mary's feet. He was fine. He simply stood up and walked away but Mary was much worse for wear. I had to leave her sitting in the ward office with a cup of tea and collected her on my way back later in the afternoon. It was then that I knew how much I had learned and how far I had come, and while I wished the best for Mary, I knew that I was ready to go.

Luckily I was able to see Delia before I left, as she happened to be up in St. Ita's for an appointment. She loved living in the hostel at Garrylough Mill but it wasn't for lack of trying. She told me that the community had protested the arrival of the new residents in the village and the protest had been loud and unsettling. She couldn't understand it. She said that she had gone out to address them, to let them know that they had nothing to fear. "This is my home," she said. Then she asked me, "Why do they do this, Chris? We never did nothin' to them." I could only suggest that when you try something new, sometimes you are the one who has to take the first step. To the village, the new residents' home was different, unfamiliar to them. Delia and her housemates might have to do the teaching. I could certainly empathize with her adjustment to her new surroundings. I wished her well and encouraged her to hold on to her new home. We said goodbye and I knew that I would miss her a great deal. I had my concerns, but it was best to say nothing.

On Haddington Road, everything was changing. Paddy had taken his redundancy and abandoned the little bedsit at the very end of the hallway. He was gone. Just like that. We fantasized that he had run away with Mrs. Enright, his housekeeper and paramour, and was now being minded at her home in the wilds of Tipperary. At least we hoped that was where he had gone. Tess from across the hall and the other side of the phone box had accepted a job in Prague. She would be the manager of a new Irish bar that was to open in the center of the city. Prague had become the newest and most popular EU destination and we envied her chance to start over in a booming European country. As it happened, her part-time job of managing the rugby club had put her in contact with some wealthy investors and so her love of ruggers had given her a career change and an exotic relocation. I tidied up my little bedsit and filled up boxes for donations and boxes for friends. To be fair, there wasn't all that much to organize with the exception of the loo. The recent overly damp winter had produced a bumper crop of lino toadstools that I now skillfully removed and cleaned up for the next bedsit inhabitant. With No. 292 all tidied up, I made an arrangement with my upstairs neighbor from Minnesota to sell her the little red Golf. That deal done, I drove around contentedly in the time that was left.

In Portrane, I busied myself with the Christmas concert and helped where I could or wherever I was needed. It was fascinating to think that this time last year I was wary of the concert only to see the incredible staff effort that created a prelude to an event that was as worthwhile and important as the event itself. This year there would be two performances. Emer would star in one and Kitty would star in the other. I was away for part of the holidays so I missed the first concert, the one with Kitty, but I was there on the second night to see the show with Emer. When I asked one of the nurses how the first night had gone, she hesitated and then she spoke; the opening performance went very, very well; everyone knew their songs and the audience loved it. But later in the evening, Kitty suffered a severe seizure and died that very night. I was broken hearted that I hadn't seen the first performance and I was surprised at how deeply I felt her loss. I feel it still. I will always regret that I missed that final opportunity to see her dance; she is the best reason for telling this story.

So just like Delia, for me, leaving Portrane was also bittersweet. I often thought of Leo who told me to say "nothing," and how his wise advice taught me to always look and listen. But what haunted me most was my brother's cavalier prediction when I announced my move to Dublin now several years ago; "Ireland," he had chided, "where's the challenge in that?"

CPSIA information can be obtained
at www.ICGtesting.com
Printed in the USA
FSHW011939280619
59557FS